EARLY BUDDHIST MYTHOLOGY

Early Buddhist Mythology

J.R. HALDAR

Foreword by
D.C. SIRCAR

MANOHAR
2022

First published 1977
Reprinted 2022

ISBN 978-93-88540-80-3

Published by
Ajay Kumar Jain *for*
Manohar Publishers & Distributors
4753/23 Ansari Road, Daryaganj
New Delhi 110 002

Printed at
Replika Press Pvt. Ltd.

Foreword

The present work embodies Dr. J. R. Haldar's thesis which earned for him the degree of Ph.D. of the University of Calcutta. Four years ago I introduced to the public a small part of it entitled *Links Between Early and Later Buddhist Mythology*, reprinted from the proceedings of a seminar on 'Religious Life of Ancient India' held under my chairmanship at the Centre of Advanced Study in Ancient History and Culture, Calcutta University, in Feburary 1971. In my foreword to that tiny work, I expressed the hope that students interested in the subject may find the author's exposition interesting and useful. The said expectation seems to have come true since I find that a reputed periodical of one of the foremost oriental societies of the West says as follows about it in its review: "Dr. Haldar has produced a useful monograph which can suggest many topics for further exploration."

I shall be glad if Dr. Haldar's bigger work, now published, gets the same kind of favourable reception from the students of Indian religious life as the small part of it, referred to above, has been tasting for sometime.

D. C. Sircar

645 New Alipore,
Calcutta 700053
November 10, 1976

Formerly Carmichael Professor
and
Head of the Dept. of Ancient Indian
History and Culture and Director of the
Centre of Advanced Study in A.I.H. and C.,
University of Calcutta

Preface

It is difficult to define mythology in a way that would satisfy all. It is a cultural complex which can be approached from various and complementary viewpoints. However, we may say that mythology records the primitive peoples' accounts of supernatural beings and their activities associated with the moral and cultural beliefs of a people concerned. It also speaks of primitive beliefs regarding creation and destruction of the universe. Mythology may be regarded as the background of religions, and Buddhism is no exception to this. Although the Buddha based his teachings upon reason, the Pali works dealing mainly with the ethical doctrines of early Buddhism also give us mythological details from its own sources and from sources often borrowed from earlier traditions—Vedic, anti-Vedic or pre-Vedic.

A careful examination of Pali works does not support the contention that early Buddhism is free from mythology. Buddhism changed its course in different ages, though the fundamental mythological ideas, as found in Pali literature, continue in Sanskrit Buddhist works. The present work deals with early or Hīnayāna Buddhist mythology as depicted in Pali literature and also as it is reflected in later (Mahāyāna) literature in certain respects.

Here I have dealt with early Buddhist mythology in seven chapters. It begins with cosmological speculations of the early Buddhists, which have not been adequately treated so far. The importance of the subject lies in the fact that the early Buddhist mythology does not acknowledge any creator-god. Another point of interest is that the Buddhist theory of destruction and renovation of the universe remind us of some of the theories of modern science. The theory of the decay and reorientation of the universe as found in early Buddhist literature resembles the myths regarding cosmic cataclysms extremely widespread among the primitive peoples.

The Buddhist ideas of heavens and hells, forming the subject matter of the second and the third chapters, are the ethical consequences of the aforesaid notions of creation and destruction. Since the nature of individual virtue and vice varied, the number of heavens and hells eventually increased. In describing the heavens and hells, Buddhist mythology has evidently followed the existing traditions which were however influenced by the Buddhist goal of escape from the cosmic cycle.

The myths about higher beings including gods and goddesses, spirits and semi-divine beings, are relatively simple. By far the most complex and dramatic category of myths includes those that are concerned with the cosmic changes which took place at a certain time in the primordial past.

However, the celestial beings of the higher category were never active. According to the early Buddhists, the gods and Brahmā are neither supreme deities nor are they creators of the universe. They are inferior to the Buddha (see Chapter V) who is regarded as omnipresent, omniscient and omnipotent. This conception of the early Buddhists was the forerunner of the deification of the Buddha in the later period. Likewise, Lakkhī of the earlier mythology, the symbol of the earned merit to the way to *nibbāna* tends to become eventually the female principle of the Ādi-Buddha in later Buddhism.

The concluding chapter entitled "Links Between Early and Later Buddhist Mythology" is meant to throw significant light on the origin of Mahāyāna mythology from a source which has not been broached before. It shows that Mahāyāna mythology is indebted to Hīnayāna because supernatural characteristics of the Buddha mentioned in the Pali texts point out that the Buddha was considered a supreme God even by the Hīnayānists. Both Pali and Sanskrit Buddhist texts regard the Buddha as superior to all gods and goddesses of the *Deva* and *Brahma-lokas*. Apart from this, as regards the constitution of the universe, its destruction and renovation, gods and goddesses, spirits and semi-divine beings, *Devāsurasaṅgrāma*, heaven and hell, etc., there is a link between Brāhmaṇical and Hīnayāna mythologies, and it has also a conspicuous connection with the mythological ideas of the Mahāyānists.

So far as the question of methodology is concerned, I have followed the policy of textual documentation in order to present things as they really are. I have intentionally avoided the temptation of speculating on different aspects of early Buddhist mythology or of making a comparative study of Brāhmaṇical, Buddhist and Jain mythology, which could, however, create a different appeal. But since early Buddhist mythology is not yet fully explored, I have given wholesale emphasis on this point.

I am grateful to Dr. D.C. Sircar for his kind and valuable guidance that has enabled me to complete my thesis for the Ph.D. degree of the University of Calcutta. I am extending my thanks to Dr. Nalinaksha Dutt who kindly allowed me to consult the valuable books in his library.

Ramchandrapur,
Dakshin Barasat,
24-Parganas, West Bengal.

J.R. Haldar

List of Abbreviations

PTS Published by the Pali Text Society.

SHB Published by the Simon Hewavitarne Bequest Series (Colombo).

SBT Sanskrit Buddhist Text.

Aṅg. Aṅguttara Nikāva (PTS).

Aṅg. Com. Manorathapūraṇī, Aṅguttara Commentary. (PTS and SHB)

Abhs. Abhidhammatthasaṅgaha (PTS Journal, 1884).

Ap. Apadāna (PTS).

BCS Buddhist Conception of Spirits, ed. B.C. Law.

Bud. Buddhavaṁsa (PTS).

Bud Com. Buddhavaṁsa Commentary (PTS).

BME Buddhism and Mythology of Evils, ed. T.O. Ling.

CN. Culla Niddesa (PTS).

CN. Com. Culla Niddesa Commentary (SHB).

CV. Culavaṁsa (PTS).

Dīg. Dīghanikāya (PTS).

Dīg. Com. Sumaṅgalavilāsinī, Dīghanikāya Commentary (PTS).

DPPN Dictionary of Pali Proper Names by G.P. Malalasekera.

Dvy. Divyāvadāna.

Dāṭh. Dāthāvaṁsa (PTS Journal, 1884).

Dham. Dhammapada (PTS).

Dham. Com. Dhammapādaṭṭhakathā, Dhammapada Commentary (PTS).

Dhs. Dhammasaṅgaṇī (P.T.S.)

Dhs. Com. Atthasālinī, Dhammasaṅgaṇī Commentary (PTS).

DB Dialogues of the Buddha (PTS).

ERE Encyclopaedia of Religion and Ethics.

GS Gradual Sayings (PTS).

HHBP Heaven and Hell in Buddhist Perspective, ed. B.C. Law.

GNB Gods of Northern Buddhism, ed. Alice Getty.
HIL History of Indian Literature, ed. M. Winternitz.
Itv. Itivuttaka (PTS).
Itv. Com. Itivuttaka Commentary (PTS).
JAIH Journal of Ancient Indian History, ed. D.C. Sircar
Jāt. Jātaka, ed. Fausboll.
JPTS Journal of the Pali Text Society.
JRAS Journal of the Royal Asiatic Society.
Khud. Com. Khuddakapāṭha Commentary (PTS).
KS Kindred Sayings, (PTS).
Kv. Kathāvatthu (PTS).
LTB The Legends and Theories of the Buddhists, 1881, ed. R. Spence Hardy Hon. *MRAS.*, 2nd edition.
Maj. Majjhimahikāya, 3 vols. (PTS).
Maj Com. Majjhimanikāya Commentary (PTS and SHB).
MAR Mythology of All Races by A.B. Keith and A.J. Carnoy
MB A Manual of Buddhism, ed. Spence Hardy.
Mbv. Mahabodhivaṁsa (PTS).
Mil. Milindapanha, ed. Treckner (Williams and Norgate)
MN Mahā Niddesa (PTS).
MN Com. Mahā Niddesa Commentary (SHB).
Mtu. Mahāvastu, ed. Senart, 3 vols.
MṬ. Mahāvaṁsa Ṭīkā (PTS).
Mv. Mahāvaṁsa, ed. Geiger (PTS).
Nd. Niddesa (PTS).
PED Pali English Dictionary (PTS).
Pat. Paṭisambhidāmagga (PTS).
Pat. Com. Paṭisambhidāmagga Commentary (PTS).
Pet. Petavatthu (PTS).
Pet. Com. Petavatthu Commentary (PTS).
PB Psalms of the Brethren, by Mrs. Rhys Davids (PTS).
PS Psalms of the Sisters, by Mrs. Rhys Davids (PTS).
Saṁ. Saṁyuttantkāya (PTS).
Saṁ. Com. Saṁyuttanikāya Commentary (SHB & PTS).
Sut. Suttanipāta (PTS).
Sut. Com. Suttanipāta Commentary (PTS).
Thera. Theragāthā (PTS).
Thera. Com. Theragthā Commentary, 2 vols. (SHB).
Theri. Therīgāthā (PTS).

Theri. Com. *Therigāthā Commentary* (PTS).
Ud. *Udāna* (PTS).
Ud. Com. *Udāna Commentary* (PTS).
Vibh. *Vibhaṅga* (PTS).
Vibh. Com. *Vibhaṅga Commentary* (PTS).
Vin. *Vinaya Piṭaka*, ed. Oldenberg, 5 vols. (Williams and Norgate).
Vin. Com. *Vinaya Pitaka Commentary*, (PTS).
Vim. *Vimānavatthu* (PTS).
Vim. Com. *Vimānavatthu Commentary* (PTS).
Vis. *Visuddhimagges* (PTS).

Contents

CHAPTER I

Cosmogony And Cosmology

The Pali Buddhist literature does not speak of any Creator-God. It lays more emphasis upon the attainment of *nibbāna*[1] than the knowledge of the origin of the universe. According to the Buddha the question on speculation about the world (*loka-cintā*)[2] is unprofitable[3] because it is not conducive to reaching the state of *nibbāna*. Though Pali literature does not generally speak of the creation theory, it deals with the never-ending cycles of destruction and renovation of the universe, produced by the endless cycles of fixed causes.[4]

The Universe

The Buddhists believe that the universe consists of innumerable *cakkāvāḷas* (world-systems or spheres)[5], scattered throughout the infinite space,[6] in groups of three, and touching each other and causing a dark region called *Lokantarika* hell in the triangular space of the three *cakkavāḷas*.[7] These *cakkavāḷas* are grouped in different kinds of *chiliocosms,* which, according to the *Aṅguttaranikāya*[8], are of the following three kinds:

(1) *Sahassī cūḷanikā lokadhātu*—a small group consisting of 1,000 *cakkavāḷas*;

(2) *Dvi-sahassī majjhimikā lokadhātu*—a middle one consisting of 1,000,000 *cakkavāḷas*; and

(3) *Tisahassī-mahāsahassī-lokadhātu*—a large one consisting of 1,000,000,000 *cakkavāḷas*.

The *Visuddhimagga*[9] states that there are three kinds of the Buddha's field—the field of his birth, the field of his authority and the field of his sphere. The field of his birth comprises the 10,000 world-systems which trembled at the time of the Tathāgata's conception. His authority domain comprises the great universe, i.e., 1,000,000,000 *cakkavāḷas*, while the field of his sphere is infinite and boundless.

Each *Cakkavāḷa* is made of 5 great elements,[10] namely, the earth, water, air, fire and ether or space—the first four being the substance of all material things. The extent of it is 12,03,-450 *yojanas* in length and breadth. In the circumference of each *cakkavāḷa* (3,610,350 *yojanas*) lies the earth of 240,000 *yojanas* in thickness,[11] surrounded by a region of water of 4,80,-000 *yojanas* in volume; the water is surrounded by air, the thickness of which is 9,60,000 *yojanas*, and the air rests on space.[12] The Buddhist conception of the earth being supported by a world of air is, as Spence Hardy[13] thinks, more scientific than the Hindu one of the earth borne upon a tortoise.

Mountains, Seas and Islands

The centre[14] of each *cakkavāḷa* is occupied by Mount Sineru (also called Meru, Sumeru,[15] Hemameru[16] and Mahāmeru[17]). It is 1,68,000 *yojanas* in height,[18] half of which is submerged in the sea. Its length and breadth are 84,000 *yojanas* each. It is the king of mountains[19] and its chief characteristic is that it is unshakable,[20] though a time comes when it is destroyed.[21]

Mount Sineru is surrounded by seven circles of rocks namely, the Yugandhara, Īsadhara, Karavīka, Sudassana, Nemindhara, Vinataka and Assakaṇṇa (horse-ear), each being half the height of the preceding one, commencing from Sineru; thus the Yugandhara rock encircles Sineru and stands half the latter's height; the Īsadhara rock half the height of Yugandhara and so on. The seven rocks therefore stand in due succession encircling Sineru. The Yugandhara is submerged in the sea to a depth of 42,000 *yojanas* and rises above the surface to the same height; Īsadhara 21,000 *yojanas* beneath the surface of the sea, and as much above it; and in this order the others encircle Sineru by half their heights. These seven celestial ranges are beautified with many gems[22]. They are inhabited by the Regent Gods (Mahārājas), the Yakkhas, and deities.[23] The Buddha covered the distance of 6,800,000 *yojanas* in three strides, from the earth to the *Tāvatiṁsa Devaloka*, and reached there (*Tāvatiṁsa*), setting his right foot down on the top of the Yugandhara and his left one on Sineru.[24] This reminds us, as D.C. Sircar points out, of the three steps of the Ṛgvedic Viṣṇu.[25] The sun rises first on Yugandhara, and for this, an expression "like the morning sun over Yugandhara" is found in the *Petavatthu Commentary*.[26] The highest point of the universe is *Bhavagga*[27] and the lowest is *Avīci*.[28]

Between every two ranges there is a sea called *Sidantarasamudda* where the Nāgas live.[29] The *Mahājanaka Jātaka* mentions *Yugandhara sāgara* which seems to be a sea between the Yugandhara and the next mountain range.[30]

Texts,[31] however, mention other seas namely,

(1) Khuramāla. It is called 'diamond sea' because diamonds are found in this ocean. The fishes of this ocean have the form of men. They have sharp razor-like snouts.

(2) Aggimāla. It is full of gold and sends forth radiance like the sun at midday, like a blazing bonfire.

(3) Dadhimāla. It is so called because it gleams as white as milk or curd. In this sea an abundance of silver is found.

(4) Nīlavaṇṇakusamāla. It is full of precious emeralds and looks like an expansion of dark Kusa-grass, or a field of green and grassy corn. Its colour is blue.

(5) Nalamāla. It is full of coral, in colour like the bamboos and looks like an expanse of reeds or a grove of bamboos. According to the commentaries, the sea was red like the scorpion-reeds or crab-reeds.[32]

(6) Vaḷabhāmukha. The water in this sea is sucked away and rises on all sides in precipices leaving a great pit. It is fearful because it produces a terrific roar which seems as if it would burst the ear and break the heart.

Of the seas, the Dadhimāla reminds us of *Dadhisamudra* of the *Purāṇas*.[33] In spite of rain and heat the waters of the seas do not increase or diminish.[34]

The seas abound in six monster-fishes namely, Ānanda, Timanda, Ajjhohāra, Titimiti, Miṅgala and Timirapiṅgala. Of them, the first three are of five hundred *yojanas* in length, while the last three are thousand *yojanas* long. The fishes themselves appointed Ānanda as the king to rule over them all.[35] He lives on one side of the ocean and all the fishes come to him, morning and evening, to pay their respects.[36]

In each *cakkavāḷa*, between the seven rocky circles and the *cakkavāḷasilā*, there are four great island continents, each of which is surrounded by 500 smaller islands.[37] They are Jambudīpa to the south, Aparagoyāna to the West, Pubbavideha to the east and Uttarakuru to the north of Mahāmeru.[38] The great earth consists of these four continents[39] and they are ruled by a Cakkavattī[40] whose chief queen comes either from Madda or Uttarakuru;[41] in the latter case, however, her good fortune urges her to appear before him of her own accord.[42] It is needless to say that this Buddhist conception is similar to the Purāṇic conception of the four-continent earth (*caturdvīpā vasumatī*).[43] In Jambudīpa, the Himavā[44] mountain is 500 *yojanas* in height and crowned with eighty-four thousand peaks. Its length and breadth are three thousand *yojanas*.[45]

Jambudīpa

In extent, Jambudīpa is 10,000 *yojanas*, of which 4,000 *yojanas* are covered by the ocean and 3,000 *yojanas* each are occupied by the Himalayan mountain and human habitation.[46] The Cittakūṭa is a part of the Himalayan mountain and is supposed to provide one with the entrance or gateway to the *Tāvatiṁsa-devaloka*,[47] which is surrounded by statues of Indra. It is said that the great island continent Jambudīpa derives its name from the mythical Jambu (or Nāga) tree, which is of extraordinary size.[48] Jambudīpa is also called Jambusaṇḍa.[49]

It is prophesied that Jambudīpa will be pervaded by mankind, even as a jungle of reeds and bushes, when Metteyya Buddha will appear on earth. On account of this, it is said, there will be 84,000 cities with Ketumatī (Banaras) at the head,[50] though this number is variously given as 60,000, 40,000 or even 20,000.[51]

Four interesting sounds are associated with four important events happening in Jambudīpa. They represent the shout uttered by Puṇṇaka, proclaiming his victory over Dhananjaya Koravya in a game of dice; the bark of Vissakamma in the guise of a dog threatening to devour all wicked beings, after the decay of Kassapa's *sāsana*;[52] the roar of Kusa challenging to battle the seven kings who sought the hand of Pabhāvatī;[53] and the yell of Āḷavaka[54] proclaiming his name from the top of Kelāsa.[55]

Jambudīpa, the southernmost of the four great continents, includes India[56] where the *Buddhas* and the *Cakkavattīs* are born.[57]

The Buddha declared that the people of this continent excelled those of both Uttarakuru and Tāvatiṁsa in three respects namely courage, mindfulness and righteousness.[58]

Uttarakuru

The island continent Uttarakuru is 8,000 *yojanas* in extent[59] and ruled by Kuvera, also known as Vessavaṇa.[60] There is in it a lake named Dharaṇī and a hall called Bhagalavatī where the Yakkhas, the inhabitants of Uttarakuru, hold their assemblies.[61]

Those who live in Uttarakuru are regarded as bhūmisayā since they have to sleep on earth. The cities of this continent, which are built in the air, include Āṭānāṭā, Kusināṭā, Nāṭapuriyā, Parakusināṭā, Kapīvanta, Janogha, Navanavatiya, Ambara-Ambaravatiya and Āḷakanandā, the last being the royal residence of Kuvera.[63] The men who live in Uttarakuru have no wives or property, and do not have to work for their living. There the corn ripens by itself and sweet-scented rice is boiled on hot oven-stoves.[64] Food never runs short in Uttarakuru.[65] Satulakāyī,[66] a woman of Uttarakuru, brought along with her a pint-pot of rice and three crystal firestones when she was brought by the gods as a wife to Jotika, the treasurer of Rājagaha who later became an *arahant*. The rice-pot was inexhaustible; wherever they wished to eat, they would put rice in the boiler and set it over the crystals. The stoves would immediately become alight and the rice was cooked; the same thing happened with curries.[67] The clothes the inhabitants wore resembled divine robes.[68] The inhabitants move about riding on cows, on men and women, on maids and youths. Their king rides on elephant, horse, in celestial cars and in state palanquins.[69]

Trees in Uttarakuru have the peculiar characteristic of bearing perpetual fruit and foliage,[70] and there is in this continent a *Kapparukkha* which lasts for a whole *kappa*.[71]

The people of Uttarakuru surpass the gods of Tāvatiṁsa and the men of Jambudīpa in three qualities,[72] viz., (1) they have no selfishness (*amamā*),[73] (2) they have no greed (*apariggahā*),[74] and (3) they have a definite term of life (niyatāyukā).

Pubbavideha and Aparagoyāna

Pubbavideha is seven thousand *yajonas* in extent[75] and its chief tree is the acacia (*śirīsa*).[76]

Aparagoyāna is seven thousand *yojanas* in extent.[77] It is inhabited by men;[78] but they have to sleep on the ground,[79] because they have no house. In the centre of the continent is a *Kadamba* tree which lasts for a whole *kappa*.[80] Its trunk is fifteen *yojanas* in girth, while its trunk and arms taken together are of fifty *yojanas* in length.

Sun, Moon, Stars and Planets

In each *Cakkavāḷa*, there is a sun,[81] a moon,[82] and a multitude of stars.[83] They move in their orbits around Mount Sineru causing the divisions of time into days, nights, months, years, etc.[84] The sun can illuminate only one *cakkavāḷa*, whereas all the *cakkavāḷas* are illuminated by the rays of light from the Buddha's body.[85] The commentary on the *Aggañña Sutta*[86] describes the habitation and movement of the sun and the moon. The sun lives within the palace of gold, the outside of which is covered with crystal, both being hot and standing one *yojana* above the abode of the moon. In size, the sun is 50 *yojanas* in diameter and 150 *yojanas* in circumference.[87] A distance of 100 *yojanas* lies between the lowest part of the moon and the highest part of the sun. The morning, midday, evening and midnight are not observed in the four different continents at the same time. When the sun rises in Jambudīpa, it is midday in Pubbavideha, evening in

Uttarakuru, and midnight in Aparagoyāna. When it is rising in Pubbavideha, it is midday in Uttarakuru, evening in Aparagoyāna and midnight in Jambudīpa. When it is rising in Uttarakuru, it is midday in Aparagoyāna, evening in Jambudīpa, and midnight in Pubbavideha. When it is rising in Aparagoyāna, it is midday in Jambudīpa, evening in Pubbavideha, and midnight in Uttarakuru.

The moon lives in a palace of gem, the outside of which is covered with silver, both being cold. In size, the moon is 49 *yojanas* in diameter, and 147 *yojanas* in circumference.[88] The moon travels slowly when her course is straight; when it is cross-wise, she moves swiftly; the planets move on her two sides and they do not change their position. The moon travels towards them as a cow to her calf. The movement of the sun is opposite to that of the moon. He moves rapidly when he is in a straight line and slowly when he is cross-wise.

On the day after the new moon, when the moon appears like a line, the sun is in the distance of 100,000 *yojanas* from the moon; on the second day 100,000 *yojanas* more, thus increasing gradually till the full-moon day when the distance between the sun and the moon increases at the rate of 100,000 *yojanas* per day. At the same rate daily, the sun moves closer to the moon till the day of the new moon (*uposatha*), when she becomes totally invisible, being covered by the sun, i.e., the moon being below and the sun above, as the covering of a small vessel by a larger one.

There are three paths along which the sun and the moon travel, viz., the goat-path, the bull-path and the elephant-path. When the sun and the moon are in the goat-path, there is no rain because the goats hate water; when they are in the elephant-path, the rain pours down as if the heavens were opened, because the elephants love water; when they rise up to the bull-path, both rain and heat are moderate.

During six months of the year (from July to December) the sun and the moon travel from Mahāmeru towards the *cakkavāḷa* rocks; and during the other six months (from January to June) from the *cakkavāḷa* rocks towards Mahāmeru.

Although the rays of the sun are always powerful and burn fiercely, they appear at some seasons to be specially fierce, and at others, mild. The derangement arises on account of the following four causes: (1) clouds acting like a screen; (2) fog arising out of the ground; (3) clouds of smoke; and (4) the asura Rāhu.[89]

The heat of the sun is more clear in winter than in summer. This anomally is thus accounted for: In summer, the dust is blown up into clouds, and pollens agitated by the winds rise up into the sky, and clouds multiply in the heavens, and gales blow with exceeding force. All these shut off the rays of the sun. In this way, by the dust, clouds, and wind, the sun's activity is interfered, and his rays diminish. In the cold season, the face of the earth is calm, the rains above are in reserve, the dust is quiet, the pollens wander gently through the air, the sky is free from clouds, and breezes blow gently. Thus, in winter, the sun's rays face no obstruction.[90]

The *nakkhattas* (stars or lunar mansions) are called heavenly bodies of the night. The *Abhidhānappadīpikā*[91] enumerates the 27 lunar mansions or constellations, their names being practically the same in both Sanskrit and Pali. The twenty-seven *nakkhattas* are: (*1*) *Assayujo*, (*2*) *Bharaṇī*, (*3*) *Kattikā*, (*4*) *Rohiṇī*, (*5*) *Magasiraṁ*, (*6*) *Addā*, (*7*) *Punabbasu*, (*8*) *Phusso*, (*9*) *Asilesā*, (*10*) *Maghā*, (*11*) *Pubbaphaggunī*, (*12*) *Uttaraphaggunī*, (*13*) *Hattho*, (*14*) *Cittā*, (*15*) *Sāti*, (*16*) *Visākhā*, (*17*) *Anurādhā*, (*18*) *Jeṭṭhā*, (*19*) *Mūlā*, (*20*) *Pubbāsāḷho*, (*21*) *Uttarāsāḷho*, (*22*) *Savaṇo*, (*23*) *Dhaniṭṭhā*, (*24*) *Satabhisaja*, (*25*) *Pubbabhaddapadā*, (*26*) *Uttarabhaddapadā*, and (*27*) *Revatī*. It is interesting to note that the *Mahāniddesa*[92] speaks of 28 *nakkhattas* (stars) instead of 27, but does not give us their names.

People would perform different types of work after consulting the *nakkhattas*.[93] Those who were conversant with the ways of the *nakkhattas* were known as *Nakkhattapāṭhakās*[94] or astrologers. They would look at the stars for ascertaining a person's destiny.[95] Some conjunctions between the moon and the lunar mansions (*nakkhattayoga*) were considered to be lucky, while others were deemed unlucky.[96] The *nakkhattapiḷana* or the occultation of a person's star implies his death.[97] Curiously enough, there were also people who were averse to the activities of the astrologers. Thus, the *Nakkhatta Jātaka* (No. 49)[98] says that trouble arises due to the foolish habit of consulting stars. The *Dīghanikāya*[99] also asserts that astrology is a base science and a false means of livelihood. The *Suttanipāta*,[100] accordingly, forbids a monk to devote himself to the study of *nakkhattas*.

Some of the *nakkhattas*, e.g., *Āsāḷhā*,[101] *Uttarāsāḷho*,[102] *Kattikā* and *Rohiṇī*,[103] are more familiar and important than others, and are frequently mentioned in Pali literature. On the full moon day of Āsāḷhā an assembly of the gods was held in the *Tāvatiṁsa devaloka*.[104]

The star *Osadhi*, otherwise called 'Morning Star', is mentioned in the literature, though it is not included in the above list of *nakkhattas*. This star is white,[105] bright and pure[106] in character. Its name *Osadhi* is due to the fact that people collect medicines and take them, when it appears in the sky.[107] The *Itivuttaka Commentary*[108] explains that it issues bright rays of light and imparts efficacy to various medicines. It maintains constancy. In all seasons, it keeps to the same path and never deviates therefrom.[109]

According to the Buddhists there are nine planets, viz., (1) Ravi (the sun), (2) Sukra (Venus), (3) Kuja (Mars), (4) Rāhu, *asura*, (5) Sani (Saturn), (6) Candra (the moon), (7) Budha (Mercury), (8) Guru (Jupiter) and (9) Ketu (the *asura*)[110]

The *Biḷārikosiya Jātaka*[111] describes the heavenly bodies as gods who are associated with Sakka in the Tāvatiṁsa heaven, but are lower in position. The moon, the sun, and the constellations are believed to be present when the *Mahāsamaya Sutta*[112] is preached. At times the *asura* Rāhu would seize the moon-God and the Sun-God, but the Buddha would be moved by their prayer and command the *asura* to free them from his clutches.

The word *nakkhatta*, which means 'a star', seems in some cases to refer to a planet as well.[113]

In each *cakkavāḷa* there are thirtyone abodes of living beings which are scattered below, upon and above Mount Sineru. They are situated one above the other according to the merits and demerits of their inhabitants, commencing from hell (the lowest place), and are divided into four groups: (1) abodes of unfortunate sense-experience, (2) abodes of fortunate sense-experience, (3) *Rūpaloka* and (4) *Arūpaloka.* Each of these four groups has again various sub-divisions. The first group has a four-fold division, viz., (1) purgatory, (2) animal kingdom, (3) Petaloka and (4) Asura-loka.[114] The second group has seven divisions which consist of one realm for human beings and six for gods (*devalokas*).[115] Since the first two groups of abodes pertain to sense-experience, they are often considered 'one' and referred to as *Kāmaloka*, and the number of its sub-divisions is eleven (4+7). Consequently, it is said that the whole abodes of living beings generally belong to three groups: (1) *Kāmaloka* (world of sense-experience), (2) *Rūpaloka* (material world) and (3) *Arūpaloka* (immaterial world).

The last two groups of abodes are devoid of sense-desires. The *Rūpaloka* consists of sixteen celestial abodes which are divided into four classes:

Abodes of the first *jhāna* to which belong the first three heavens, namely, (1) the heaven of Brahmā's retinue (*Brahmapārisajja*), (2) that of Brahmā's ministers (*Brahmapurohita*), (3) that of the great Brahmās (Mahābrahmā).

Abodes of the second *jhāna* to which belong the next three heavens, namely, (4) the heaven of minor lustre (Parittābha), (5) that of infinite lustre (*Appamāṇābha*), (6) that of radiant gods (*Ābhassara*).

Abodes of the third *jhāna* to which belong another three heavens, namely, (7) heaven of minor beauty (*Parittasubha*), (8) that of immeaurable beauty (*Appamāṇasubha*), (9) that of complete beauty (*Subhakiṇha*).

Abodes of the fourth *jhāna* to which belong the following seven heavens, namely, (10) heaven of the gods of great reward (*Vehapphala*), (11) that of the unconscious beings *Asaññasatta*), (12) that of the immobile beings (*Avihā*), (13) that of the serene beings (*Atappā*), (14) that of the beautiful beings (*Sudassā*), (15) that of the clearsighted (*Sudassī*), (16) that of the supreme beings (*Akaniṭṭha*). Of these heavens, 12 to 16 are called pure abodes (*Suddhāvāsa*).

The *Arūpaloka* consists of the following four spheres (heavens) which are of different grades: (1) the sphere of the conception of infinite space (*Ākāsānañcāyatanaṁ*); (2) the sphere of the conception of infinite consciousness (*Viññāṇañcāyatanaṁ*); (3) the sphere of the conception of nothingness (*Ākiñcaññāyatanaṁ*); and (4) the sphere of the conception of neither consciousness nor unconsciousness (*Nevasaññānāsaññāyatanaṁ*).[116]

Since, according to Buddhist doctrine, an individual's upliftment or downfall depends on his *Kamma* (activity), the lowest being may, by progressing in virtuous deeds, rise to the highest rank, while the most elevated persons can suffer a downfall with the exception of the Buddhas, Pacceka Buddhas and Arahants, who are destined to get *nibbāna*—the final goal of the Buddhists. However, the beings are classified in the following order: (1) the Supreme Buddhas, (2) the Pacceka Buddhas, (3) the Arahants, (4) the Brahmās, (5) the Devas, (6) the Gandhabbas (celestial musicians), (7) the Garuḍas (winged beings flying through the sky like lightning), (8) the Nāgas (snake-like beings resembling clouds), (9) the Yakkhas, (10) the Kumbhaṇḍas (goblins), (11) the Asuras (demons), (12) the Rakkhasas (monsters), (13) the Petas (ghosts), and (14) the inhabitants of hell.

Cycles of Dissolution and Evolution

The *Visuddhimagga*[117] says that the universe undergoes many cycles of dissolution and evolution.

The cycle of dissolution is the descending cycle and that of evolution is the ascending one. Dissolution may be effected by three elements, namely, fire, water and air. When fire effects dissolution, the worlds below the Ābhassara heaven are all burnt down. When destruction is wrought by water, the places below Subhakiṇha are dissolved. Similarly, when air is the cause of destruction, worlds below Vehapphala are blown to pieces.

When the world is destroyed by fire, a great world-destroying rain-cloud appears and causes heavy rain. But, after sometime no more rain falls and the rain-cloud entirely disappears, and there are no rains for many years. As a result, the water dries up and the inhabitants, including the denizens of hell, being unable to live, are reborn in the Ābhassara Brahma-world.[118] 'There they are made as if of mind, feeding on joy, self-radiant, faring through the sky, in splendour abiding, for a long, long time they stand fast.'[119]

After a long period, a second sun appears in the sky; and with its appearance the break up of time into night and day ceases, and day alone manifests itself. The world receives the sun's heat uninterruptedly, for with the setting of one sun another rises. The world-destroying sun (*Kappavināsakasuriya*) causes small streams to dry up,[120] and renders the sky free from vapour and cloud, and makes it spotless like the disc of a mirror, unlike when the natural sun rises filling up the space with clouds and crests of vapour.

In course of time the third sun appears and burns up the great rivers.[121] Similarly with the appearance of the fourth sun the seven great lakes, Sīhapātana, Haṁsapātana, Kaṇṇa-muṇḍaka, Rathakāra, Anotaṭṭa, Chaddanta, and Kuṇāla—being the sources of the great Himalayan rivers—are dried up.[122] The fifth sun vapourises the water of the great ocean,[123] and the sixth[124] and seventh[125] suns render the whole world-system a mass of vapour without even leaving the ashes. As a result, the space from the *Avīcimahāniraya* (Great Hell) to the place below the *Ābhassara Brahmaloka* form a mass of darkness.

When the world is destroyed by water, the great world-destroying rain pours down alkaline (*Khārodaka*) water and causes total destruction. It starts with small drops which gradually turn to great torrents, filling the hundred thousand myriad world-systems (*Koṭisatasahassa cakkavāḷa*). The utter acridness of the rain not only dissolves the earth but also all things connected with it. The water rises from the earth to the second Jhāna-plane and dissolves the places below the Subhakiṇha abode. The rising water affects all material substances and stops only after the destruction of their smallest particle. Ultimately, places below the Subhakiṇha abode is engulfed in a mass of darkness.

In the process of destruction by wind, it first rises fine dust, then thick dust, refined sand, thick sand, gravel, rocks, and so on until it raises rocks of the size of a storied building, and big trees. Without letting them fall the wind finally grinds them and reduces them to fine powder so that they lose their existence. Then, gradually, the wind rises from underneath the earth, turns it upside down and throws it into space, as a result of which the earth, broken into one to five hundred *yojanas* in size, is finally reduced by the impact to fine powder and entirely disappears. The wind then lifts mountains including Sineru and hurls them into space, and, as a result, they strike one another and destroy themselves. This way, the wind destroys earthly and airy mansions and the six deva-worlds in the realm of sense. Then it dashes one world-system against another, the Himālaya against other Himālayas, and Sineru against other Sinerus, so that they are all reduced to fine powder and destroyed. The wind reaches the third Jhāna plane and destroys the places below the Vehapphala abode. In this way, the great wind, after destroying the hundred thousand myriad world-systems, itself perishes, and the lower sky together with the upper one forms a single mass of darkness.

Long after its destruction[126] by fire the world-system begins to re-evolve[127] with the power of the united merit of all orders of existing beings.[128] A great rain-cloud appears and pours down water which fills up all the burnt places of the hundred thousand myriad world-systems. Then wind rises from below and across the water, and holds it in a mass, rounding it like a water-drop on a lotus leaf. The water, collected together and held in a mass by the wind, in receding, begins to descend. When the water gradually descends, the lower Brahma-worlds and Deva-worlds are formed in the place of those destroyed. In descending to the former site of the earth, the water is caught by strong winds, like water kept in a water-bag whose mouth is closed. The sweet water in receding gives rise to a tasty earth above, which looks like a film on undiluted rice-porridge, being endowed with colour, flavour and taste. Then beings who were born in the Ābhassara Brahma-world during destruction pass away thence, either on account of the inferiority of their merit or because their period of residence in that *loka* is complete, and appear on the earth.[129] As these beings are self-illuminated, they can traverse the firmament. But their self-illumination disappears when they lick the tasty earth and, overcome by craving, try to eat in mouthfuls. As a result they fall into darkness and become frightened. But they become glad and delighted when the sun appears. As the sun (fifty *yojanas* in size), after shining during day, sets, the moon (forty-nine *yojanas* in size) appears for removing the darkness at night. After the appearance of the sun and moon, the stars and constellations come into sight. From that time day and night appear, and gradually the month, the half-month, the seasons, and the year also appear. On the full-moon day of the month of phagguna, Sineru, the world-system, and the Himālaya mountain appear simultaneously. When millet is cooked, a number of bubbles are formed on the surface of the water, and some parts of that surface are elevated, while others are low and level; in like manner, at the formation of the world-system, the elevated places are mountains, the low places are oceans and the level places islands.

Those who have eaten the tasty earth are beautiful; they despise the ugly ones who have not eaten it. Due to this, the tasty earth disappears, and an earthly outgrowth appears. For the same reason, that also disappears, and a creeper called *bodālatā* appears. Again for the same reason, that too disappears. Then there appears paddy cooked without the aid of fuel, free from the coating of red powder, yielding huskless, pure, sweet-smelling rice. Then vessels appear and when the people rut the paddy in these vessels and place them on rocks, a flame of fire, rising of its own accord, cooks it. When they eat that food they develop urine and excrement. In order to let them go out, holes like the mouths of wounds open up on their bodies. Then masculinity and femininity appear; in the female appear the distinctive features of the female and in the male those of the male. Now man and woman begin to gaze at each other, and lust arises. Following their sensual instincts they practise evil and, to conceal their sin, they make houses wherein they dwell. At one stage of the process, following the practice of an unknown lazy man, they hoard up their grains. Then setting up of boundaries, acquisition of private property, crime and imorality, law and state appear. The people choose a man from among themselves to be their king who would maintain law and order in the State. For expenses, the king is given a share of grains and he becomes *khettānaṁ patī* (lord of the fields) and is called Khattiya. Thus the class of Khattiya arises and in due course the other castes, namely Brāhmaṇa, Vessa, Sudda are also formed.

When the world is renovated after its destruction by fire, water and wind, the process of evolution is the same in each case except for this little difference: when the world appears after its destruction by fire the beings from the Ābhassara Brahma-world pass away (as mentioned above) and are reborn in the lower Brahma-lokas and other places; in the case of its destruction by water creation begins with the Ābhassara Brahma-world and the beings come from the Subhakiṇha abode to be reborn in the Ābhassara and other places; and when renovated after its destruction by wind, creation begins with the Subhakiṇha Brahma-world, and the beings passing away from the Vehapphala abode are reborn in the Subhakiṇha and other places.

The world is destroyed seven times by fire and the eighth time by water. In this procedure it is destroyed seven times by water, and seven times again by fire. 'By so much are passed sixty-three cycles. Within this limit, although the turn to perish by water is arrived, it is inhibited, and the wind which takes its turn destroys the world, crushing the Subhakiṇha whose term of life is full sixty-four cycles.'[130]

In each case, i.e., when the world is under destruction by fire, water, and wind, there is a great cycle made of four aeons.[131] The first aeon, from the great world-destroying rain to the cessation of the flames, is called dissolution (*saṁvaṭṭo*). The second, from the cessation of the world-destroying flames to the great rain flooding up the world-system (*koṭisatasahassa cakkavāḷaparipūraka*) is called the process of dissolution (*saṁvaṭṭaṭṭhāyī*). The third aeon, from the great world-flooding rain to the appearance of the sun and the moon, is called evolution (*vivaṭṭo*). The fourth, from the appearance of the sun and the moon to the great world-destroying rain, is called the process of evolution (*vivaṭṭaṭṭhāyī*).

Notes

Chapter I

1. *Nibbāna*—Cessation of existence. It is all bliss. There is no intermingling of pain in it (*Mil.*, pp. 313-15; *SBE*, Vol. XXXVI, pp. 182-85).
2. 'Who made the moon and sun, who made the earth, the ocean, beings, mountains, mangoes, coconuts, etc.?' (*KS*, Vol. V, p. 377, note 2).
3. *Saṁ.*, Vol. V, p. 447; *KS*, Vol. V, p. 378.
4. See below, pp. 11 ff.
5. Cf. *anantāni cakkavālāni, anantā lokadhātuyo* (*Vis.*, Vol. I, p. 207; *Vin. Com.*, Vol. I, p. 120; *Sut. Com.*, Vol. II, p. 443.
6. *Maj.*, Vol. III, p. 103; *Aṅg.*, Vol. I, p. 267; *LTB*, p. 80.
7. *Vin. Com.*, loc. cit.; *Sut. Com., loc. cit.; Vis.* loc. cit; *KS*, Vol. V, p. 382 (*Lokantarikā aghā*); cf. *LTB*, loc. cit.
8. Vol. I, p. 228; *GS*, Vol. I, p. 207. It is not consistent with the arrangement of the Lokantarika hell because if the great universe of 1,000 *cakkavālas* appears grouped in triads, the number of Lokantarika hells would be 333 and one *cakkavāḷa* would remain excluded. Cf. McGovern, op. cit., p. 48.
9. Vol. II, p. 414.
10. *Aṅg.*, Vol. I, p. 176; *JPTS*, 1884, p. 27; see map of the *Cakkavāḷa* in D.J. Gogerly, *Ceylon Buddhism*, Vol. II.
11. *Jāt.*, Vol. III, p. 42; *MB*, p. 3.
12. *Vin. Com.*, Vol. I, p. 119; *Sut. Com.*, Vol. II, p. 442; *Vis.*, Vol. I, pp. 205-06; *Dhs. Com.*, pp. 297-98; see also *Dīg.*, Vol. II, p. 107; *Aṅg.*, Vol. IV, p. 312; *Mil.*, p. 68 (*mahāpaṭhavī udake patiṭṭhitā, udakaṁ vāte patiṭṭhitaṁ, vāto ākāsaṭṭho hoti*); when the wind blows, the water shakes and as a result, the earth quakes (*yaṁ mahāvātā vāyanti... udakaṁ kampenti, udakaṁ Kampitaṁ, paṭhaviṁ Kampeti*). Cf. D.J. Gogerly, op. cit., pp. 19, 21; *ERE*, Vol. IV, p. 131; *LTB*, pp. 85-86; McGovern, op. cit., p. 49.
13. *MB*, p. 12, note.
14. *Aṅg.*, Vol. I, pp. 227; Vol. V, p. 59; *LTB*, p. 81.
15. E.g., CV. Ch. 42, Verse 2.
16. Ibid., Ch. 37, Verse 79.
17. *Maj.*, Vol. I, p. 338. It is also mentioned as Neru in the *Jāt.*, Vol. III, pp. 247-48.

18. *Sut. Com.*, Vol. II, p. 443; Vin. Com., Vol. I, p. 119; *Vis.*, Vol. I, p. 206., *Dhs. Com.*, p. 298; *Aṅg.*, Vol. IV, p. 100.
19 *Aṅg.*, Vol. IV, p. 100.
20. *Jāt.*, Vol. I, p. 229. ; *Dīg. Com.*, Vol. III, p. 864.
21. *Aṅg.*, Vol. IV, p. 103; *Vis.* Vol. II, p. 416.
22. *Vis.*, Vol. I, p. 206., *Dhs. Com.*, p. 298; *Vin. Com.*, Vol. I, p. 119; *Sut. Com.*, Vol. II, p. 443. Although the Yugandhara forms the first of the seven ranges around Sineru, it is mentioned as the fourth range in the *Jāt.*, Vol. VI, p. 125. Cf. *LTB.*, p. 89; D.J. Gogerly, op. cit., p. 20, note.
23. *Vis.*, loc. cit.; *Dhs. Com.*, loc. cit.; *Vin. Com.*, *loc. cit.*; *Sut. Com.*, *loc. cit.*
24. *Vis.*, p. 391; *Dham. Com.*, Vol. III, p. 216.
25. *Cosmography and Geography in Early Indian Literature*, p. 40.
26. See p. 137.
27. *Vibh.*, p, 426.
28. E.g., *Jāt.*, Vol. IV, p. 182; Vol. VI, p, 354; *Mil* , p. 336 (*SBE*, Vol. XXXVI, p. 221).
29. *Jāt.*, Vol. VI, p. 125. See *LTB*, pp. 84-85 where it is said that the water of the seas do not increase with rain or diminish due to heat.
30. E.g., *Jāt.*, Vol. I, p. 64; Vol. VI, p. 43; *MB*, p. 12.
31. *Jāt.*, Vol. IV, pp. 139-41; *MB*, p. 13; D.C. Sircar, op. cit., p. 51. See *LTB*, pp. 90-91.
32. E.B. Cowell, *Jāt.*, Vol. IV, p. 89, note 3.
33. D.C. Sircar, op. cit., p. 51.
34. *LTB*, pp. 84 f.
35. *Jāt.*, Vol. I, p. 207; Vol. II, p. 352; Vol. V, p. 462.
36. *Ibid.*, Vol. V, loc. cit.
37. *Vis.*, Vol. I, p. 207; *Vin. Com.* , Vol. I, pp. 119-20; *Sut-Com.*, Vol. II, p. 443 (*ettha mahādīpo pañcasata pañcasata parittadīpaparivāro)*.
38. Cf. *LTB*, p. 85; D.J. Gogerly, op. cit., p. 20.
39. *Dīg.*, Vol. II, p. 173; *Dīg. Com.*, Vol. II, p. 623.
40. There are three types of sovereign rulers namely, *Cakkavāla-cakkavattī* (ruler of a *cakkavāla*), *Dīpa-cakkavattī* (ruler of a *dvīpa* or island) and Padesa-Cakkavattī (ruler of the part of a dvīpa). See Childers, *PED*, s.v. *Cakkavātti.*
41. *Dīg. Com.*, Vol. II, p. 626.; *Khud. Com.*, p. 173.
42. Loc. cit.
43. D.C. Sircar, op. cit., p. 40.
44. Himavā, also called Himācala, Himavanta, etc., is identified with the Himālaya.
45. *Dhs. Com.*, p. 288; *Vis* , Vol. I, p. 206; *Vin. Com.*, Vol. I, p. 119; *Sut. Com.*, Vol. II, p. 443 (*yojanānaṁ satān ucco Himavā pañca pabbato yojanānaṁ sahassāni tīṇī āyāmavitthato caturāsīti sahassehi kūṭehi paṭimaṇḍito*).

46. *Vin. Com.*, Vol. I, p. 119; *Vis.*, Vol. I, p. 207; *Dīg. Com.*, Vol. II, p. 623; *Sut. Com.*, Vol. II, p. 443.
47. *Jāt.*, Vol. VI, pp. 125f.
48. *Vin.*, Vol. I, p. 30; *Sut. Com.*, Vol. II, p. 443; *Vis.*, Vol. I, p. 206; *Dhs. Com.*, p. 298; *The Expositor*, (*PTS*), Vol. II, p. 393; *Vin. Com.*, Vol. I, p. 119.
49. *Sut.*, verse 552; *Sut. Com.*, Vol. I, p. 121.
50. *Dīg.*, Vol. III, pp. 74f.
51. *Sut. Com.*, Vol. I, p. 59; *Pet. Com*, p. 111. *Jāt.*, Vol. IV, p. 84, says sixty-three thousand.
52. To scare the people into virtue, Sakka and Mātali came to the city where king Usīnara was ruling, in the guise of a forester and a dog respectively. Barking loudly, the dog devoured all those who worked in unrighteousness (*Mahākaṇha Jātaka*, No. 469; *Jāt.*, Vol. IV, p. 182).
53. See *Jāt.*, Vol. V, pp. 310-12, where it is mentioned that king Kusa was the *Bodhisatta* in his previous birth.
54. Āḷavaka was a tree-demon, who claimed sacrifice of one victim every day (E.B. Cowell, *Jāt.*, Vol. IV, p. 112, note 3).
55. *Sut. Com*, Vol. I, p. 223. See *Jāt.*, Vol. IV, p. 182, where only three sounds of the Buddha are mentioned—(1) the cry of king Puṇṇaka in the Puṇṇaka Birth, (2) the cry of Snake-king Sudassana in the Bhūridatta Birth (*Jāt.*, Vol. VI, p. 157), (3) the roar of Mātali as a dog in the Mahākaṇha Birth.
56. *GS.*, Vol. I, p. 207, note 1.
57. *Bud. Com.*, SHB, p. 48; *Maj. Com.*, Aluvihāra Series, Colombo, Vol. II, p. 913.
58. *Aṅg.*, Vol. IV, p. 396; KV., Vol. I, p. 99.
59. *Vin. Com.*, Vol. I, p. 119; *Vis.*, p. 207; *Sut. Com.*, Vol. II, p. 443; *Dīg. Com.*, Vol. II, p. 623.
60. *Dīg.*, Vol. III, p. 201.
61. Loc. cit.
62. *Thera. Com.*, *SHB*. Vol. II, pp. 187-88.
63. *Dīg.*, Vol. III, pp 200-01. Elsewhere Āḷakanandā is described as a city full of Gods (*Dīg.*, Vol. II, p. 170; *Mil.*, p. 2; *SBE*, Vol. XXXV, p. 31).
64. *Dīg.*, Vol. III, pp. 199-200.
65. *Vin.*, Vol. III, p. 7.
66. *Dham. Com.*, Vol. IV, pp. 209 ff.
67. Loc. cit.
68. See e.g., *Pet. Com.*, p. 76.
69. *Dīg.*, Vol. III, p. 200.
70. Ibid., p. 201.
71. *Aṅg. Com.*, *PTS*, Vol. II, pp 34f.; *Vis.*, Vol. I, p. 206; *Dhs. Com.*, p. 298.
72. *amamā apariggahā niyatāyukā visesabhūṇo* (*Aṅg.*, Vol. IV. p. 396; *GS.*, Vol. IV, p. 265. G.P. Malalasekera translates *Visesabhūṇo* as

'great elegance' and says that the men of Uttarakuru excel the Gods of Tāvatiṁsa in four qualities (*DPPN, SV*. Uttarakuru).

73. The people of Uttarakuru are *acchandikā* (*Vibh. Com.*, p. 461).
74. *Dīg.*, Vol. III, p. 201.
75. *Sut. Com.*, Vol. II, p. 443; *Vin. Com.*, Vol. I, p. 199; *Vis.*, Vol. I, p. 207.
76. *Vis.*, Vol. I, p. 206; *Dhs. Com.*, p. 298.
77. *Vin. Com.*, Vol. I, p. 119; *Vis.*, Vol. I, p. 207; *Sut. Com.*, Vol. II, p. 443.
78. *Khud. Com.*, p. 123.
79. *Thera. Com.*, Vol. II, pp. 187-88.
80. *Vis.*, Vol. I, p. 206; *Dhs. Com.*, p. 298.
81. *Aṅg.*, Vol. I, p. 227; Vol. V, p. 59. See *LTB*, pp. 87-89.
82. Loc. cit.
83. *MN*, Vol. II, p. 382.
84. McGovern, op. cit., p. 56.
85. *Saṁ.*, Vol. I, p. 47; *Maj.*, Vol. III, p. 120.
86. *Dīg. Com.*, Vol. III, pp. 866ff.
87. Cf. *Vis.*, Vol. I, p. 207; *Vin. Com.*, Vol. I, p. 119; *Sut. Com.*, Vol. II, p. 443.
88. Loc. cit.
89. *Mil.*, p. 273; *SBE*, Vol. XXXVI, pp. 111-12.
90. *Mil*, p. 274; *SBE*, Vol. XXXVI, pp. 112-13.
91. See Verses 56-59.
92. Vol. I, p. 382 (*aṭṭhavīsati nakkhattāni*).
93. Loc. cit.
94. Loc. cit.
95. *Dham. Com.*, Vol. I, pp. 166-67, 174; *Jāt.*, Vol. I, pp. 257ff.
96. Loc. cit.
97. *Dham. Com.*, Vol. I, pp. 166-67.
98. *Jāt.*, Vol. I, pp. 257 ff.
99. Vol. I, p. 10.
100. See Verse 927.
101. *Jāt.*, Vol. I, p. 50.
102. Ibid., pp. 63, 82.
103. *Sut. Com.*, Vol. II, pp. 456.
104. *Dīg.*, Vol. II, pp. 200 ff.
105. Cf. *Odātā*, *odātavaṇṇā*, etc., in *Dīg.*, Vol. II, p. 111; *Maj.*, Vol. II, p. 14.
106. *Dīg. Com.*, Vol. II, p. 451; cf. *Vis.*, Vol. II, p. 412; *Itv.*, p. 20.
107. *Maj. Com.*, Aluvihara Series, Colombo, Vol. II, p. 714.
108. *Itv.*, Vol. I, p. 90.
109. *Bud. Com.*, p. 110.
110. *Abhidhānappadīpikā*, Verse 60; *MB*, p. 24.
111. *Jāt.*, Vol. IV, pp. 63-65.
112. *Dīg.*, Vol. II, p. 259.
113. See *ERE*, Vol. XII, p. 72.

114. *Pet.*, p. 66; cf. *Aṅg.*, Vol. I, p. 37; Vol. V, pp. 269-70.
115. See below, Ch. II.
116. E.g., *Aṅg.*, Vol. I, p. 41; cf. Kern, *Manual of Indian Buddhism*, pp. 57-59.
117. See pp. 414-22; see also *Dīg.*, Vol. III, pp. 84-96; cf. *MB*, pp. 28-35.
118. Cf. *Aṅg.*, Vol. V, p. 60; *GS*, Vol. V, p. 41, note 4; *Dīg.*, Vol. III, p. 84.
119. *GS*, Vol. V, p. 41.
120. Cf. *Aṅg.*, Vol. IV, p. 100.
121. The great rivers are the Ganges, Yamuna, Aciravatī, Sarabhu and Mahī (ibid., p. 101).
122. Cf. loc. cit., where Mandākinī is mentioned for Haṁsapātana.
123. *Aṅg.*, Vol. IV, p. 101.
124. Cf. ibid., Vol. IV, p. 102; *Saṁ.*, Vol. III, p. 150.
125. Cf. *Aṅg.*, Vol. IV. p. 103.
126. *Vis.*, Vol. II, pp. 414-17, 420-21.
127. Loc. cit.; *Dīg.*, Vol. III, pp. 28-30, 84-95.
128. *MB*, pp. 34-35.
129. *Dīg.*, Vol. III. p. 30.
130. *Path of Purity*, Vol. II, p. 488; *evaṁ vinassanto pi ca nirantaram eva satta vāre agginā, vinassati Aṭṭhame vāre udakena, puna satta vāre agginā aṭṭhame vāre udakena ti evaṁ aṭṭhame aṭṭhame vāre vinassanto sattakkhattuṁ udakena vinassitvā puna sattavāre agginā nassati. Ettāvatā tesaṭṭhi kappā atītā honti. Etth'antare udakena nassanavāraṁ sampattam pi paṭibāhitvā laddhokāso vāto paripuṇṇacatusaṭṭhikappāyuke Subhakiṇhe viddhaṁsento lokaṁ vināseti* (*Vis.*, Vol. II, pp. 421-22).
131. It is not easy to count aeons. There are so many aeons, so many hundreds, so many thousands, so many hundred thousand aeons (*KS*, Vol. II, p. 123).

CHAPTER II

The Heaven

The Buddhist heaven, as mentioned in Pali literature, is divided into two worlds—(1) *Devaloka* (Heaven of the gods) or the world of enjoyment and (2) *Brahmaloka* (Heaven of the Brahmās) or the world in which the enjoyment is of a more intellectual character, verging on supreme tranquility, the state which is of neither consciousness nor unconsciousness.

The celestial worlds stand one above another like the storeys of a building, which one can reach only through progress in meritorious deeds. In fact, Pali texts prescribe various qualifications for a rebirth in heaven. Thus, the *Samaññaphalasutta* of the *Dighanikaya*[1] states that those who are righteous in body, speech and thought, are of right view and do right work are reborn in heaven after death. The *Aṅguttaranikāya*[2] adds that those who are believers[3], have morality, and are grateful, ardent, energetic, and strong in wisdom are able to reach heaven. The *Sekhavulavagga*[4] states that people who are blameless and have insight will attain heaven. According to the *Tikaṇḍakivagga*[5], those who abstain from destruction of life, theft, lust, falsehood and liquor can reach heaven. The *Caravagga*[6] states that one who does not transgress *dhamma* (righteousness) being led by desire, ill-will, delusion and fear is entitled to enjoy heaven. The *Sumanavagga*[7] states that those who are almsgivers[8] and liberal are eligible for a place in heaven. The *Akodhana*, *Anupanahi*, *Anissuki*, *Amaccharī*, *Anaticāri*, *Sīlavā*, *Bahussuto*, *Viriya*, and *Sati suttas* of the *Saṁyuttanikāya*[9] state that a woman who is faithful, modest, scrupulous, not wrathful, not grudging, not envious, not stingy, not adulteress, moral, having wide knowledge (*bahussuta*), energetic, not muddleheaded, and rich in wisdom is destined for heaven. The same *Nikāya*[10] informs us how people who hush their passions and follow 'the Aryan Truths are entitled to reach heaven. It also says[11] that one can go to heaven if one has unwavering loyalty to the Buddha, the Norm, the Order and the virtues dear to the Aryans. The *Sumaṅgala Jātaka*[12] says that a king who does not abandon the goddess Sirilakkhī and becomes free from anger and fear will reach heaven. The *Dhajavihetha Jātaka*[13] states that the persons who follow the precepts of a meritorious saint will see the path of heaven. According to the *Pañcagatidīpana*,[14] one would reach *Devaloka* by observing disciplinary rules and *Brahmaloka* by meditation.

The *Visuddhimagga*[15] says that the persons who perform meritorious deeds for the attainment of celestial bliss are sure to enjoy it in heaven. It also states that observers of the precepts formulated by the great teacher can enter into the celestial palaces.[16] Even a frog who attentively listened to the teachings of the Buddha was reborn in a golden mansion, twelve *yojanas* in size,[17] in the Tāvatiṁsa heaven and was named Mandukadevaputta having a company of apsarases. He appeard before the Buddha with his *vimāna* (mansion) and listened to a religious discourse.

The *Aṅguttaranikāya*[18] says that lay disciples who could thoroughly understand and grasp the teachings of the great Buddhist teacher Sunetta would be entitled to reach the Brahma-world; but those who failed to appreciate them fully would go to the six lower heavens.

Devaloka

The *Devaloka* is called *kāmaloka*, the world of desire,[19] and it is lower than the *Brahmaloka*. The exact number of the *Devalokas* is six, and they are from the lowest position to the highest—*Cātummahārājika*, *Tāvatiṁsa*, *Yāma*, *Tusita*, *Nimmānarati* and *Paranimmitavasavatti*.[20] According to the *Aṅguttaranikāya*,[21] those among the denizens of the six *Devalokas* who have acquired strong devotion in the *Buddha*, the *Dhamma* and the *Saṅgha* are not subject to hell and are destined to attain *sambodhi*.

CĀTUMMAHĀRĀJIKA. It is the lowest of the 6 *Devalokas* and stands half-way up Mount Sineru.[22] This world is so called because there live four great kings (*cattāro Mahārājāno*) who are the guardians of the four quarters, namely, Dhataraṭṭha of the East, Virulhaka of the South, Virūpakkha of the West and Vessavana or Kuvera of the North.[23] Their retinues are, respectively, Gandhabbas, Kumbhandas, Nāgas and Yakkhas. These kings are the protectors[24] of the Buddha from the moment of his conception in his mother's womb, and the *Āṭānāṭiyasutta* says that they protect not only the Buddha but also his followers.[25]

The assembly of the said gods is *Cātummahārājikaparisā*. The records of the happenings in this assembly are kept by the four kings.[26] In the bright half of the month these kings send to the human world their councillors on the 8th and their sons on the 14th, while they themselves come down on the 15th to discover whether many men pay reverence to mother and father, to recluses and Brāhmaṇas, and show deference to the elders of the clan, observe the sabbath, keep the vigil and do good deeds. Then the four great kings report the matter to the gods of the *Tāvatiṁsa*, who sit in the *Sudhammāsabhā* (Hall of Righteousness) and rejoice or lament at the news whether men cultivate righteousness or not.[27]

Having created the bases of meritorious action founded on gifts and virtue to a very high degree, the four kings surpass[23] other dwellers of their realms in term of divine beauty, life, happiness, pomp, power, shapes, sounds, perfumes, tastes and touch.

Apart from these four great kings and their followers, other denizens of the Cātummahārājika-world are the *Khiḍḍāpadosikā, Manopadosikā, Sītavalāhakā, Uṇhavalāhakā* and the devaputtas Candima and Suriya.[29]

The *Aṅguttaranikāya*[30] states that those who observe the *Uposatha* (sabbath) day in all its eight parts are reborn in this world. The *Pañcagatidīpana*[31] says how the persons who do not seek their own happiness and do not feel joy in taking possession of other's proprety will reach the Cātummahārājika-world. According to the *Majjhimanikāya*,[32] the bhikkhus who are pious, faithful, learned, charitable and wise are reborn in it. The Cātummahārājika *devas* live for 90,00,000 years[33] in human computation.

TĀVATIMSA. According to the *Saṁyuttanikāya Commentary*,[34] *Tāvatiṁsa* was named after Magha and his thirty-two companions who were reborn there as a result of their good deeds in Macalagāma.[35] The commentaries on the *Therīgāthā*[36] and *Vibhaṅga*[37] explain *Tāvatiṁsa* as the world of thirty-three. It is difficult to say if the number of the chief denizens of this world always remained thirty-three, though some passages, e.g., in the *Janavasabhasutta*,[33] lead us to suppose so. Some say that the idea of the Tavatimsa-devas is borrowed from the Vedic conception of 33 *devas* (12 Ādityas, 8 Vasus, 11 Rudras and 2 Asvins[39]). Often *tidasa* (thirty) is substituted for *tāvatiṁsa*.[40] Sometimes it is called *Tidiva*[41] which the *Pañcagatidīpana*[42] explains as devaloka, i.e., heaven for the gods.

The Tāvatiṁsa-world is situated at the top of the Mount Sineru.[43] It was originally the abode of the Asuras. But, when Magha[44] was born as Sakka and dwelt with his companions in Masakkasāra,[45] the capital city[46] of Tāvatimsa, as a ruler of it and of the Cātummahārājika, he, having disliked the idea of sharing his kingdom with the Asuras, made them intoxicated and hurled them down to the foot of the Sineru where the Asurabhavana soon developed. The existence of the Pāricchattaka tree in the Tāvatiṁsa and Cittapāṭali (pied trumpet-flower) tree[47] in Asurabhavana makes a difference between the two worlds.

To defend Tāvatiṁsa from a possible attack by the Asuras Sakka built five walls around it, which were guarded by the Nāgas, Supaṇṇas, Kumbhandas, Yakkhas and the Cātummahārājikadevas.[48] The Cittakūṭadvārakoṭṭhaka was the entrance to the Tāvatiṁsa around which statues of Indra (*Indapaṭimā*) stand.[49]

The Tāvatiṁsa is of ten thousand *yojanas* in extent.[50] It is adorned with the *Vejayanta* and other palaces, with parks—*Phārusaka, Cittalatā, Missaka* and *Nandana*, with the Nandā[51] and other lakes and filled everywhere with heavenly beings.[52] The *Pāricchattaka* tree[53] with its flower described as *koviḷāra*, the divine *kakkāru* flower,[54] the elephant king Erāvaṇa and the Assembly-hall Sudhammā are the chief features of the Tāvatiṁsa.[55]

Of the parks, mentioned above, the *Nandanavana* is regarded as the chief one because the denizens of the *Tāvatiṁsa-devaloka* headed by Indra go there for amusement.[56] It is so called because it delights the hearts of all who visit it.[57] It is said[58] that there is *Nandanavana* in each *deva*-world. The *devas* go there just before their death. The Bodhisatta went to the *Nandanavana* in the Tusita-world before his 'descent' into Mahāmāyā's womb.[59] There is a palace *Ekapuṇḍarīkavimāna*[60] in *Nandanvana.* Ascetics[61] possessed of great iddhi-power used to spend their siesta in the shadow of the grove. There is a lake named *Nandana*[62] variantly called *Nandāpokkharaṇī,*[63] *Nandanapokkharaṇī*[64] and *Nandanavanapokkharaṇī.*[65] The lake is five hundred *yojanas* in extent which came into being in the Nandanavana through the meritorious acts of Nandā, wife of Magha.[66] It is of great splendour, having one hundred bathing-places (*satatittham*) and one thousand inlets (*sahassavaṁkaṁ*), and covered with the five kinds of lotus (*pañcavaṇṇapaduma*[67]).

Magha planted a *Koviḷāra*-tree outside the Sudhammā-sālā.[68] As a result, the Pāricchattaka tree grew in the Nandanavana. According to the commentaries, this tree is described as *Koviḷāra.*[69] Its circumference is one hundred *yojanas* and a *Paṇḍukambalasilāsana* is found at its foot.[70] It lasts throughout a *kappa.*[71]

The Pāricchattaka-koviḷāra flower is described as Pārijāta.[72] When the celestial tree (Pāricchattaka) of the *Tāvatiṁsa-devaloka* is in full bloom, its effulgence pervades full fifty *yojanas* and the perfume travels one hundred *yojanas.* The flowers shine like the morning sun. The flowers and leaves are fully open after passing through different stages of development, each stage being watched eagerly by the *devas* and marked by rejoicing. They are not plucked. The wind sweeps away the faded flowers and scatters fresh ones on the seats of Sakka and other gods of the Tāvatiṁsa in the Sudhammā hall. Their bodies are covered with sweetly scented pollen of lotuses. Thus, the *Tāvatiṁsa devas* sport for four divine months at the foot of the celestial tree, indulging in the five pleasures of the senses.[73]

The park *Cittalatāvana* is five hundred *yojanas* in extent. It arose in the Tāvatiṁsa as a result of good deeds performed by Magha's wife, Cittā.[74] It is so called[75] because of its association with Cittā as well as for various creepers that grew in it bearing flowers of different colour. In this pleasure-garden a creeper named *Āsāvatī*[76] grows. In its fruit a divine drink is produced. Those who drink it once are intoxicated for four months. It bears fruit only once in a thousand years, and the sons of the gods patiently wait for that period for a drink of the fruit.

According to the custom, all the Buddhas spend the *vassas* (rainy seasons) in the *Tāvatiṁsa* following the performance of *Yamakapāṭihāriya* (twin-miracle).[77] Gotama, the Buddha, was born there and preached the Abhidhamma to his mother. He covered in three strides the distance of sixty-eight hundred thousand *yojanas* from the earth to the Tāvatiṁsa placing his right foot down on the top of the Yugandhara and his left on Sineru.[78] In the 7th year after his enlightenment,[79] the Buddha sat on Sakka's throne, the *Paṇḍukambalasilāsana*, at the foot of the Pāricchattaka tree, preached to the *devas* for three months.[80] The ascetics possessing of iddhi-power spent the afternoon in the *Tāvatiṁsa*.[81]

The palace *Vejayanta* is so called because it was built by Sakka in the Tāvatiṁsa just in the hour of his victory over the Asuras.[82] According to Buddhaghoṣa, it arose on the virtue of Sakka who built a rest-house, in his previous birth as Magha, for the use of the multitude.[83] It is one thousand *yojanas* high and is adorned with banners, each of which is 3 hundred *yojanas* long. The banners made of jewels are placed on golden staffs. On the coral staffs stand the banners made of pearl. The next banners are made of seven kinds of gems and placed on the staffs made of the same gems. The whole palace is decorated with the seven precious substances. It has one hundred towers each seven storeys high, with seven nymphs in each storey, waited on by seven attendants. It was shown to Moggallāna who with his big toe made the palace quake and rock.[84] In this palace Sakka dwelt.[85] His crimson-footed (*kakuṭapādiniyo*) nymphs came forward to greet the Buddha who visited the Tāvatiṁsa with Nandā. The nymphs had given oil for massaging

Kassapa Buddha's feet.[86] When king Sādhīna of Mithilā went to the Tāvatiṁsa, he lived in *the Vejayantapāsāda* for seven hundred years according to human computation.[87] This palace is depicted on the Bhārhut Stūpa.[88]

The *Janavasabhasutta*[89] describes an assembly of the Tavatiṁsa gods, which was held in the Sudhammā Hall.[90] It is a jewelled mansion and looks like a sky of autumn. It is nine hundred *yojanas* in extent,[91] and supported by finely wrought columns and is eight-sided.[92] It arose in the Tāvatiṁsa as a result of meritorious deeds done by Sudhammā, the wife of Magha, and was so called according to her name.[93] The *Dīghanikāya Commentary*[94] states that in the middle of the assembly there is a jewelled throne (seat) for the Enlightened one, canopied by a three-yojana long white umbrella, after which follow the seats of Sakka and other gods. In the assembly of the gods of the Tāvatiṁsa, the Cātummahārājika gods were present and acted as guards. Sometimes, denizens of other deva- and brahma-worlds were present as guests, e.g., Brahmā Sanaṅkumāra who came in the disguise of Pañcasikha. In this assembly the *devas* held their meetings on the eighth day of each month, or when the Dhamma was preached, and also on their important festivals and gatherings. All the Buddhas preach the *Abhidhamma* in the Sudhammā hall.[95] It is said that every *devaloka* has a *Sudhmmā-sabhā*.[96]

According to the *Janavasabha sutta*, all the denizens of the *Tāvatiṁsa-devaloka* seem to have been devotees of the Buddha and followed his teachings.[97] They deposited their offerings in the Cūlāmaṇi-cetiya, where Sakka laid the hair of prince Siddhattha, cut off by him when he renounced the world and put it on the garments of a recluse on the banks of the Narañjarā.[98] Sakka also deposited here the eye-tooth of the Buddha which Doṇa hid in his turban, hoping to keep it for himself.[99]

The gods of the *Tāvatiṁsa-devaloka* took part in human festivities on earth.[100] Thus Sakka, Vissakamma and Mātali visited the earth on various occasions.[101] The goddesses from the Tāvatiṁsa also came to bathe in the Anotaṭṭa and spent time on the Manosilātala.[102] In this connection, it may be noted that there were evidently no goddesses among the Thirty three *devas*. Both Māyā and Gopikā[103] became *devaputtas* at their birth in the Tāvatiṁsa. It seems that the women worked there as the attendants of the gods[104] as each *deva* had numerous attendants. As mentioned above, the dove-footed (*kakuṭapādiniyo*) nymphs (*accharā*) of the Tāvatiṁsa are famous in the Pali literature for their beauty.[105]

According to human computation, the life-term of a denizen of the *Tāvatiṁsa-devaloka* is 3,60,00,000 years.[106] The gods of the Tāvatiṁsa are handsome. They live in gold mansions.[107] A mansion would appear in the Tāvatiṁsa when a man performs an exceptionally good deed, but it would remain unoccupied till his human life came to an end.[108] The *Pañcagatidīpana*[109] states that the persons who are charitable (*cāgavā*), pay reverence to their parents, and who are ready to pardon others and find no delight in quarrels are born in the Tāvatiṁsa.

Sometimes the gods of the Tāvatiṁsa invited human beings to their world. According to the *Jātakas*,[110] Sakka invited some human beings to the Tāvatiṁsa, e.g., Nimi, Guttila, Mandhātā and the queen Sīlavatī.[111] During the life-period of thirty-six Sakkas[112] Mandhātā reigned as co-ruler of the Tāvatiṁsa.

The Tāvatiṁsa gods excel both the men of Northern Kuru and Jambudīpa in terms of life, beauty and happiness.[113] The king of the Tāvatiṁsa gods is Sakka.[114]

YĀMA. This world stands between the Tāvatiṁsa and Tusita.[115] The denizens of it are called *Yāmā*. The commentators[116] explain Yāmā as those who have attained divine bliss. Other explanations of this word are 'misery-freed' and 'governing gods.'[117] *The Khuddakapāṭha Commentary*[118] states that the name was derived from Yama, king of the under world. But the author of the *Compendium of Philosophy*[119] says that the word 'Yama' should not be confounded with Yama, the mythical king of death.

Sometimes the Yāma gods are born as men. The *Hatthipāla Jātaka*[120] mentions four such gods.

The *Pañcagatidīpana*[121] adds that those who are not fond of fights and dissensions are born in the Yāma-world. Sirimā, sister of Jīvaka, was born in the Yāma-world after death, and became the wife of Suyāma.[122] She visited the Buddha with five hundred other denizens of this heaven.[123]

In human computation, the life-period of the Yāma gods is 14,40,00,000 years.[124]

TUSITA. The dwellers of this world are called Tusita. They are so called because they are satisfied in their heavenly property.[125] They were present at the preaching of the *Mahāsamaya-sutta.*[126] Sometimes Sakadāgāmins (e.g. Purāṇa and Isidatta) are born there.[127] There is a rule that all the Bodhisattas are born in the Tusita in their last life but one, when the *devas* of the ten thousand world-systems assemble and request the Bodhisatta to be born among men as the time is ripe for the appearance of a Buddha in the world.[128] Dhammika, Anāthapiṇḍika, Mallikā, the Thera Tissa, Mahādhana and Duṭṭhagāmaṇi[129] were reborn in the Tusita.

The *Pañcagatidīpana*[130] states that those who are wise, religious and endowed with much knowledge of sacred lore and always find delight in good things are reborn in the Tusita-world. The king of the Tusita-world is Santusita.

In human computation, the life-term of a Tusita-deva is 57,60,00,000 years.[131]

NIMMĀNARATI. The denizens of this world are called Nimmānaratī. They are so called because they rejoice in their own creation.[132] They can change their forms at pleasure.[133] Their king is Sunimmita.[134]

The *pañcagatidīpana*[135] states that the persons who are moral, observe the disciplinary rules and are enthusiastic about them can live with the *Nimmānaratī-devas* whose life-term is 230,40,00,000 years.[136]

PARANIMMITAVASAVATTI. It is the highest stage of the sensuous universe (*Kāmaloka*). The *devas* of this world are called Paranimmitavasavattī because they have desire for the creation of others and get them into their control.[137] According to the commentary,[138] the objects of their desire are created by other *devas* who know their weakness, just as a cook, knowing the king's favourite dishes, would prepare them for him. As mentioned in the *Pañcagatidīpana,*[139] one who is intent upon self-control and whose mind is open is reborn in this world.

In human computation, the life-term of a *Paranimmitavasavatti deva* is 921,60,00,000 years, each day being equal to sixteen hundred human years on earth.[140]

Brahmaloka

The Buddhist Brahma-world mentioned in Pali literature is quite different from that of the Brāhmṇical literature. The conception of Brahmā as the creator of the universe[141] and the philosophic idea of one's union with Brahman for the highest good were discarded by the Buddha. He speaks of many Brahmās; but none of them is regarded as the highest being in all creation.[142] According to him, the union with Brahman is but an association with him in his world,[143] and this sort of union is not of the highest good.[144] In fact, as already seen, the highest good of the Buddhists lies in the attainment of *nibbāna*.[145]

The Brahma-world, the abode of the Brahmās, has been regarded as the highest of the celestial worlds.[146] It consists of twenty heavens,[147] which are divided into two classes (1) *Rūpaloka* (the material world) and (2) *Arūpaloka* (the immaterial world).

All the denizens of *Brahmaloka* are free from sensual desires.[148] Here there is no woman.[149] But developing *jhānas* on earth, the woman can be born in the first material world Brahmapārisajja.[150]

Those who give up their attachments to sense-desires and meditate on *mettā* (love), *karuṇā* (pity), *muditā* (sympathy) and *upekkhā* (equanimity) are reborn in the Brahma-world.[151] According to the *Jātakas*, the Bodhisattas practised meditation and consequently were born in the Brahma-world.[152]

For preaching to the gods of the Brahma-worlds, the Buddhas and their more eminent disciples frequently visited these regions.[153]

The sole food[154] of the Brahmās is meditation which is full of bliss (*sappītikajjhāna*). As said above,[155] in connection with the different grades of dwelling places, the Brahma-worlds belong to four kinds of *jhānas*. The Brahmās belonging to the first *jhāna* are different in body, but uniform in intelligence.[156]

Tudu, Nārada, Ghaṭikāra, Baka, Sanaṅkumāra and Sahampati are described as Mahābrahmās.[157] Besides these, there is mention of several Brahmās. Baka speaks of seventy-two Brahmās, living, apparently, in his world as his companions.[158] Seven Anāgāmins,[159] viz., Upaka, Phalagaṇḍu, Pakkusāti, Bhaddiya, Khaṇḍadeva, Bāhuraggi and Piṅgiya, dwell in the Avihā and other Brahma worlds. The *Vinaya Commentary*[160] mentions a Mahābrahmā who was a *khiṇāsava*[161] living for sixteen thousand *kappas*. When the Buddha was born, this Brahmā assured him that none was greater than he. Names of the Pacceka Brahmās[162] are also mentioned in the texts. Of them, Subrahmā and Sudhāvāsa went to see the Buddha. When they saw that the Buddha was in meditation, they went to visit another Brahmā who was infatuated with his own power and glory, and challenged him to the performance of miracles; they excelled him and converted him to the faith of the Buddha.[163] Tudu is sometimes described as a Pacceka Brahmā.[164] He is spoken of as exhorting Kokālika to put his trust in Sāriputta and Moggallāna.[165] The designation *Pacceka-Brahmā* was apparently coined after *Pacceka-Buddha*.

The Pali texts represent the Brahmās as visiting the earth and taking an interest in human affairs. Nārada, the great Brahmā, descends from the Brahma-world to dispel the heresies of king Aṅgati.[166] Illuminating Jetavana with the effulgence of his body, Sahampati visited the Buddha on several occasions. When the Buddha hesitates to preach his doctrine because of its profoundity, Sahampati requests him to preach it for the welfare of the world.[167]

The Brahmās are also represented as visiting the deva-worlds. Sanaṅkumāra, assuming the form of Pañcasikha,[168] was present at an assembly of the Tāvatiṁsa gods, where he praised the Buddha and exposed his teaching

As stated above,[169] of the twenty Brahma-worlds, nine are subject to change and destruction[170] while the regions from the *Vehapphala* to the *Nevasaññānāsaññāyatana* are saved.[171]

The twenty heavens of *Brahmaloka* are described below from the lowest to the highest.[172]

Brahmapārisajja. The beings born there are called Brahmapārisajjā,[173] the retinue of Brahman. Their life-term is one-third of an *asaṅkheyya-kappa.*[174] Those who slightly meditate in the first stage of meditation (*paṭhama-jhāna*) will be born among the Brahmapārisajja gods.[175] We have already mentioned[176] that women who are otherwise not seen in *Brahmaloka* can be born there through meditation.

Brahmapurohita. The denizens of this world are called *Brahma-purohitā*, i.e. the priests or ministers of Brahman, who live for half an *asaṅkheyya-kappa.*[177] Those who reach the midway of the first stage of meditation are born among the Brahma-purohita gods.[178] Brahman has no distinct abode. But there is a high storeyed tower in the middle of the purohita-heaven, which is regarded as his residence.[179]

Mahābrahma. Those who can meditate fully in the first stage of meditation will be born in the realm of Mahābrahmā (great Brahmā), who live there for a whole *asaṅkheyya-kappa.*[180] They are mighty and powerful, but they are subject to the laws of *kamma.*[181]

Parittābha (Heaven of minor lustre).[182] The denizens of this world are classed as Ābhā gods. Those who slightly meditate in the second plane of *Jhāna* (meditation) are born among the parittābha-gods. Their life-term is two *kappas.*[183] One becomes a Parittābha-deva if he dies after finishing meditation on a small circle of light.[184]

Appamāṇābha. This world is of immeasurable splendour.[185] Those who reach midway in the plane of the second *jhāna,*[186] absorbing the idea of boundless brilliancy (or light)[187] or possessing faith, virtue, learning, munificence and wisdom,[188] are born in this world. Their life-term is four *kappas.*[189]

Ābhassara. It means radiant. There live the radiant *devas* from whose body rays of light are emitted, like lightning.[190] Buddhaghoṣa[191] says that the Ābhassara-world is so called because radiance spreads in all directions from the bodies of the gods of this world, like flames from a torch. This world is the third station of consciousness.[192] Those who can fully meditate in the second stage of meditation are born among the Ābhassara gods.[193] Their life-term is eight *kappas*[194] and there is no guarantee that a person who has been born there may not later be reborn in an unhappy condition.[195] Their bodies are uniform, but their perceptions are diverse.[196]

The commentary[197] adds that their bodies are of the size of lightning flashes and 'their minds differ with their efficiency in the second and third musings.'

The Ābhissara gods appear in Pali texts, not as the names of the third category of the second *jhāna*, but as the general name of the gods of the first rank[198] above Brahmā, and as the general name of the gods of the second stage of meditation.[199] When the world is under dissolution, beings are generally reborn as radiant ones (*Ābhassara-vattanika*). The *devas* of this world are regarded as the highest during the period of destruction.[200] This world is saved,[201] while the rest of the world is destroyed by fire at the end of a *kappa*, and the first beings to be born on the earth come from the Ābhassara Brahma-world.[202]

The devas of this world are described as *manomayā* (made of mind), *sayaṁpabhā* (self-radiant), *antalikkhacarā* (traverser in the air) and *subhaṭṭhāyi* (enjoyer of glory). They are also called *pītibhakkhā* because they subsist on joy.[203] As joy flows and overflows in them, they, from time to time, utter the cry of *aho sukhaṁ, aho sukhaṁ* (joy, oh joy!) which is the best of all sounds.[204] According to the *Aṅguttaranikāya*,[205] the Sayaṁpabhā class of *devas* enjoy five-fold pleasures of the sense in the *Nandanavana* and become happy and contented.

Sometimes the Bodhisattas are born in the Ābhassara-world.[206] After having passed through the *Vehapphala* and *Subhakiṇha*, when Baka Brahmā was born in the Ābhassara-world and conceived the idea that he was eternal, the Buddha met him and convinced him of his error.[207]

When the world begins to re-evolve (*vivaṭṭati*), after its destruction by fire, an empty *Brahmavimāna* (abode of the Brahmās) appears first. Then a being is reborn in the *Brahmavimāna* leaving the Ābhassara-world either because he has finished his life there or because his merit is exhausted. Others follow his course. The first person who is reborn in the *Brahmavimāna* thinks of himself as Brahmā, the eternal, etc.[208]

When the denizens of the Ābhassara-world are reborn in the human world, their existence will be the same as they had in the Brahma-world. But with the passage of time they lose their qualities and they develop the physical and mental characteristics of human beings.[209] According to Buddhaghoṣa,[210] their birth on the earth is *opapātika* (by spontaneous regeneration) and they are mind-born (*manomayā*).

Parittasubha (heaven of minor beauty). This belongs to the world of *Subha* gods.[211] Those who slightly meditate in the third stage of meditation are born in this world of limited beauty.[212] They enjoy a life of sixteen *kappas*.[213]

Appamāṇasubha. This is the world of immeasurable beauty.[214] The denizens of this world are *Appamāṇasubha* who enjoy a life-span of thirty-two aeons (*kappas*).[215] Those who reach the midway in the third stage of meditation[216] and possess of faith, virtue, learning, munificence or relinquishment and wisdom[217] are born in this world.

Subhakiṇha. It means complete beauty. According to the commentaries, it is so called because the denizens of it are covered with lustre. The beauty, radiance and colour of their bodies are so glorious that it looks like a golden ball burning and resplendant and placed on a golden casket. The radiance which is emitted from their bodies is neither intermittent nor in flashes like that of the *Ābhassara devas*.[218]

Those who fully meditate in the third stage of meditation will be born in this world and enjoy a life-term of 64 *kappas*.[219] The denizens of it are blissful and happy. They rejoice in quiet and feel the best of joys.[220] They are uniform both in body and in mind.[221]

Vehapphala. According to Buddhaghoṣa,[222] *Vehapphala* means abundant fruits (*vipulā phalā*). It may mean great reward, because it is connected with the *jhāna* practice. Those who reach the plane of the fourth *jhāna*[223] are entitled to obtain a great reward. Hence the denizens of this world are called the gods of great reward.

F.L. Woodward[224] says that Vehapphala 'possibly means a refined form of ether of the tenth Brahmaloka'. It is one of the three great worlds in a whole *cakkavāḷa*, where the *Anāgāmins* are born. Those *Anāgāmins* who become the denizens of the Vehapphala world have not to go elsewhere for attaining *nibbāna*.[225] The *Puthujjanas* can also be born in this world.[226]

Baka Brahmā was once the dweller of it.[227] The *devas* of this world enjoy a life-term of five hundred *kappas*.[228] When the world is destroyed by wind, *Vehapphala* forms the limit of destruction.[229]

Asaññasatta. The world is so called because the dwellers of it are unconscious and experience nothing.[230] As soon as an idea occurs to them, they fall from the state of unconsciousness.[231] Their life-term, according to some texts,[232] is 500 *kappas*. The *Abhidhammatthasaṅgaha*[233] states that they belong to the fourth stage of meditation and are placed only below the highest denizens of the *Rūpaloka*, namely, the beings of the Pure Abodes (*Suddhāvāsa*) According to the *Dīghanikāya Commentary*[234] the Brāhmaṇa ascetics who attain by practice of meditation the plane of the fourth *jhāna*, and after having seen the disadvantages attached to consciousness (thinking), decide mistakenly that consciousness must be eliminated if release is to be attained. When they die in this state of mind, they are reborn in the *Asaññasatta* world. They take birth there with form only, and not with sensations, ideas, pre-dispositions and consciousness. They die straightway when an idea occurs to them.[235]

The Kathāvatthu[236] raises the controversy as to whether there is or there is not consciousness among the denizens of the *Asaññasatta*. According to the Andhakas, the *devas* of this world are sometimes conscious and sometimes unconscious; and sometimes they have five-fold organic life and sometimes only a single organic life. They are conscious at death and at rebirth and unconscious during life. But this view is discarded by the *Theravādins*. Once the Elder Sobhita was born in this world and could remember that existence.[237]

The next five worlds, i.e. Nos. 12 to 16, are called *Suddhāvāsa*, the 'pure Abodes'[238] of the *Rūpa Brahmaloka* which belong to the fourth stage of meditation.[239] The *Suddhāvāsā* are described as *buddhānaṁ khandhāvāraṭṭhānasadisā*.[240] The *Anāgāmins* are born there and attain arahantship; such *Anāgāmins* are divided into twentyfour classes.[241] The Bodhisattas are never born there.[242] Sometimes these worlds remain empty [243] for many *asaṅkheyyas* of *kappas* when no Buddhas are born there. When a Buddha is about to be born, the *devas* of the Suddhāvāsa insert a knowledge of the signs of a Great Being in the Vedas and teach this among men in the guise of Brāhmaṇas. Learning this, men are able to recognize a great Being.[244] The *Devas* of the Suddhāvāsa know the number of Buddhas to be born in any particular *kappa* after an observation of the number of lotuses blossomed on the site of the *Bodhi-pallaṅka* when the earth gradually emerges after the destruction of the world.[245] The four omens which lead to a Bodhisatta's renunciation in his last lay life[246] are provided by the *Suddhāvāsa Brahmās*. If one is reborn anywhere in the *Suddhāvāsa*, he enters into complete *nibbāna* without reaching the middle of his life and he is called *antarāparinibbāyi.*[247] *Suddhāvāsakāyikā-devā* appeared before the Buddha and recited some verses in praise of the *Saṅgha.*[248]

Avihā. It means 'not falling from prosperity'.[249] The following seven persons became *arahants* immediately after being born in the Avihā-world—Upaka, Phalagaṇḍa, Pakkusāti, Bhaddiya, Khaṇḍadeva, Bāhuraggi and Piṅgiya.[250] The denizens of this world enjoy a life-term of one thousand *kappas.*[251] The *Uddhaṁsotas*[252] start their career from the *Avihā* and end in the *Akaniṭṭha.*[253] The Avihā-world was once visited by the Buddha who received praise from several thousands of the Avihā gods.[254]

Atappā. They are *Anāgāmins.*[255] According to Buddhaghoṣa, the world is so called because they torment no one.[256] The life-term of the *Atappā* gods is two thousand *kappas.*[257] The *Majjhimanikāya*[258] states that the householders who are virtuous are reborn there.

Sudassā. It is so called because the denizens of it are beautiful and charming.[259] They enjoy a life-span of four thousand *kappas.*[260] Five kinds of *Anāgāmins* are born there.[261]

Sudassī. The world is so called because the gods of this world are well seeing or clear sighted.[262] Their lease of life is 8,000 *kappas.*[263]

Akaniṭṭha. This is the highest of the five Suddhāvāsa (Pure Mansions).[264] According to Buddhaghoṣa,[265] the world is so called because the denizens of it are supreme in virtue and in happiness and because there are no juniors among them.

The *Akaniṭṭha-bhavana* is the upper limit of the *rūpa*-worlds,[266] which is also considered to be the highest point of the universe. In the *Sakkapañhasutta*,[267] Sakka speaks of this heaven as the highest one and desires that he, too will be born there in his last life. Its position as the highest of all material worlds is due to the fact that all its denizens lead glorious lives and they enjoy a life span of 16,000 kappas.[268] It is one of the three highest worlds, mentioned in the *Vibhaṅga Commentary*,[269] where *Anāgāmins* are born and enter into complete *nibbāna* (*antarāparinibbāyi*) without reaching the middle of his life. As mentioned above,[270] *Anāgāmins* of the Avihā heaven end their existence, in a subsequent birth, in the *Akaniṭṭha*-world. The Buddha visited this world and conversed with the beings who were born there in consequence of the holy lives they had lived under various Buddhas.[271] The quarrel among the Kosambi monks reached even up to the *Akaniṭṭha*-world,[272] like the shouts of the assembly at the severing of the branch of the Bodhi tree.[273] The next four, i.e., Nos. 17 to 20, are *Arūpa Brahmalokas* and they belong to the fourth stage of meditation.

Ākāsānañcāyatana. It is the world of the infinity of space, where one is reborn who passes completely over all perceptions of inertia (sense reaction), and ceases to dwell on perceptions of diversity.[274] According to the *Visuddhimagga*,[275] the persons who desire to enjoy happiness in fôrmless existence are born in this world. The denizens of this world enjoy a life-span of twenty thousand cycles (*kappas*)[276] and their minds become conscious and unconscious in a moment's time.[277]

Viññāṇañcāyatana. It is the realm of the infinite consciousness. One who completely passes over the realm of the infinity of space and says to himelf "consciousness is infinity", dwells in such a realm.[278] The lease of life in this world is forty thousand *kappas*.[279]

Ākiñcaññāyatana. This is the third Arūpa-world,[280] where "nothing exists". One who completely passes over the realm of the infinity of consciousness is born in the world of nothingness. It is the best of all conscious states[281] and the dwellers of it enjoy a life-span of sixty thousand *kappas*.[282]

Nevasaññānāsaññāyatana. It is the highest of the Arūpa Brahmalokas. It has neither consciousness nor unconsciousness. Those who pass completely over the realm of nothingness,[283] go there and enjoy a life-span of the devas of the *Nevasaññānāsaññāyatana*, i.e. 80,000 *kappas*.[284] The lives they enjoy are the best of lives.[285]

Notes

Chapter II

1. Vol. I, p. 82; cf. *Aṅg.*, Vol. II, pp. 226, 237; *Itv.*, pp. 14, 99.
2. Vol. II, pp. 226-27.
3. *Ibid.*, Vol. III, p. 3.
4. Loc. cit.
5. *Aṅg.*, Vol. III, pp. 171, 204, 432; cf. *Saṁ.*, Vol. IV, p. 245, where it is said that a woman possessing these qualities is reborn in heaven.
6. *Aṅg.*, Vol. II, p. 19.
7. Ibid., Vol. III, pp. 39-40.
8. Cf. *Saṁ.*, Vol. I, p. 92; *Jāt.*, Vol. III, p. 472.
9. Vol. IV, pp. 243-44.
10. Vol. I, p. 30.
11. Vol. V, p. 366.
12. *Jāt.*, Vol. III, p. 443.
13. Ibid., p. 306.
14. *JPTS*, 1884, p. 160; *sīlena tidivaṁ yāti jhānena Brahmasaṁpadaṁ.* Here *tidiva* is translated as *Devaloka.*
15. Vol. I, p. 199.
19. Ibid., p. 9.
17. Ibid., pp. 208-09.
18. Vol. III, pp. 103-04.
19. *Vibh. Com.*, p. 521; *Tāvatiṁsā ca Yāmā ca || Tusitā cāpi devatā || Nimmānaratino devā || Ye deva Vasavattino || kāmabandhanabaddhā te ||* (*Saṁ.*, Vol. I, p. 133); L. de La Vallee Poussin translates *kāmaloka* as the world of concupiscence (*ERE*, Vol. IV, p. 134).
20. *Aṅg.*, Vol. I, pp. 210, 227-28; Vol. III, p. 287; Vol. IV, pp. 119, 240 ff.; *Dīg.*, Vol. I, pp. 215-223; *Maj.*, Vol. I, p. 289; Vol. III, pp. 100-03, 147.
21. Vol. III, pp. 332-33.
22. *Paṭ. Com.*, Vol. III, p. 613; *Vibh. Com.*, p. 519.
23. *Dīg.*, Vol. II, pp. 207f., 257-58; Vol. III, pp. 194f; *Paṭ. Com.*, Vol. III. p. 613; for details see below pp.
24. *Dīg.*, Vol. II, pp. 257f.
25. Ibid., Vol. III, pp. 194-204; *Dham. Com.*, Vol. II, pp. 96, 146.
26. *Dīg.*, Vol. II, p. 225.
27. *Aṅg.*, Vol. I, pp. 142f.

28. Likewise, Sakka of the Tāvatiṁsa, Santusita of the Tusita, Śuyâma of the *Yāma*, Sunimmita of the *Nimmānarati* and Vasavatti of the *Paranimmitta* vasavatti *devalokas* surpass other dwellers of their worlds (*Aṅg.*, Vol. IV, p. 242; cf. *Dīg.*, Vol. III, p. 146).
29. *Vibh. Com.*, p. 519; *Paṭ. Com.*, Vol. III, p. 613.
30. Vol. I, pp. 213-14. On account of such meritorious deeds, human beings can be born also in the Tāvatiṁsa, Yāma, Tusita, Nimmānarati and Paranimmitavasavatti worlds.
31. *JPTS*, 1884, p. 160.
32. Vol. III, p. 100; similarly, as a result of their exertion, they are born in other *lokas* commencing from the *Tāvatiṁsa* heaven to the *Nevasaññānāsaññāyatana* heaven (*ibid.*, pp. 101-103).
33. *Mānusakāni paññāsa vassāni Cātummahārājikānaṁ devānaṁ eso eko rattindivo, tāya rattiyā tiṁsarattivo māso, tena māsena dvādasa masiyo sāṁvaccharo, tena saṁvaccharena dibbāni pañca vassa satāni Cātummahārajikānaṁ devānaṁ āyuppamāṇaṁ.* Fifty years of human life are a single night and day to the *Devas* of the Cātummahārājika-world. Thirty such days and nights make a month. Twelve of such months make a year. Five hundred of such years are the life-period of the *Devas* (*Aṅg.*, Vol. I, p. 213; Vol. IV, p. 252; *Vibh.*, p. 422); cf. *KV*, pp. 207-08; *Dīg. Com.*, Vol. II, pp. 472, 647; *CP*. p. 140.
34. Vol. I, PTS, p. 29.
35. Macalagāma in Magadha (*Magadharaṭṭhe Macalagāma—Sut. Com.*, Vol. II, p. 484).
36. See p. 169 (*tettiṁsa janā yattha uppannā taṁ thānaṁ Tāvatiṁsaṁ ti*).
37. See p. 519 (*tettiṁsa janā tattha uppannā ti Tāvatiṁsa*).
38. In an assembly of the gods in Tāvatiṁsa, they rejoiced that their number was increasing because many people on the earth were following the teachings of the Buddha. Brahmā Sanaṅkumāra appeared there in the guise of Pañcasikha who, assuming thirty-three forms, took his place by each god of Tāvatiṁsa and confirmed the glad tidings of the increasing number of *devas* (*Dīg.*, Vol. II, pp. 207-12; cf. *ibid.*, pp. 221 f., 226).
39. *Ṛgveda*, Vol. IX, pp. 24, 92.
40. E.g., *Nandanaṁ rammaṁ tidasānaṁ mahāvanaṁ* (*Vim. Com.*, p. 94; *Pet. Com.*, p. 173); *Saṁ.*, Vol. I, p. 5; Vol. V, p. 342; *Sakko'ham asmī tidasānaṁ indo* (*Jāt.*, Vol. V, pp. 20, 390).
41. E.g., *Aṅg.*, Vol. III, p. 40 (*to dīgharattaṁ tidive patiṭṭhitā devānaṁ sahavyagatā ramanti te*).
42. JPTS, 1884, p. 160. See also above, p. 37 note 3.
43. *Sut. Com.*, Vol. II, p. 485.
44. For details see below, p. 108.
45. *Jāt.*, Vol. V, p. 167; Vol. VI, pp. 272, 289; *Vim. Com.*, p. 350. According to some scholars, the Masakkasāra is really the name of Mount Sineru, and so called because it is immovable (*Masakkasāro vuccati*

osakkanaparisakkanābhāvena ghanasāratāya ca Sinerupabbatarājā), and *Tāvatiṁsa* is known as Masakkasāra because it is built on Sineru (*Jāt.*, Vol. V, p. 168; Vol. VI, p. 271). The *Vin. Com.*, (Vol. I, p. 49) mentions Amarāvatī as the city of Sakka; cf. *CV.*, Ch. 80, Verse, 5; it is described in the *Mahābhārata*, Vol. III, pp. 1714 ff; see also Hopkins, *Epic Mythology*, pp. 140 f.

46. *Jāt.*, Vol. V, p. 400.
47 This tree lives for a whole aeon (*Saṁ.*, Vol. V, p. 238) and reveals the whereabouts of the Asuras (*Jāt.*, Vol., I, p. 202; *Sut. Com.*, Vol. II, p. 485; *Dham. Com.*, Vol. I, p. 272); when the Cittapāṭali blossomed, the Asuras thought of the *Pāricchattaka*-tree which was left behind by them in the *Tāvatiṁsa* and started making preparation for a war against Sakka (see *Jāt.*, Vol., p. 202).
48. *Jāt.*, Vol. I, p. 204; *Dham. Com.*, Vol. I, p. 280.
49. *Jāt.*, Vol. VI, pp. 125-26; *Sut. Com.*, Vol. II, p. 485.
50. *Jāt.*, Vol. V, pp. 385-86; *Dham. Com.*, Vol. I, p. 272; *Vis.*, Vol. I, p. 207; *Vin. Com.*, Vol. I, p. 119; *Sut. Com,*, Vol. II, p. 443, 485.
51. *Jāt.*, Vol. I, p. 204.
52. Ibid., Vol. VI, pp. 131-32, 278-79.
53. *Aṅg.*, Vol. IV, p. 117 (*Pāricchattaka* is a celestial tree and described here as *Pāricchattaka-kovilāra*.
54. *Jāt.*, Vol. III, p. 87.
55. Ibid., Vol. VI, p. 278.
56. E.g., *Dham. Com.*, Vol. II, p. 266; *Aṅg.*, Vol. III, p. 40 (The *Sayaṁpabhā* (self-radiant) class of *devas* enjoy five-fold pleasures of the sense in the *Nandanavana* and become happy and contented). Cf. *Saṁ.*, Vol. I, p. 5, where a *deva* of the *Tāvatiṁsa-devaloka*, while wandering in the *Nandanavana*, was attended by a troop of apsarases, and was provided with five-fold celestial sensuous enjoyments. He uttered a verse—
Na te sukhaṁ pajānanti ye na passanti Nandanaṁ
āvāsaṁ naradevānaṁ tidasānaṁ yasassinan ti
Cf. Ibid., Vol. V, p. 342.
57. *Jāt.*, Vol. V, p. 158.
58. *sabba-devalokesu hi Nandanavanaṁ atthi yeva* (ibid., Vol. I, p. 49).
59. Ibid., 50; VI, p. 144.
60. *Mt.*, 568.
61. *Jāt.*, Vol. V, p. 392.
62. Ibid., Vol. II, p. 189.
63. *Jāt.*, Vol. I, pp. 204-05; Vol. VI, p. 132; *Dham. Com.*, Vol. I, p. 275.
64. *Jāt.*, Vol. II, p. 189.
65. Ibid., Vol. VI, p. 333.
66. Ibid., Vol. I, pp. 204-05; Vol. VI, pp. 132, 232, 531; *Dham. Com.*, Vol. I p. 275.
67. *Jāt.*, Vol. I, p. 189.
68. *Dham. Com.*, Vol. I, p. 270.

69. E.g., *Vim. Com.*, p. 174.
70. *Dham. Com.*, Vol. I, p. 273.
71. *Jāt.*, Vol. I, p. 202.
72. *Vim. Com.*, p. 174.
73. *Aṅg.*, Vol. IV, pp. 117 f; *Dig. Com.*, Vol. II, pp. 649-50.
74. *Dham. Com.*, Vol. I, pp. 271-75; *Jāt.*, Vol. I, p. 204.
75. *Vim. Com.*, p. 94.
76. *Jāt.*, Vol. III, pp. 250-51.
77. *Vis.*, Vol. I, p. 391.
78. Loc. cit.; *Dham. Com.*, Vol. III, p. 216; *Jāt.* Vol. IV, p. 265.
79. *Jāt.*, Vol. IV, p. 265; *Dham. Com.*, Vol. III, pp. 216 ff.
80. It is said in the *Mahākaṇha Jātaka* (*Jāt.*, Vol. IV, p. 180) that the Buddha dwelt three months in the *Tāvatiṁsa* heaven and taught full comprehension of the Law to eight hundred millions of deities. Cf. Spence Hardy, *MB*, p. 298.
81. E.g., Kāladevala (*Jāt.* Vol. I, p. 54), brāhmaṇatāpasa Nārada (Ibid., Vol. V, p. 392).
82. *Ibid.*, Vol. I, p. 203.
83. *Dham. Com.*, Vol. I, p. 273; cf. *Dīg. Com.*, Vol. III, p. 698.
84. *Maj.*, Vol. I, pp. 253 f. The palace was also made to rock by the novice Saṅgharakkhita on the day he joined the Order (*Dīg. Com.*, Vol. II, p. 558).
85. *Dīg.*, Vol. II, p. 296; *Saṁ.*, Vol. I, pp. 234-36.
86. *Sut. Com.*, Vol. I, p. 274.
87. *Jāt.*, Vol. IV, p. 357.
88. Alexander Cunningham, *The Stūpa of Bharhut*, 1877, pp. 141-42.
89. *Dīg.*, Vol. II, pp. 207 ff.
90. See above, p. 31.
91. *Jāt.*, Vol. I, p. 204, where it is said that the *Sudhammā maṇisabhā* is of *Pañcayojanasatikā*.
92. Ibid., Voi. VI, pp. 126-27.
93. *Dham. Com.*, Vol. I, pp. 269 f., 274 f., *Jāt.*, Vol. I, pp. 201f. In a previous birth, Sakka was named as Magha on the earth, where he with his companions built a rest-house for travellers. When the building was constructed, Sudhammā, one of his four wives, desired to have a share in the work; but as the woman was not allowed to get a share in it, she bribed a carpenter who made a pinnacle of seasoned wood and laid it aside with the words: *Sudhammā nāma ayaṁ sālā*. At the time of erection of the pinnacle, he told Magha and his companions that it was difficult to make a pinnacle then because it must be of seasoned wood. Then Sudhammā declared to give her pinnacle. Though the men were at first unwilling, they at last took her pinnacle.
94. Vol. II, p. 649; cf. Alexander Cunningham, op. cit., p. 142, p, where the hall is illustrated.

95. See, e.g., *Dīg.*, Vol. II, p.268; *Maj.*, Vol. II, p. 79; *Saṁ.*, Vol. I, p. 221; *Jāt.* Vol. VI, pp. 97, 126; *Thera.*, Verse, 1198; *Dīg. Com.*, Vol. II, p. 650.
96. *Thera. Com.*, SHB, Vol. II, p. 185.
97. *Dīg.*, Vol. II, pp. 207 ff.
98. *Jāt.*, Vol. I, p. 65.
99. *Dīg.*, *Com.*, Vol. II, p. 609.
100. *Jāt.*, Vol. III, p. 87.
101. See below, Ch. IV.
102. *Jāt.*, Vol. V, p. 392.
103. Loc. cit.
104. But see, e.g., Jālinī and the various stories of the *Vimānavatthu Commentary*.
105. *Jāt.*, Vol. II, p. 93.
106. *Dham. Com.*, Vol. I, p. 364; *Ang.*, Vol, I, p. 213; Vol. IV, pp. 252-53; *Vibh.*, p. 422; *CP.*, p. 140; *Dīg. Com.*, Vol. II, p. 472..
107. *Dham. Com.*, Vol. III, p. 7.
108. Ibid., p. 291.
109. *JPTS*, 1884, p. 160.
110. E.g., Vol. VI, p. 95; Vol. II, p. 312.
111. For details, see *Jātaka* Nos. 243, 258 and 541.
112. *Jāt.*, Vol. II, p. 312.
113. *Aṅg.*, Vol. IV, p. 396.
114. Ibid., Vol. I, p. 242.
115. E.g., loc. cit., p. 228; Vol. III, p. 287; Vol. IV, p. 240; *Maj.*, Vol. II, p. 194; Vol. III, p. 100, etc.
116. *Dibbaṁ sukhaṁ yātā payātā sampattā ti* (*Vibh. Com.*, p. 519); *Therī. Com.*, p. 169.
117. *CP.*, p. 136, note 2.
118. Vol. I, p. 166 (*Yāmato yāva Akaniṭṭhaṁ*) (from the under world to the highest heaven).
119. See p. 136, note 2.
120. Vol. IV, pp. 475-76.
121. *JPTS*, 1884, p. 160.
122. He is the king of the Yāma gods.
123. *Sut. Com.*, Vol. I, pp. 244 f; see also *Vim. Com,*, p. 246 for the birth of an *upāsaka* in the Yāma-world.
124. *Aṅg.*, Vol. I, p. 213; Vol. IV, p. 253; *Vibh.*, pp. 422-23; *CP*, pp, 140-41.
125. *Dibbāya sampattiyā tuṭṭhā pahaṭṭhā ti Tusitā* (*Therī. Com.*, p. 169; also *Paṭ. Com.*, Vol. III, p. 613; *Vibh. Com.*, p. 519.
126. *Dīg.*, Vol, II, p. 261.
127. *Aṅg.*, Vol. III, p. 348; Vol. V, p. 138.
128. *Vis.*, Vol. I, pp. 391; *Aṅg.*, Vol II, p. 130; Vol. IV, p. 312; *Dham. Com.*, Vol. I, pp. 69 f.

129. For details, see *Dīg. Com.*, Vol. III, p. 740; *Dham. Com.*, Vol. III, pp. 119 ff., 341 ff., 429f.; *MV.* Chs. xxii—xxxii; *DV.*, xviii, 53; xix. 1ff.
130. *JPTS*, 1884, p. 160.
131. *Aṅg.*, Vol. I, p. 214; Vol. IV, p. 253; *Vibh.*, p. 423; *CP.*, pp. 140-41.
132. E.g., *Dīg.*, Vol. III. p. 218.
133. *Pakatipaṭiyattārammaṇato atirekena ramitukāmakāle yathāruci te bhoge nimminitvā nimminitvā ramanti ti Nimmāṇaratī* (*Paṭ.*, *Com.*, Vol. III, p. 613; *Vibh. Com.*, p. 519).
134. *Aṅg.*, Vol. IV, p. 243.
135. *JPTS*, 1884, p. 160.
136. *Aṅg.*, Vol. I, p. 214; Vol. IV, p. 253; Vibh., p. 423; *CP*, pp. 240-41.
137. E.g., *Aṅg.*, Vol. I, p. 210, etc.; *Dīg.*, Vol. III, p. 218; *Maj.*, Vol. I, p. 289.
138. Cf. *cittacāraṁ ñatvā parehi nimmitesu bhogesu vasaṁ vattentī ti Paranimmitavasavattī* (*Vibh. Com.*, p. 519; *Paṭ. Com.*, Vol. III, p. 613; *Therī. Com.*, p. 169) (here *cittaruci* is mentioned instead of *cittacāra*, *Dīg. Com.*, Vol. III, p. 1001).
139. *JPTS*, 1884, p. 160.
140. *Aṅg.*, Vol. I, p. 214; Vol. IV, p. 254; *Vibh.*, p. 423; cf. *CP.*, pp. 240-41.
141. E.g., *Dīg.*, Vol. I, p. 18, where Brahmā is described as *vasavattī issaro kattā nimmātā* etc., Vol. III, p. 28.
142. See however, *Aṅg.*, Vol. V, pp. 59 f., where Mahā-Brahmā is spoken of as the highest denizen of the *Sahassalokadhātu*; but he, too, is impermanent.
143. The denizens of *Brahmaloka* are called *Brahmakāyikā* (see, e.g., *Aṅg.*, Vol. I, p. 210) and this term, according to Buddhaghoṣa, is applied to those beings who are ready to live with Brahmā [*Brahmakāye brahmaghaṭāya niyuttā' ti Brahmakāyikā* (*Paṭ. Com.*, Vol. III, p. 613)].
144. E.g., see *Aṅg.*, Vol. V, *loc. cit.*
145. See above, p. 1, note 1.
146. See above, pp. 11 f.
147. *Maj.*, Vol. I, p. 289; *CP*, p. 142; *Vibh.* pp. 422-26.
148. *Vibh. Com.*, p. 437; see *Jāt.*, Vol. IV, p. 378, where Diṭṭhamaṅgalikā is spoken of as Mahābrahmabhariyā; reading the *Mātaṅga Jātaka* some one may consider that the Mahābrahmās had wives.
149. *Dham. Com.*, Vol. 1, p. 270.
150. *Vibh., Com.*, pp. 437f.
151. Maj., Vol. II, pp. 194-95; Vis., Vol. I, pp. 199-200, 415 ; JPTS, 1884, p. 160.
152. E.g., *Jāt.*, Vol. II, pp. 43, 69, 90, etc.
153. E.g., *Maj*, Vol. I, pp. 326ff.; Abhibhn and the disciple of the Buddha Sikhi also visited the Brahma-world (*Aṅg.*, Vol. I, pp. 227 f.).

The Buddha could visit this world in his mind-made and physical bodies (*Saṁ.*, Vol. V, pp. 282 f.)

154. *Saṁ. Com.*, (PTS), Vol. I, p. 207. According to the same commentary, Vol.I, pp. 158f., Mahābrahmā is invited to partake of food and drinks, but not of sacrifices.
155. See p. 11.
156. *Dīg.*, Vol.II, p. 69; Vol. III, p. 253; *Aṅg.*, Vol. IV, p. 401.
157. For details, see below, Ch. IV.
158. *Saṁ.*, Vol. I, p. 142.
159. Ibid., pp. 34 f., 59 f.
160. Vol. I, p. 131.
161. I.e. whose mind is free from the four mental obsessions.
162. *Sam.*, Vol. I, pp. 146 ff.
163. Loc. cit.
164. Ibid., p. 149.
165. DPPN, s.v. Sāriputta and Moggallāna.
166. *Jāt.*, Vol.VI, pp. 242 f.
167. E.g., see *Dīg.*, Vol. II, p. 36; *DB*, Vol. II, p. 30, note 4.
168. *Dīg.*, II, pp. 211 ff. Pañcasikha, Five-crest, 'which became a famous name in Indian legends, and was adopted by Saivite and Sāṅkhya writers. It is nowhere explained what, or how disposed, his five crests were' (*DB*, Part. II, p. 244, note 2).
169. See pp. 11 f.
170. *Maj.*, Vol. I, pp. 327 ff.
171. See above, p. 13.
172. E.g. *Maj.*, Vol. I, p. 289.
173. *Vibh. Com.*, pp. 519 f.
174. Loc. cit.; Vibh., p. 424; *CP*, p. 142.
175. E.g. *Vibh.*, loc. cit.
176. See p. 37.
177. *Vibh.* loc. cit; *Vibh.*, *Com.*, loc. cit; *CP*, loc. cit.
178. *Vibh.* loc. cit.
179. E.R.E., Vol. IV, p. 135.
180. *CP*, p. 142; *Vibh.*, p. 424; *Vibh. Com.*, p. 520.
181. E.g., see *Saṁ.*, Vol. V. p. 410; *Aṅg.*, Vol. IV, pp. 76 f., 104 f.
182. *Vibh. Com.*, loc. cit.
183. Loc. cit.; *CP*, loc. cit.; *Vibh.*, loc. cit.
184. *Maj.*, Vol. III, p. 147.
185. *Vibh. Com.*, loc. cit.
186. *Vibh.*, loc. cit.
187. *Maj.*, loc. cit.
188. *Maj.*, Vol. III, p. 102.
189. *Vibh.*, p. 424; *CP*, p. 142.
190. *CP*, p. 138, note 4.
191. *Daṇḍadīpikāya acciviya tesaṁ sarīrato ābhā chijjitvā chijjivā patanti viya sarati vlsarati ti Ābhassarā* (*Vibh. Com.*, p. 520).

192. *Aṅg.*, Vol. IV, pp. 40, 401; *Dīg.*, Vol. II, p. 69; Vol. III, p. 253.
193. *Vibh.*, loc. cit; *Vibh. Com.*, loc-cit.
194. *CP*, p. 142; *Vibh*, loc. cit.
195. *Aṅg.*, Vol. II, pp. 127, 129, where their life-span is given as two *kappas* (*Ābhassarāṇaṁ ...devānaṁ dve kappā āyuppamāṇaṁ*).
196. *Aṅg.*, Vol. IV, pp. 40, 401; *Dīg.*, Vol. II, p. 69; Vol. III, p. 253.
197. *GS*, Vol. IV, p. 23, note 1.
198. *Aṅg.*, Vol. IV, p. 89; Vol. V, p. 60; *Dīg*, Vol. I, p. 17.
199. *Aṅg.*, Vol. II, p. 127.
200. Ibid., Vol. V, p. 60.
201. *Khud. Com.*, p. 121; *Vis.*, Vol. II, p. 415.
202. *Vis.*, loc. cit., p. 417.
203. *Dīg.*, Vol. I, p. 17; Vol. III, pp. 28, 84 f.; *Aṅg.*, Vol. V, p. 60; *Saṁ.*, Vol. I, p. 114; *Dham. Com.*, Vol. III, p. 258; *Jāt.*, Vol. VI, p.55.
204. *Aṅg.*, Vol. III, p. 202; *Dīg.*, Vol. III, p. 218.
205. Vol. III, p. 40.
206. Ibid., Vol. IV, p. 89; *Maj.*, Vol. I, p. 326; *Jāt.*, Vol. I, p. 406. The Bodhisattas are never reborn in the Formless (Arūpa) world even though they attain to the highest state, because they are incapable of passing beyond the realm of Form (Rūpa) (ibid., pp. 473-74).
207. *Jāt.*, Vol. III, p. 359.
208. *Dīg.*, Vol. III, p. 29.
209. Ibid., pp. 84 ff.
210. *Dīg. Com.*, Vol. III, p. 865; *DB*, Vol. I, p. 201, note 3; *Dīg.*, Vol. III, p. 85.
211. *Maj.*, Vol. III, p. 102.
212. *Vibh.*, p. 424; *Vibh. Com.*, p. 520.
213. *Vibh*, p. 520; *CP*, p. 142.
214. *Vibh. Com.*, p. 520.
215. *Vibh.* p. 425; *CP*, loc. cit.
216. *Vibh.*, p. 424.
217. *Maj.*, Vol. III, p. 102.
218. *Subhena okiṇṇā vikiṇṇā, subhena sarīrappabhāvaṇṇena ekaghanā suvaṇṇamañjusāya ṭhapitasampajjalita-kañcanapiṇḍasassirīkā ti Subhakiṇhā, etesaṁ hi na ābhassarāṇaṁ viya chiijjitvā chijjitvā pabhā gacchati* (*Vibh. Com.*, p. 520).
219. *CP*, p. 142; *Vibh.*, p. 425; *Vibh. Com.*, loc. cit.; but see *Aṅg.*, Vol. II, pp. 127, 129, where their life is stated given as four *kappas.*
220. *Dīg.*, Vol. III, p. 219; *Aṅg.*, Vol. III, p. 202.
221. *Aṅg.*, Vol. IV, pp. 40, 401; *Dīg.*, Vol. II, p. 69; Vol. III, p. 253.
222. *Vibh. Com.*, p. 521.
223. *Vibh.* p. 425.
224. *GS.*, Vol. II. p. 131, note 4.
225. *Vibh. Com.*, p. 522, where *Vehapphala* is mentioned with the other two great worlds, i.e., the *Akaniṭṭha* and *Nevasaññānāsaññāyatana.* The *Anāgāmins* being born in these three worlds have not to go elsewhere for the acquisition of *nibbāna.*

226. *Vibh. Com.*, p. 376; *Aṅg.*, Vol. II, p. 129.
227. *Jāt.*, Vol. III, p. 358.
228. *Vibh.*, p. 425; *Aṅg.*, Vol. II, pp. 128-29; also see Vol. III, p. 358.
229. *Vis.*, Vol. II, p. 414.
230. *Aṅg.*, Vol. IV, p. 401; the *Vibh. Com.*, p. 520 explains that *Asaññasattānam ti saññāvirahitānam sattānaṁ*.
231. *Dīg.*, Vol. I, p. 28.
232. *Vibh.*, p. 425; *CP.*, p. 142.
233. The *Vibh.*, p. 425 and its commentary, p. 520 place *Asaññasatta* above *Vehapphala*.
234. Vol. I, p. 118.
235. Loc. cit.; *Dīg.*, Vol. III, p. 33.
236. See p. 262.
237. *Thera. Com.*, SHB, Vol. I, p. 291.
238. *Dīg.*, Vol. III, p. 237; Vol. II, p. 52; cf. *PC*, p. 74, note 2.
239. E.g., *CP*, p. 139.
240. Saṁ, Vol. I, p. 26; cf. *Dīg.*, Vol. II, pp. 153 f.
241. See, e.g., *Khud. Com.*, Vol. I, pp. 182 f.
242. *Sut. Com.*, Vol. I. p. 50.
243. *Aṅg. Com.*, Vol. II, p. 808; *Maj. Com.*, Aluvihara Serles, Colombo, Vol. I, p. 30.
244. *Sut. Com.*, Vol. II, p. 448.
245. *Dīg. Com.*, Vol. II, pp. 411-12.
246. See, e.g., *Dīg. Com.*, Vol. II pp. 455 f.
247. *Vis.*, Vol. II, p. 710; cf. *PC*, pp. 77-78; *antarāparinibbāyī* is an Anāgāmin.
248. *Saṁ.*, Vol. I, p. 26; cf. *Dīg.*, Vol. II, pp. 353 f.
249. *Attano sampattiyā na hāyantīti Avihā* (*Vibh. Com.*, p. 521; *Dīg. Com.*, Vol. II, p. 480).
250. *Saṁ.*, Vol. I, pp. 35, 60.
251. *Vibh.*, p. 425; *CP.*, p. 142; *Dīg. Com.*, Vol. III, p. 740.
252. I.e. one who strives 'upstream'. He is one of the five *Anāgāmins* (*Dīg.*, Vol. III, p. 237).
253. Loc. cit.; *Dham. Com.*, Vol. III, pp. 289-90.
254. *Dīg.*, Vol. II, pp. 50-51.
255. *Itv. Com.*, p. 40.
256. *Na kiñci sattam tappentīti* (*Vibh. Com.*, p. 521; *Dīg. Com.*, Vol. II p. 480). Cf. *DB*, Vol. II, p. 41, note 1.
257. *Dīg. Com.*, Vol. III, p. 740; *Vibh.*, p. 425; *CP.*, p. 142.
258. Vol. I, p. 289.
259. *Dīg.*, Vol. II, p. 52; *Vibh. Com.*, p. 521.
260. *Vibh.*, p. 425; *Dīg. Com.*, Vol. III, p. 740; *CP*, p. 142.

261. Five anāgāmins (never-returners) are (1) *Antarāparinibbāyī* (one who passes away before middle age in that world in which he has been reborn); (2) *Upahacca-parinibbāyī* (one who passes after middle age); (3) *asaṁkhāra-parinibbāyī* (one who passes without much toil, with ease); (4) *sasaṁkhāraparinibbāyī* (one who passes with

toil and difficulty) and (5) *Uddhaṁsoto* (one who strives 'upstream'). They are also reborn in the Akaniṭṭha-world (*Dīg.*, Vol. III, p. 237; cf. *Aṅg.*, Vol. IV, pp. 14 f.). *Khud. Com.*, Vol. I, p. 183; *Vibh. Com.*, p. 521.

262. *Dīg.*, Vol. II, p. 52 (*DB.*, Vol. II, p. 41, note 3); Vol. III, p. 237; *Maj.*, Vol. III, p. 103; *Khud. Com.*, Vol. I, p. 120; *Vis.*, p. 473; *Vibh. Com.*, p. 521 (*suṭṭhupassanti, sundaram etesam va dassanam ti sudassī*).
263. *Vibh.*, p. 425; *Dīg. Com.*, Vol. III, p. 740; *CP*, p. 142.
264. *Dīg.*, Vol. III, p. 237.
265. *Dīg. Com.*, Vol. II, p. 480 (*sabbehiyeva guṇehi ca bhavasampattiyā ca jeṭṭhā natth' ettha kaniṭṭhā ti); āyunā ca paññāya ca Akaniṭṭhā jeṭṭhakā sabba-devehi paṇītatarā devā* (ibid., Vol. III, p. 739); cf. *Vibh. Com.*, p. 521.
266. *Paṭ.*, Vol. I, p. 84.
267. *Dīg.*, Vol. II, p. 286.
268. *KV.*, p. 208; *Vibh.*, p. 425; *CP.*, p. 142; *Dīg. Com.*, Vol. III, p. 740.
269. See p. 522; *Vis.*, Vol. II, p. 710; *Dīg. Com.*, Vol. III, p. 740.
270. See note 252.
271. *Dīg.*, Vol. II, pp. 50 ff.
272. *Jāt.*, Vol. III, p. 487.
273. *Mil.*, p. 284.
274. *Dīg.*, Vol. II, p. 69; Vol. III, p. 253; *Aṅg.*, Vol. I, pp. 40-41; Vol. IV, pp. 401-02; *Maj.*, Vol. III, p. 103; *Saṁ.*, Vol. IV, p. 266.
275. Vol. I, p. 200.
276. *Aṅg.*, Vol. I, p. 267; *CP.*, p. 143; *Vibh.*, p. 425.
277. *KV*, p. 208.
278. *Dīg.*, Vol. II, p. 69; Vol. III, p. 253; *Aṅg.*, Vol. I, p. 41; Vol. IV, pp. 40, 401; *Saṁ.*, Vol. IV, p. 266.
279. *Vibh.*, p. 425; *CP.*, p. 143.
280. *Maj.*, Vol. III, p. 103.
281. *Dīg.*, Vol. II, p. 69; Vol. III, p. 253: *Aṅg.*, Vol. I, p. 41; Vol. III, p. 202; Vol. IV, pp. 40, 401.
282. *Vibh.*, p. 426; *CP.*, p. 143.
283. *Paṭ.*, p. 84.
284. *Vibh.*, p. 426; *CP.*, p. 143.
285. *Aṅg.*, Vol. III, p, 202.

CHAPTER III

The Hell

As we have said above,[1] hell is the lowest of the thirty-one abodes of living beings. It is meant for punishment and lies below the earth.[2] There is no happiness[3] or refreshment in hell.[4] The *Mūgapakkha Jātaka* states that, in hell there is no laughter or joy; the torture is more severe than the fire produced from a houseful of palm leaves. The pain suffered in hell is also greater than the torments caused by an elephant and by cutting off a limb with a sword. If a man smears his whole body with molasses and is attacked by flies, his suffering is lesser than that suffered in hell; will also be lesser than that of a man put on a pan of fire.

The persons who are sinful in action, speech and thought are reborn in hell[5] and suffer from various sorts of punishment. The *Nirayasutta* of the *Aṅguttaranikāya*[6] states that one is led to hell for the following: (1) destruction of life,[7] (2) theft, (3) lust, (4) falsehood, (5) consumption of liquor, (6) evil desires, and (7) wrong views.[8] The same *Nikāya*[9] adds that ungrateful persons are reborn in hell. The *Dīghanikāya*[10] says that the defamers of the Noble are thrown into hell. The *Duppaññasutta*[11] says that one who is an unbeliever, immoral, indolent and unwise, will be destined to suffer in hell. According to the *Kodhana, Upanāhi, Issukī, Maccherena, Aticārī, Dussīla, Appassuta, Kusīta* and *Muṭṭhassati Suttas,*[12] a woman who is faithless, shameless, unscrupulous, wrathful, grudging, envious,[13] stingy, adulterous, immoral, ignorant, indolent, muddleheaded and unwise is led to hell. The *Devatā Saṁyutta* of the *Saṁyuttanikāya*[14] adds that persons who are miserly and averse to liberality are liable to suffer in hell.

The *Majjhimanikāya*[15] states that the monks and Brāhmaṇas who hold the view that there is no harm in sensual pleasures are sure to suffer in hell. The *Sekhabālavagga*[16] adds that hell is the place for a monk who is faithless, shameless, reckless, indolent and insightless.

The *Theragāthā*[17] states that, if a man induces sensual, misanthropic, or confused ideas in others and causes them to lose their earnestness he will have to go to hell. According to the *Visuddhimagga*,[18] the persons who misconduct owing to their attachment to sensual desires and commit sin in word and thought are reborn in hell. The *Itivuttaka*[19] states that hell is the ultimate abode of those who are conceited for their wealth and fame.

Pali literature does not speak of one consistent system of hell. It describes various types of punishment for which different kinds of hell are conceived. The earliest is the hell where seven kinds of torture, as mentioned in the *Aṅguttara*[20] and *Majjhima*[21] *Nikāyas*, are inflicted. First, the guardians of *Niraya* torment a sinner with fivefold pinions.[22] They drive a hot iron stake each through his hands and feet and a fifth one through the middle of his chest. Second, they put him down and flay him with hatchets. Third, they place him with head downwards and plane him with knives. Fourth, they fix him to a chariot and drive it to and fro over the burning ground, Fifth, they lift him up on a great heap of burning coal. Sixth, they take him with feet up and head down and cast him into a blazing copper cauldron (*lohakumbha*)[23] and seventh, they throw him into the Great Hell (*Mahāniraya*).[24] According to the *Majjhimanikaya,*[25] those who have seen the five deva-messengers (birth, old age, disease, etc.) and do not abstain from evil deeds, are subject to such torments.

In the *Patavatthu Commentary,*[26] these seven tortures have been modified and are called *Sattusada* (seven *ussadas*). Ambasakkhara,[27] a Licchavi who performed an evil deed, was reborn in the hell where a sinner is tormented with fivefold fetters. Hot iron is placed upon him. He is laid on a mountain of burning charcoal, is thrown into a copper cauldron,[28] is made to enter a forest which has swords for leaves of trees, is compelled to cross the river *Vetaraṇī*[29] and is finally led to the Great Hell.

Eight major hells are often described in Pali Buddhist literature.[30] They are *Sañjīva, Kāḷasutta, Saṅghāta, Jālaroruva,*

Dhūmaroruva, Avīci, Tapana and *Patāpana.* Each of these hells has four corners and four doors and is divided into four equal parts. It is surrounded by iron walls and has an iron roof. Its floor is made of burning iron, one hundred *yojanas* around.[31] To each great hell are attached sixteen minor hells (*ussadas*).[32] These hells are full of horrors and terrible misery. The sinners are tortured in the *ussadas* by flames. Those who have committed outrage on saints or holy men are thrown into hell with their feet up and heads down. On account of their misdeeds they are roasted in hell for countless years like mangled fish cooked in a pot. Although they are eager to escape from hell, they never find a way in the east, west, north and south. Thus they dwell in hell for many thousand years and lament always for their pain.

The *Saṁkicca Jātaka*[33] describes the eight major hells as follows:

1. *Sañjīva.* The hell is so called because sinners are cut to pieces with various weapons by the guardians of the *nirayas* and come frequently to life to suffer the same punishment.[34] Those who kill living beings and cause them to be killed out of greed (*lobha*), delusion (*moha*), fear (*bhaya*) and anger (*krodha*) are reborn in the Sañjīva hell and have to suffer for one thousand years.[35]

2. *Kāḷasutta.* The guardians of the *nirayas* place the sinners[36] on a floor of hot iron, mark them with a black thread and then cut them into pieces with burning saws like the carpenters who mark the wood with black thread for cutting it into pieces.[37] Murderers of great sages are reborn in the *Kāḷasutta* hell and suffer torture for a long time. The son who slays his father out of greed and hatred suffers in hell. The keepers of the hells boil him in an iron cauldron.[38] They pierce him with spears and pluck his eyes. Then they feed him with filth and plunge him in brine. The goblins sometimes feed him with a hot iron ball; and in case he closes his mouth they open it with a hot ploughshare and put filth into it. Black and brown vultures, ravens, birds with iron beaks, and a motley crew tear his tongue into fragments and devour that quivering morsel soaked with blood. The goblins assail him with blazing iron clubs. The *Pañcagatidīpana*[39] states that

those who injure or harm their friends, speak falsehood and backbite others are subjected to such suffering.

3. *Saṅhgāta*. The hell is so called because the forgers are reborn there and are crushed by massive burning mountains of iron. As a result, they vomit and eat that filth. Crows, ravens, vultures and jackals eat the flesh and blood of the quivering wretches. The *Pañcagatidīpana*[40] states that the slayers of goats, sheep, jackals, hares, deers, pigs, etc., are reborn in the *Saṅghāta* hell where they are huddled up in one place and beaten to death.

4. *Jālaroruva*. It is one of the divisions of the *Roruva* hell, the other being *Dhūmaroruva*. The term *Roruva* is derived from the name *Ruru*. Unwise people who cast aspersions on the *Aryan norm* fall into this dreadful hell.[41] The *Mahānārada Kassapa Jātaka*[42] says that those who go after other man's wives are reborn in the *Roruva* hell. According to the *Pañcagatidīpana*,[43] miserly persons who are apt to cause mental and bodily pain to others and cheat them are subject to suffer in this hell. The *Jālaroruva* is so called because it is full of flames which enter the body of a sinner through his nine openings.[44]

5. *Dhūmaroruva*. It is a *Roruva* of smoke. The caustic smoke enters the body of a sinner through his nine openings.[45] In the *Saṁyuttanikāya*,[46] a hell is mentioned as *Mahārruva*, where a person is reborn for destroying life. The *Pañcagatidīpana*[47] states that those who misappropriate the property of others kept in trust with them and those who destroy the things entrusted to their care are reborn in the *Mahāroruva* hell, where they are consumed by a dreadful fire fiercer than that in the *Roruva*.

6. *Tapana*. It is so called because the victims of it have to suffer from terrible heat. The king who tortures his subjects is reborn in the *Tapana* hell and is surrounded by flames. His body burns and he roars in pain like a goad-stricken elephant. If a woman despises her husband and does not serve her relations, she is reborn in the *Tapana*. Her tongue is wrenched out with a hook and cord and it gets infested with worms. She has to endure awful pain without any complaint. The *Jātaka* commentator[48] says that in the *Tapana* the sinners are asked to sit upon a burning iron stake. The *Pañcagatidīpana*[49] states

that those who cause death of living beings by throwing them into fire, etc., are reborn here and burnt in the dreadful fire.

7. *Patāpana.* It is so called because its heat is excessive.[50] The commentary on the *Saṁkicca Jātaka*[51] says that the sinners who have been tormented in the *Tapana* are beaten in the *Patāpana* with burning weapons and have to climb up blazing iron mountains, from the top of which they fall with heads downwards on burning iron stakes on the ground. Those who are nihilists and cause death of living beings by throwing them into a big fire and represent *dhamma* as *adhamma* and vice versa are reborn here and are burnt in the fire,[52] which is more dreadful than that of the *Tapana* hell.

8. *Avīci.* It is the most fearful of the *nirayas,* According to the commentators, the name, *a-vīci,* means 'without rest or cessation'. The hell is so called because there is no cessation of either the fire or the pain.[53] The *Pañcagatidīpana,*[54] however, states that as there is no wave of happiness, it is called *Avīci* or waveless. It also says that those who injure men of great virtue and slay arahants, parents or preceptors are reborn in it and are burnt in a terrific fire.[55]

Avīci occurs as *niraya* in the *Itivuttaka,*[56] *Vinaya*[57] and *Dhammasaṅgaṇi.*[58] The word occurs once in the four *Nikāyas.* In the *Cakkavatti-Sīhanāda Sutta* of the *Dighanikāya,*[59] it is mentioned in connection with the tremendous growth of population which would occur in *Jambudīpa* in the future age when houses would be so close to one another that a cock could fly from any one to the next, and one would think it *Avīci.* According to Rhys Davids,[60] the word might have been originally used to denote density of population.

Spence Hardy[61] thinks that Avīci refers to absence of refuge. It is a place which 'affords no way of escape; it allows of no intermission to its misery'.

Buddhaghoṣa[62] explains the words *Avīci* as *nirantarapūrita* probably in the sense that it is filled with fire. The word appears in the *Visuddhimagga*[63] as a synonym for *jarā* (disintegration) and is used in connection with the disintegration of earth, water, mountains, sun, moon, etc. One who ridicules an *ārya*,[64] a disciple of the Buddha of Paccekabuddha must suffer in the Avīci hell.[65]

The *Avīcimahāniraya* is ten thousand *yojanas* in extent and forms a part of a *cakkavāḷa*.[66] The *Jātaka* commentator says that it is 1800 *yojanas* in diameter and 5400 *yojnaas* in circumference.[67] It is often referred to as the lowest point of the universe.[68] Heat is its chief suffering.[69]

According to the *Milindapañha*,[70] it is one hundred *yojanas* in depth and covered with blazing fire. The *Dhammapada Commentary*[71] places it under the earth because the earth opens wide to allow the flames of the *Avīci* to drag down sinners into its bowels. The following persons who committed grievous crimes were dragged into the *Avīci*—Devadatta; Cunda; Ānanda, who raped his cousin, the Therī Uppalavaññā; the ascetic Jambuka who in a previous birth insulted an arahant; Sivali who in a former birth blockaded a city for seven years; Snuppabuddha who insulted the Buddha; Mallikā, because of her misbehaviour with a dog (she was there for seven days only); Ciñcā-Mānavikā, because she falsely accused the Buddha; and Kapila, brother of Sodhana, for reviling pious monks.[72]

Being cursed by a sage, the king of Ceti who once could tread the air was lost and swallowed by *Avīci*.[73] The *Visuddhimagga*[74] states that the Buddha, having divided the earth into two parts at Sāketa by his supernatural power, showed his disciples the Avīci hell. Spence Hardy[75] mentions a tradition according to which *Avīci* is seven hundred miles directly under the Bodhi Tree and Gayā. Edkins says that *Avīci* is twenty thonsand *yojanas* (280,000 miles) below the Jambu continent.

The following tortures that await an entrance to the *Avīci* are described in the *Dhammapadaṭṭhakatha*.[77] When Devadatta entered the hell, his body became one hundred *yojanas* in height, his head as far as the outer ear entered into an iron skull; his feet sank up to the ankles in iron; an iron stake as thick as the trunk of a palmyra tree came from the west wall, pierced his back and penetrating his chest entered into the east wall. Similar stakes came from the south and the north and transfixed him. Another stake came out from the skull and piercing the head entered the earth.

The fire of *Avīci* is so powerful that it flames up one hundred *yojanas* [78] and destroys in a moment a rock as large as a gabled house, yet beings born there remain undestroyed.[79] It destroys the eyes of anyone looking at it from a distance of one hundred *yojanas*.[80]

The inhabitants of this hell have to suffer for periods of varying length. Devadatta passed 100,000 *kappas*,[81] while Mallikā, Pasenadi's queen remained only for seven days.[82] The *Saṁyutta*[83] and *Aṅguttara*[84] *Nikāyas* and the *Suttanipāta*[85] describe some hells which, according to Buddhaghoṣa,[86] are not separate *nirayas* but specified periods of suffering in the *Avīci*. They are Abbuda, *Nirabbuda, Ababa, Aṭaṭa, Ahaha, Kumuda, Sogandhika, Uppala, Puṇḍarīka* and *Paduma* and counted in a geometrical progression of twenty (i.e., twenty *Abbudas*=one term of *Nirabbuda*, twenty *Nirabbuda*=one term of *Ababa*, etc.), an *Abbuda* being reckoned as the time taken to remove twenty *Kośalan khāris* (equal to a cartload) of tila-seeds, taking one seed at the end of each century.[87] The monk Kokālika was born in the *Paduma* purgatory on account of hardening his heart against Sāriputta and Moggallāna.[88] 'Some say that the names of the purgatories are representations of the lamentations (e.g., *ahaha, ababa, aṭaṭa*) or occupations of their inmates. Others think that they are cold purgatories (and presumably these words represent the chattering of teeth, etc.).[89]

Sarājitā is another mode of suffering in the *Avīci*. The *Saṁyuttanikāya*[90] mentions it as a purgatory in which those who die in battle are reborn. According to the commentary,[91] it is not a distinctive purgatory, but a part of *Avīci*, where sinners are tormented like the fighters who fight on the battlefield, being armed with five weapons, riding on elephants, horses and chariots and taking ploughshares in hand.

We have said above that *Avīci* is one of the eight major hot hells and, according to Buddhaghoṣa,[92] it is identified with *Mahāniraya*, probably that of the *Aṅguttara* and *Majjhima Nikāyas*. The constitution of *Mahāniraya*[93] is also the same as that of the eight major hells of the *Saṁkicca Jātaka*. The remaining part of its description, according io the *Suttas*, is as following: Flames leap up from each of the four walls (eastern, western, southern and northern), and from the top to the bottom of the *Mahāniraya*. When the eastern, western, southern and northern gateways are opened, the sinners rush there. While they are rushing, their skin, flesh and tendons burn and their eyes are filled with smoke. The next time when the eastern gateway is opened, they go out by it. But, adjacent to this great hell, there are other hells,[94] wherein the sinners fail and suffer. They are (1) *Gūtha*, (2) *Kukkula*, (3) *Simbalivana*, (4) *Asipattavana* and (5) *Khārodakanadī*. Of these, Nos. 2, 4 and 5 a rementioned as *ussada-nirayas*[95] in the *Pañcagatidīpana*.

1. *Gūtha*. It is so called because the inhabitants of it have to eat filth. It is compared to a mother's womb.[96] According to Buddhaghoṣa,[97] those who insult their parents have to suffer in this hell. The *Pañcagatidīpana*[98] states that a man who leads a wrong life is reborn there. *Miḷhakūpa* (one of the *ussadas* of a *Mahāniraya*) may be compared to the *Gūtha* hell because both the names carry a common meaning and apply the same torture to the sinners.[98a] The needle-mouthed creatures (worms) pierce the sinner's bodies, cut away their skin, hide, flesh, tendons and bones and then devour the marrow of their bones.[99]

2. *Kukkulaniraya*. It is so called because it is full af embers. King Daṇḍaki was born here for his heinous crimes.[100] He was overwhelmed with a mass of glowing coals, one hundred *yojanas* deep; huge glowing sparks fell on him and entered his body through the nine wholes.[101] The *Pañcagatidīpana* says that those who do not adopt and follow moral precepts are born in the *Kukkulaniraya*, where they are boiled[102] and fried[103] like mustard seeds.

3. *Simbalivana* (great forest of silk-cotton trees).[104] It is one *yojana* in height and is full of thorns with sharp iron-spikes. It always burns and looks like a mass of fire from a distance. The *Jātaka*[105] commentator says that branches of the Simbali trees hang on both sides of the Vetaraṇī river. Unfaithful husbands, guilty wives and adulterous people have to climb up and down the trees, driven on by the servants of Yama bearing spears in their hands. When the sinners climb up the silk-cotton trees, they are covered with blood, their bodies gashed

and flayed, sick and racked with pain, panting and sighing. They are then beaten with stripes and fall on the ground, revolving in their flight with mangled limbs and there they pass sleepless nights. According to the *Jataka* commentary[106], when they fall with head downwards their bodies are pierced by stakes rising from the earth. At dawn, they hide themselves in a great iron cauldron (*lohakumbha*) which is as a big as a mountain[107] and is full of hot water. The *Suttanipāta Commentary*,[108] however, describes *lohakumbha* as a separate *niraya*, where beings suffer from excessive heat.[109] It extends under the earth and is four *nahutas* and two hundred thousand *yojanas* in depth. The hell is so called because it looks like a cauldron filled up to the brim with molten metal.[110] The *Dhammapadaṭṭhakthā*[111] says that it is 60 *yojanas* in extent.

Those who spend their money and time by indulging in vices, such as aduletry, kidnapping, etc., have to suffer in the *Lohakumbhiniraya*.[112] The *Nimi Jātaka*[113] says that those who hurt the Brāhmaṇas and bhikkhus fall in the blazing iron cauldron with their heads downwards.

The *Lohakumbi Jātaka*[114] describes how four princes of Sāvatthi in their previous existence did evil deeds and were born in the *Lohakumbhiniraya*. These princes were guilty of gross misconduct with the carefully guarded wives of their neighbours near Vārāṇasī and, as a result, were born in four iron cauldrons. Being tortured for thirty thousand years in a thick corrosive and boiling liquid in the iron cauldrons, when they at one time sank and reached the bottom, and at another time rose to the top like a foam bubble,[115] though after that period they found the mouth of the cauldron, looked over the edge, and wanted to proclaim their misery in four stanzas, but failed to do so owing to their sin. After uttering one syllable of each, namely *Du*, *Sa*, *Na* and *So*, they sank again in the cauldrons. The complete stanzas are :

(1) *Dujjīvitaṁ ajīvmha ye sante na dadamhase, vijjamānesu bhogesu dīpaṁ nākamha attano ti.*

(2) *Saṭṭhivassasahassāni paripuṇṇāni sabbaso, niraye paccamānānaṁ kadā anto bhavissatīti.*

(3) *N'atthi anto kuto anto na anto patidissati, tadā hi pakataṁ pāpaṁ mama tuyhañ ca mārisā'ti*

and

(4) *So hi nūna ito gantvā yoniṁ taddhāna mānusīṁ vadaññū sīlasampanno kāhāmi kusalaṁ bahunti.*

4. *Asipattavana* (sword-leafed forest). The *Mahānārada Kassapa Jātaka*[116] says that the hell is so called because it is a lofty forest like heaps of clouds, covered with swords-like leaves with iron knives which sack the blood from men. When a sinner climbs up the tree with iron leaves, he is wounded with the sharp swords. According to the *Suttanipāta Commentary*,[117] the hell appears as a mango grove in the distance, and when the sinners enter it to eat the mangoes, leaves which are sharp like swords, stirred by the wind, cut off their limbs. The *Pañcagatidīpana*[118] states that a treacherous person is subject to such sufferings.

5. *Khārodakanadī* (river of caustic water). Here the sinners are carried with and against the stream, but do not get across.[119] Fishermen, robbers, hunters, knaves; slayers of sheep, swine and cows are assailed and pursued with swords, iron clubs, spears and arrows and thrown into the caustic river[120] with their heads downwards. Buddhaghoṣa[121] identified it with river Vetaraṇī. In the *Āditta Jātaka*,[122] Vetaraṇī is referred to as a separate *niraya*. The *Suttanipāta*[123] regards it as a river in the *Mahāniraya*. Its waters are sharp and bitter (*tiṇadhārā, Khuradhārā*).[124] In the *Saṁkicca Jātaka*,[125] *Khuradhārā* is mentioned as a different niraya, where adulterers are reborn and cut into pieces with the sharp blazing razors. The *Pañcagatidīpana*[126] states that those who foster disunion in the Buddhist Saṅgha will have to suffer in this hell.

However, though it is hard for sinners to flee from the *Khuradhārā* hell, some of them do so after having drank a medicine of brine and fall in the *Vetaraṇīnadī*.[127] Oppressors of the weak are reborn in it.[128] The *Nimi Jātaka*[129] says that the Vetaraṇī river is stinking, full of corrosive brine, and hot. It is covered with flames. The *Jātaka* commentator[130] gives a long description of this region. Its waters are covered with spears, cane creepers and thorns which are sharp like razor and are ablaze. On the banks of this river the guardians of *niraya* stay with burning swords, spears. clubs, etc. They strike the sinners with these weapons and cast them into the unbearable Vetaraṇī, where they are covered with the thorns of canes. The thorns are sharp like blazing razors by which they are cut into pieces. Then they are pierced with the blazing stakes. Next they have to fall on the sharp iron leaves of lotuses, where their limbs are cut.[131] Below it there are burning caustic waters. Sinners cannot seek peace even in the bed of this river because it is covered with sharp razors. They run in pain with and against the stream. When they get up on the shore, the keepers of hell strike and spear them. The *Pañcagatidīpana*[132] states that those who slay aquatic animals like fish are born in the Vetaraṇī, where they suffer for a long time. The Vetaraṇī flows by the Simbalivana[133] and *Asipattavana*[134] *nirayas*. The *Suttanipāta Commentary*[135] states that the river is full of sharp razors. People going to the river to bathe and drink water are hecked by swords and other sharp weapons that stand concealed along the banks of the river.

Having tortured the victim in the river of *Mahāniraya* the keepers of hell haul him out with a fish hook, set him on dry ground and ask him, "My good man, what do you want?" When he replies that he is hungry and thirsty, the guardians of the *niraya* open his mouth with a glowing iron-spike, and push into it a blazing copper pellet (*lohagulam*) and sprinkle into it burning copper and bronze. These burn his lips, mouth throat, chest and pass out through the bowels and intestines.[136]

The *Dīghanikāya Commentary*[137] states that Devadatta bore malice against the Buddha, tried to take his life, brought disunion in the Saṅgha and performed many other evil deeds. As a result, he after being devoured by the earth, had to suffer in the *Mahāniraya.*

Besides the eight major hells, the commentary on the *Sarabhaṅga Jātaka*[138] mentions a *Mahāniraya* called *Sunakha*, where the sinners fall into the jaws of dogs. King Nāḷikīra of Dantapura, situated in the Kaliṅga kingdom, invited some saints, poured filth on their alms bowls, hurt their heads with iron clubs and caused dogs to eat their legs. As a result, he had to fall into this hell where his body becomes three *gāvutas* in height.

According to the *Jātaka* commentator, the sixteen minor hells (*ussadas*[139]) mentioned above are divided equally in four groups situated in the four doors of each great hell. In the *Ayoghara Jātaka,*[140] *Ussada* is mentioned as a separate *niraya* which is a place of great suffering. It looks like a city with four gates surrounded by a wall. While Mittavindaka arrived at the *Ussada,* he saw a man supporting a wheel as sharp as a razor, which looked like a lotus-flower. He took it from that man, and realising what it was, tried to flee, but was unsuccessful. The razor-wheel pierced him and smashed him like a pestle crushing mustard seeds. Those who smite their mothers have to undergo such suffering. Sakka, during a visit to the *Ussada,* saw Mittavindaka, but could not rescue him.[141]

Beings who promise to give a gift and fail to do it are reborn in this hell.[142] Once the Bodhisatta was born here and suffered for eighty thousand years for his cruelty when he was a king of Vārāṇasī.[143] Revatī[144] was also once born here.[117]

The commentary on the *Matakabhata Jātaka*[146] refers to the sixteen *ussada-nirayas*; but it does not mention the eight great hells to which the *ussada-nirayas* are attached.

After mentioning the *Mahānirayas* (major hells) and *ussadas* (minor hells), the *Pañcagatidīpana*[147] describes other tortures. When the sinners come out from the *Kukkulaniraya,* they go to the trees covered with beautiful leaves for relief. But there the crows, vultures, dogs, owls, boars and cranes devour their flesh. Those who destroy themselves in battle get blazing nails like swords by using which they kill one another. The persons who practise adultery have to climb up the silk-cotton-trees[148] and embrace massive and terrific women bearing iron-teeth who devour them. Thieves have to eat iron ball and drink crushed copper powder. The judges who take bribes are reborn in hell where they are cut to pieces in an iron wheel. The sinners are beaten with clubs and pressed with machines and mountains. Those who cause quarrel between friends have to go along a path as sharp as the edge of a razor.[149] Besides some persons are reborn in the *Yamaloka* for their vices, e.g., envy, anger and pleasure at the sight of the sufferings of others.

There are other kinds of tortures associated with the following *nirayas*. The *Mahānāradakassapa Jātaka*[150] says that those who hold wrong views and are addicted to sensual pleasure with other's wives are reborn in hell. They have to suffer first in the Kākola hell,[151] where they are dragged by flocks of ravens and devoured by crows, vultures and hawks. As a result, their bodies are torn. Those who are churlish and miserly, and hurt Brāhmaṇas and ascetics with their foul tongue, are reborn in this hell.

If, however, they are not reborn in it, they must be born in the *Lokantarika* series of hells.[152] Each of these is eight thousand *yojanas* in extent and is situated in the space between the three *cakkavāḷas* where darkness prevails.[153] This reminds us of the *anārambhanam tamas* (unsupported darkness) of the *Ṛgveda*.[154] It is evermore tumultuous and dreadful because the light from the sun and moon does not reach here.[155] Beings born there have their bodies three *gāvutas* in height and, cling to the *cakkavāḷa-pabbata* with their long nails. Sometimes, they find no food and fall into the world-bearing water (*lokasandhārakaüdaka*) and die of its salinity.[156] In the *Mahāniddesa*[157] and *Buddhaghoṣa's commentary*,[158] they are said to suffer from extreme cold. According to the *Buddhavaṁsa Commentary*,[159] *Lokantarika* is the hell of the *Asurakāya*. The *Dīghanikāya Commentary*[160] describes it as a great hell where the sins of violence against relatives and virtuous ascetics are punished. The inhabitants of this hell are classed as *petas* in the Sinhalese source,[161] but there is no indication of it in the Pali literature.

Besides, sinners have to suffer from the following punishments for their wrong view. The mighty dogs, giant in size, and called Sabala and Sama, devour the victims with their iron teeth.[162] The Kāḷūpakāḷās (keepers of hell) smite and wound the sinners in hell with arrows and sharp spears, keeping them on the iron-teeth. Thus they are smitten and have their entrails mangled and bodies torn. Heaven rains spears, arrows, javeline and spikes, as well as flames like burning coals and blazing stones on the head of a cruel man.[163] An intolerable hot wind blows in hell and its inhabitants do not feel even a transient pleasure; they have no refuge, and rush about in their sickness. The guardians of the *niraya* having yoked the sinners in chariots, tread along the fiery ground urging them on with goads and sticks. When the inhabitants of hell climb up a fearful blazing mountain full of razors, their bodies are gashed and dripping with blood.[164] They also have to ascend a dreadful blazing heap of coals. As they climb it, the unfortunate sinners cry. Next they have to suffer in the hells like *Simbalivana*,[165] *Asipattavana*[166] and *Veṭaraṇīnadī*.[167]

In the *Nimi Jātaka*,[168] Mātali, the charioteer of Indra, showed the tortures to king Nimi. At first were shown the river *Vetaraṇī*,[169] and the hell *Kākola*.[170] The king saw a hell wherein the bodies of sinners were burning as they lay on the blazing ground of iron. The keepers of hell struck their bodies with hot iron clubs. Those who are enemies of honest people and torment them have to fall into this hell. Next he saw a glowing pit of coals where the sinners have to fall and suffer. The guardians of hell rain burning coal on their heads. They tremble and roar in pain. Those who collect money for the benefit of the people but spend it for their own enjoyment with the support of false evidence and bribing bigger people have to be reborn in such hell.

The guardians of the *niraya* wring the victims by neck and after battering their heads, cast them in the iron cauldron[171] full of boiling water. The battered head of one goes to the neck of another. The wicked men who, in the world catch birds and destroy them by battering their heads, are subject to such sufferings.

There flows a deep river with shallow banks, easily accesible, in hell. When the victims go to it to drink for quenching their thirst, the water turns to chaff. The persons who mix grain with chaff and sell it to buyers suffer from this sort of punishment.

Those who take what is not theirs (i.e., goat, sheep, kine, bull, corn, treasure, silver and gold) are reborn in hell and pierced with spikes, spears and arrowheads by the guardians of the *nirayas*.

Somewhere in the hells the sinners are fastened by the neck and cut to pieces for the sin of slaying fishes, boars, cattle, bulls and goats for food.

There is in the hell a lake filled with stinking filth[172] and ordure. Its inhabitants have to eat ordure and filth. Malicious persons who harm their friends and hurt others are subject to such suffering.

Another stinking lake full of blood and pus is also there. Those who slay their fathers, mothers and others to whom they should pay reverence are cast into it and have to drink a draught of blood.

The tongues of persons who take bribe and do not pay the proper price of articles and practise knavery are pierced with a hook and have to flutter like a fish on the ground.

The women who, being born in a noble family, lead unclean lives, do bad deeds and leave their husbands for satisfying their lust with other persons, are reborn in hell where they are buried waist-deep in earth; the upper parts of their bodies are crushed by blazing mountains, and smeared with stains of blood; they wail like cattle in the shambles.

The man who seduces another's wife falls with his head downwards in hell. The heretics who hold wrong views have to suffer from intolerable pain. Besides, Mātali showed the king, at one flash, all the great hells in four quarters of which no description is found in the *Nimi Jātaka*.

The *Suttanipāta*[173] describes the following tortures in hell. The victims are struck with iron rods; they are led to the iron stake with sharp edges; they have to eat a red-hot ball of iron when they became hungry; they have to lie on a bed of embers and are made to enter a blazing pyre. The warders of hell cover them with net and thrash them with iron flails. Then they are cooked in a fiery copper cauldron. One who commits sin must be boiled in a mixture of pus and blood, in water full of worms, whence they cannot flee because the surface is concave. Then they suffer in the *Asipattavana*,[174] *Veraraṇī*,[175] *Kākola*[176] and *Paduma*.[177]

The Pali literature mentions other hells which are as follows :

1. *Sataporisa*.[178] Those who slay their mothers are sent to this hell and are cut with ploughshares by demons. When they become thirsty, the demons give them blood resembling

molten copper which flows from their wounds. Here they suffer from loss of sight. Enormous worms pierce the sinners' skin and devour their flesh and blood.

2. *Sattisūla.*[179] The hell is so called because here the victims are pierced with stakes. As Ajjuna pierced Aṅgirasa Gotama, he had to take rebirth here. The keepers of the hell placed him on the mountain of hot iron. Thence he was thrown by the wind on the blazing ground of iron. At the time of falling, burning stakes of iron arose from the ground and pierced his head,

3. *Mahāpariḷāha.*[180] The hell is so called because all the objects of senses, though really attractive, appear quite repulsive to the sinners who take rebirth in it.

4. *Pahāsa* (Purgatory of laughter). Those players who make people laugh on the stage or in the arena are reborn in it because such plays make people more lustful and resentful.[181] According to the *Saṁyutta Commentary,*[182] it is not a distinctive purgatory, but a section of the *Avīci,* where actors play their parts and are cooked.

5. *Saṁsavaka.*[183] It is deep and so called because it flows with stinking filth. The selfish persons who abuse religious men are cast into this hell and have to suffer for a thousand years. The inhabitants of this hell have also to endure other kinds of torture, e.g., their hands, feet, ears and noses are cut off and are devoured by ravens.

Notes

Chapter III

1. See p. 10
2. See e.g., *Jāt.*, Vol. V, pp. 135, 143-45, 270 ; *Vis.*, Vol. II, p.390 ; *Dham. Com.*, Vol. I, pp. 127, 148 ; Vol. III, p.181 ; cf. R. Spence Hardy, *MB.*, p.26.
3. *Pet. Com.*, p.52 (*natthi ettha ayo sukhan ti*)
4. *Vis.*, Vol. II, p. 427, Cf. *Jāt.*, Vol. VI, pp. 6-8.
5. *Aṅg.*, Vol. I, pp. 292-93 ; Vol. III. pp. 170, 204, 432 ; Vol. II, pp. 226, 231 ; *Maj.*, Vol. III, p.179 ; *Dīg.*, Vol. I, p.82 ; *Itv.*, pp.12, 99 ; cf. *Sut.*, p. 127.
6. Vol. III, pp. 170, 204, 432 ; cf. the *Pañcavera Sutta* of the *Saṁ.*, Vol. IV, p. 243, where it is said that a woman committing the five sins goes to hell.
7. Cf. *Jāt.*, Vol. V, p. 131.
8. Cf. *Aṅg.*, Vol. II, pp. 226, 237 ; *Dīg.*, Vol. I, p. 82 ; *Maj.*, Vol. III, p.179.
9. Vol. II. p.226.
10. *Loc. cit* ; cf. *Maj.*, Vol. III, p.179 ; *Sut.*, pp. 127-28.
11. *Aṅg.*, Vol. II, p.227.
12. *Saṁ.*, Vol. IV, pp, 240-43.
13. *Loc. cit* (*Tīhi Sutta*).
14. *Ibid*, Vol.I, p. 34.
15. Vol.I, pp. 307-08.
16. *Aṅg.*, Vol. III, p. 3.
17. *PB*, p. 369.
18. Vol. I, p. 199
19. See pp.73f.
20. Vol. I, pp. 141.
21. Vol. III, pp. 179-83.
22. Cf. *PC*, p. 346 ; *Sut. Com.*, Vol II, p. 479.
23. See below, note 109.
24. See below, pp.55-56, 59.
25. Vol. III, pp. 178-183.
26. See p. 221.
27. *Pet.*, p. 45.
28. See below, p. 71

29. See below, pp. 58-59.
30. *Jāt.*, Vol. V, pp. 266-75; *JPTS*, 1884, pp. 154-56, where *Roruva* and *Mahāroruva* are mentioned in place of *Jālaroruva* and *Dhūmaroruva*
31. Cf. *Catukaṇṇo catudvāro vibhatto bhāgaso mito*
 Ayopākārapariyanto ayasā paṭikujjito
 Tassa ayomayā bhūmi jalitā tejasā yutā
 Samantā yojanasataṁ pharitvā tiṭṭhati sabbadā ti (*Jāt.*, Vol. V, p. 266 ; *Aṅg.*, Vol. I, pp.141-142 ; *Maj.*, vol. III, p.183) ; *PC*, p. 347.
32. See below, note 109.
33. *Jāt.*, Vol. V, pp. 266-75.
34. Cf. *JPTS*, 1884, p. 154.
35. Loc. cit.
36. The body of a sinner becomes 3 *yojanas* in length (*Jāt.*, Vol.V p.273).
37. Cf. loc. cit.
38. See below, p.57.
39. *JPTS*, 1884, p.154.
40. Loc. cit., *The Saṁkicca Jāt.*, Vol. V, p. 270 states that those who hunt beast with beast, and slay birds with birds suffer terrible pain in hell.
41. *Saṁ.*, Vol. I, p. 30 ; *KS*, Vol. I, p. 41, note 1.
42. *Jāt.*, Vol. VI, pp. 236-39.
43. *JPTS*, 1884, p. 154.
44. *Jāt.*, Vol. V, p. 271.
45. Loc. cit.
46. Vol. I, pp. 92-93. Cf. *Dham. Com.*, Vol. IV, p. 79.
47. *JPTS*, 1884, pp. 154-55.
48. *Jāt.*, Vol. V, p. 271.
49. *JPTS*, 1884, p. 155.
50. *Jāt.*, Vol. V, p.271.
51. Loc. cit.
52. *JPTS*, loc. cit.
53. *dukkhassa vīci nāma n'atthi, jālānaṁ vīci nāma n'atthi* (*Jāt.*, loc. cit.).
54. *JPTS*, 1884, p.155.
55. *Loc. cit.*
56. *SBB*, Vol. IV (*DB*, Vol.III), p. 73, note 1.
57. Loc. cit.
58. Loc. cit.
59. Vol. III, p. 75. See *DB*, Vol. III p. 72, note 2.
60. *DB*, Vol. III, p. 73, note 1.
61. *MB*, 1860, p. 27.
62. *Dīg. Com.*, Vol. III, p. 855.
63. Vol. II, p. 449.
64. Ibid., pp. 425. 427
65. Cf. *Maj.*, Vol. III, p. 179.
66. *Sut-, Com.*, Vol. II, p. 443 ; *Vis.*, Vol. I, p. 207 ; *Vin. Com.*, Vol. I p. 119.
67. *ERE*, Vol.XI, p.831.

68. E.g., *Vis.*, Vol.II, pp.390, 486.
69. *MN. Com.*, *SHB*, p.8.
70. See p.357 (*SBE.*, Vol. XXXVI, p. 261, note 4).
71. Vol. I, pp. 127, 147 ; Vol. III, p. 181.
72. *Dham. Com.*, Vol. I, p. 125 ; Vol. II, pp. 49f, 52 63; Vol.III, pp. 44f. 119 ff., 178f ; *Jāt.*, Vol. IV, pp. 187f; *Itv*, *Com.*, p. 69 ; *Vin.*, Vol.III p. 35. *Mil.*, pp. 108, 301, 357.
73. *Jāt.*, Vol. III, pp. 459-60 ; Vol. V, p. 267.
74. Vol. II, p. 390.
75. *MB*, p. 27.
76. *Chinese Buddhism*, p. 225.
77. Vol. I, p. 148.
78. *Jāt.*, Vol. VI, p. 8.
79. *Dham. Com.*, Vol. I, p. 127 ; *Mil.*, p. 67.
80. *Aṅg.*, Vol. I, p. 142.
81. *Dham. Com.*, Vol. I, p. 148.
82. Ibid., Vol. III, p. 121.
83. Vol. I, pp.149-52.
84. Vol. V, p. 173.
85. See p. 126.
86. *Aṅg. Com.*, *PTS*, Vol. V, pp. 61-62.
87. *Aṅg.*, Vol. V, p. 173; *Sut.*, p. 126 ; Saṁ., Vol. I, p. 152, *KS*, Vol. I p. 190, notes 1 and 2; *Sut. Com.*, Vol. II, p. 477 gives an *Abbuda* as equal to 100,000 *ninnahutas* and its 20 times is *nirabbuda* ; *Aṅg. Com. PTS*, Vol. V, pp. 61-62.
88. *Aṅg.*, Vol. V, p. 172; *Sut.*, p. 126 ; *Jāt.*, Vol. IV, pp. 244-45 (because Kokālika reviled the chief disciples, there arose over all his body boils of the size of a mustard seed which grew to the size of a ripe seed of a Bilva tree and burst. As a result, he groaned in pain and fell into the hell by the gate of Jetavana) ; *Aṅg. Com.*, *PTS*, Vol V, p. 61 ; *Dham. Com.*, Vol. IV, p. 91 ; *Saṁ.*, Vol. 1, p. 151.
89. *GS*, Vol. V, p. 116, note 1.
90. Vol. IV; pp. 309, 311.
91. *Saṁ. Com.*, PTS, Vol. III, pp. 103-04.
92. *Aṅg. Com.*, PTS, Vol. II, p. 256 ; *Dīg. Com.*, Vol. I, pp. 138-39.
93. See above, note 31.
94. *Maj.*, Vol. III, p. 185.
95. See below, p. 60.
96. *Jāt.*, Vol.IV, p. 493.
97. *Dham. Com.*, Vol. IV, p. 34.
98. *JPTS*, 1884, pp. 155-56.

98a. Loc. cit.

99. *Maj.*, Vol. III, p. 185 ; *Jāt.*, Vol. VI, p. 8 ; *Sut. Com.*, Vol. II, p. 481.
100. *Maj.*, Vol. III, p. 185 ; *Jāt.*, Vol. V, pp. 114, 143; *JPTS*, 1884, p. 155.
101. *Jāt.*, Vol. V, p. 144.
102. *JPTS*, loc. cit.
103. *Ibid.*, p. 156.

104. Loc. cit.; *Maj.*, Vol. III, p. 185 ; *Jāt.*, Vol. VI, p. 249 ; Vol. V, p. 269
105. *Jāt.*, Vol. V. p. 275.
106. Loc. cit.
107. Cf. *Jāt.*, Vol. VI, p. 108.
108. Vol. I, p. 59.
109. *Jāt.*, Vol. III, p. 22; Vol. V, p. 269.
110. *Sut Com.*, Vol. II, p. 480; cf. *Jāt.*, Vol, V, p. 275.
111. Vol. II, pp. 5, 10 ; cf. *Jāt.*, Vol. V, p. 275.
112. *Dham. Com.*, Vol. II, pp. 10f.
113. *Jāt.*, Vol. VI, pp. 108f.
114. Ibid., Vol. III, pp. 43-48 ; cf. *Dham. Com.*, Vol. II pp. 5-11, *Pet. Com.*, pp. 279 ff.
115. Cf. *Mil.*, p. 357 ; *Aṅg.*, Vol. I, p. 141 ; *Maj.*, Vol. III, pp. 179-83.
116. *Jāt.*, Vol. VI, p. 250, p. cf. *Maj.*, Vol. III, p. 185 ; *Sut.*, verse 673.
117. Vol. II, p. 481.
118. *JPTS*, 1884, p. 156.
119. *Maj.*, loc. cit.
120. *Jāt.*, Vol. V, p. 270.
121. *Sut. Com.*, Vol. II, p. 482.
122. *Jāt.*, Vol. III, p. 473 ; cf. Vol. IV, p. 273. See also *KS*, Vol. I. p. 30 note 5.
123. Verse 674. Cf. *Saṁ.*, Vol. I, p. 21.
124. *Sut.*, verse 674.
125. Vol. V, pp. 269, 274f.
126. *JPTS*, 1884, p. 156
127. *Jāt.*, Vol. V, p. 269.
128. *Ibid.*, Vol. VI, p. 106.
129. *Ibid.*, p. 105.
130. Loc. cit.
131. Cf. *Jāt.*, Vol. VI, p. 250, where it is said that the cruel Vetaraṇī has boiling water and is covered with iron lotuses and sharp leaves.
132. *JPTS*, loc. cit., where Vetaraṇī is described as hot as molten brass. It is mentioned here as one of the four *Ussadanirayas*.
133. See above. p. 56.
134. Cf. *Sut. Com.*, Vol .II, p. 482; *Jāt.*, Vol. VI, p. 250.
135. Vol. II, p. 482.
136. *Maj.*, Vol. III, pp. 185f.
137. Vol. I, pp. 138f.
138. *Jāt.*, Vol. V, pp. 143-45.
139. *Jāt.*, Vol. V, p. 272. The *Pañcagatidīpana* (*JPTS*, 1884, pp.155f.) speaks of only four *Ussadas* belonging to each great hell, namely, (1) *Miḷhakūpa*, the hell of dung, where beings are eaten up by worms ; (2) *Kukkula*, the hell of ashes ; (3) *Asipattavana*, the forest with leaves of swords ; and (4) *Nadī* (*Vetaraṇī*), or river of bitter water, Those who are in the great hell have to pass these minor hells one after another.
140. *Jāt.*, Vol. IV, p. 493.

141. *Jāt.*, Vol. IV, pp. 3f; Vol. II, pp. 206 f.
142. Ibid., Vol. IV, p. 405.
143. Ibid., Vol. VI, p. 2.
144. *Dham. Com.*, Vol. III, pp. 290 ff; *Vim. Com.*, pp. 220 ff; *Pet. Com.*, p. 257.
145. *Vim. Com.*, p. 223.
146. *Jāt.*, Vol. I, p. 168.
147. *JPTS*, 1884, pp. 155f.
148. See above, p. 56.
149 See above, 58.
150. *Jāt.*, Vol. VI, pp. 246 50.
151. Cf. ibid., Vol. VI, p. 247; *JPTS*, p. 155 ; *Sut.*, verse 675,
152. *Jāt.*, Vol. VI, p. 247 ; *Sut. Com.*, Vol. II, p. 443.
153. *Dīg.*, Vol. II, p. 12.
154. *ERE*, Vol. IV, p. 132.
155. *Jāt.*, Vol. VI, p. 247.
156. *Aṅg. Com.*, *SHB*, Vol. III, p. 126.
157. *MN. Com.*, *SHB.*, p. 8.
158. *Sut. Com.*, Vol. I, p. 59.
159. See p. 29.
160. *ERE*, Vol. XI, p. 830.
161. *MB*, pp. 47, 58.
162. *Jāt.*, Vol. VI, p. 247.
163. *Ibid.*, p. 248.
164. *Jāt.*, Vol.VI, p.249 ; see also above, p. 62 (4th of the 7 tortures).
165. See above, p. 56.
166. See above, p. 58.
167. See above, p. 58.
168. *Jātaka* No. 541.
169. See above, pp. 53-59.
170. See above, p. 61.
171. See above, p. 57.
172. See above, p. 56.
173. See pp. 129-30.
174. See above, p. 58-59.
175. See above, pp. 58-59,
176. See above, p. 61.
177. See above, p. 55.
178. *Jāt.*, Vol. V, p. 269.
179. *Jāt.*, Vol. V, pp. 143-45.
180. *Saṁ.*, Vol. V, pp. 450-52.
181. Ibid., Vol. IV, pp. 307 ; cf. *PB*, p. 369.
182. Vol. III, PTS, p. 103 (*Pahāsanāma nirayo tivisuṁ Pahāsanāmako nirayo nāma na hoti. Avīciyaṁ yeva Pana ekasmiṁ koṭṭhāse naccantā viya gāyanīā viya ca naṭavesaṁ gahetvā paccante.*
183. *Vim.*, p. 50.

CHAPTER IV

Gods and Goddesses

The Pali literature does not speak of any Supreme God. All the gods mentioned in it[1] are inferior to the Buddha. The *Aṅguttaranikāya*[2] says that though Sakka is the ruler of the gods, he is inferior to a *bhikku* (who acquired Arahantship and was free from the defects of ordinary beings) because he is not free from *rāga, dosa* and *moha* (passion, hatred and delusion). The Brahmās[3] are the highest of all the gods; but they are neither supreme nor are they creators of the universe. They are also inferior to the Buddha. Sometimes the gods including Brahmās come on earth to worship the Buddha and to carry out his order.[4]

Beings above the human level in certain respects, are regarded as gods. According to a late classification,[5] three kings of *Devā* (gods) are found—(1) *Sammutidevā* (conventional gods, e.g., kings and princes); (2) *Visuddhidevā* (beings who are divine by the purity of their great religious merit, e.g., arahants and Buddhas); and (3) *Uppattidevā* (beings who are born divine).

Under the last category are enumerated various groups of gods, the commonest number of which is seven,[6] namely, (1) *Cātummahārājika,* (2) *Tāvatiṁsa,* (3) *Yāma,* (4) *Tusita,* (5) *Nimmānaratī,* (6) *Paranimmitavasavattī,* and (7) *Brahmakāyikā.*

The following twenty classes of Brahmās are called '*Brahmakāyikā Devā:* (1) *Brahmapārisajjā,* (2) *Brahmapurohitā,* (3) *Mahābrahmās* (4) *Parittābhā,* (5) *Appamāṇābhā,* (6) *Ābhassarā,* (7) *Parittasubhā,* (8) *Appamāṇasubhā,* (9) *Subhakiṇhā,* (10) *Vehapphalā,* (11) *Asaññasattā,* (12) *Avihā,* (13) *Atappā,* (14) *Sudassā,* (15) *Sudassī,* (16) *Akaniṭṭhā,* (17) *Ākāsānañcāyatanapagādevā,* (18) *Viññāṇañcāyatanapagādevā,* (19) *Ākiñcaññāyatanapagādevā,* and (20) *Nevasaññānāsaññāyatanapagādevā.*

Buddhist literature recognises the Vedic tradition of personification and deification of natural phenomena.[8] Some important Vedic gods have also been mentioned in Pali literature with certain changes, particularly in conformity with the Buddhist conception. Most of the gods are the followers of the Buddha and are kind to good men, whom they protect.[9] But a few gods are unkind to men because they induce them to do evil deeds.[10]

Sometimes gods take human and animal forms. The *Somanassa Jātaka*[11] says that some deities in human shape traversed the seven ranges of hills and reached the Himālaya. The *Vessantara Jātaka*[12] says that the gods took the form of red-deer and carried the chariot of the Buddha born as Vessantara when he offered four horses of his chariot to four Brāhmaṇas.

Worship of certain tutelary gods, tree-gods, hill-gods and ocean-deities[13] are also mentioned in Buddhist literature. Of them, the *Bhumma*, *Rukkha* and *Vemāna*[14] classes of gods are of lower grades.

As mentioned in the *Kakkaru Jātaka*,[15] some terrestrial deities, along with four divine beings from the Tāvatiṁsa-world who wore wreaths made of heavenly *Kakkāru* flowers, attended a great festival at *Vārāṇasī*.

The gods have their respective dwelling places which are named according to their class-names.[16] Of them, those who live in the sky and on the earth are conscious of the earth, and are subject to grief and lamentation like ordinary human beings while the gods who are free from attachment are not subject to grief, but are conscious of it and have knowledge of the impermanence of things.[17]

The six classes of devas who have strong faith in the *Buddha Dhamma* and *Saṅgha*, claim to have acquired the stage of *sotāpanna* and are destined for the attainment of *sambodhi*. They are not, therefore, liable to fall into hell.[18] They, especially the *Cātummahārājika* and *Tāvatiṁsa* gods, take interest in the doings of man. They come to the earth to show reverence to good men.[19]

Though the gods possessing miraculous power can shake the earth,[20] they are not free from death. Their lease of life varies according to the merits they earn.[21]

However, the gods are born full of youth and free from illness and remain so till the moment of their death. They die for the following reasons: (1) exhaustion of life, merit or food; (2) failing, through forgetfulness, to eat; and (3) jealousy at the glory of another which leads to anger.[22] At the time of their death five signs appear on them—(1) their clothes get soiled, (2) flowers worn by them fade, (3) sweat exudes from their armpits, (4) their bodies become colourless, and (5) they become restless on their seats.[23]

Besides the seven principal groups of gods, other classes of gods are mentioned here and there. The *Mahāsamaya sutta*[24] describes the following classes of gods who were present at the preaching of the *Sutta*:

1. *Accutadevā.*
2. *Anejakā.*
3. *Aruṇā.* They are of diverse hue, of wondrous gifts, mighty power and comeliness, and with splendid following.
4. *Ariṭṭhakā.* They were like azure flowers in hue (*ummāpupphanibhāsino*). According to Buddhaghoṣa,[25] *ummāpuphanibhāsino* is the name of another class of *devas.*
5. *Asamā.*
6. *Āpā.* The word *Āpo-devā* literally means water-gods who are mentioned with *paṭhavī* (earth)-*devā*, *tejo* (fire)-*devā*, and *vāyo* (air)-*devā*. These four classes of gods are deifications of the four elements—earth, water, fire and air. According to Buddhaghoṣa,[26] the *Āpā* gods were born as such because they practised meditation on water (*āpokasiṇa*) in the previous life.
7. *Ummāpupphā.* This class of *devas* are so called because their bodies were azure in colour, like ummā-flowers.[27]
8. *Odātagayhā.* They are described as *pāmokkhā* (eminent devas?).
9. *Kaṭṭhakā.*
10. *Karumhā:*
11. *Khiḍḍāpadosikā.* This class of *devas* dwell in the Cātummahārājika-world.[28] As they spend their time laughing and in sports of sensual lust, their self-possession is corrupted

and as a result they fall from their state.[29] On account of their subjection to corruption and destruction by sport (*khiḍḍāya padussanti vinassanti*) they are called *Khiḍḍāpadosikā*.[30] They play in such pleasances as *Nandanavana*, *Cittalatāvana* and *Phārusakavana*. While they play, they forget to eat and drink and fade away like flowers. They die owing to self-consciousness (*attasañcetanā*).[31] They are, as it were, burnt up by their infatuation.[32]

12. *Khemiyā*. They dwell both in the *Tusita* and *Yāma* heavens[33].

13. *Joti*. According to Buddhaghoṣa,[34] they are flaming deities like beacon lights on mountain tops.

14. *Vasū*.
15. *Vāruṇā* were the followers of Varuṇa.
16. *Vāsavanesī*.
17. *Vāyodevā*.
18. *Vicakkhaṇā*.
19. *Veghanasā*.
20. *Varuṇā*. They probably form the retinue of Varuṇa.
21. *Missakā*.
22. *Mettākāyikā*.
23. *Manopadosikā* (*Manopadūsikā*). They are of a low order and dwell in the *Cātummahārājika* heaven.[35] They are so called because their minds are debauched by envy (*dosassa anudahanaṭāya*).[36] They fall from their state[37] on account of their feeble bodies and polluted minds which are the results of their continuous burning with envy against others.[38]
24. *Manosattā*.[39]
25. *Rucirā*.
26. *Rojā*.
27. *Lambītakā*.
28. *Lāmaseṭṭhā*.
29. *Lohitavāsī*.
30. *Sadāmattā*.
31. *Samānā*.
32. *Sahabhū*.
33. *Sahadhammā*.
34. *Sahaḷī*.
35. *Sukkā*.

36. *Suleyyā.*
37. *Harayo.*[40]
38. *Hāragaja.*

The gods who are earth-bound were also present at the preaching of the *Mahāsamaya-sutta.* They are of the following places: (1) Kapilavatthu, (2) the Himālaya, (3) Sātāgira, (4) Vessāmitta and (5) Rājagaha[41]. The *Aṅguttaranikāya*[42] applies the name *Bhummā* to the earth-bound deities. As said above,[43] the *Bhummā* gods are of the lowest category.

The same *Nikāya*[44] mentions the *Manāpakāyikā* class of gods who possess lovely forms. One day a large number of them visited Anuruddha at the Ghositārāma and said to him that in a trice they could assume any colour they desired, produce any sound and obtain any happiness. Having tested their claims, Anuruddha found them to be true. Some of them sang, some danced, some clapped, some played on various musical instruments; but, observing that their entertainment was lost on Anuruddha, they left him. When Anuruddha told the Buddha of their visit, the latter said that the possession of eight qualities[45] enabled women to be born among the *Manāpakāyikā.*

The *Saṁyuttanikāya*[46] mentions *Valāhakāyikā devā*, a general name for the following five groups of gods called cloud-spirits of the skies, whose existence is responsible for the changes of weather. These are personified and deified.

1. *Sītavalāhakā.* They represent the cloud-spirits of cold. When they wish to regale their bodies, the weather becomes cool.[47] They live in the *Cātummahārājika* world.[48]

2. *Uṇhavalāhakā.* Being the dweller of the *Cātummahārājika* world,[49] they represent the cloud-spirits of heat. When they want to get delight, the weather becomes hot.[50]

3. *Abbhavalāhakā* who are embodied in the thunder-clouds (cumulus clouds). When they desire enjoyment, thunder-clouds appear in the sky.[51]

4. *Vātavalāhakā* who cause rain. Once one of the *Vassavalāhakā devā* went to visit an Arahant. There in the Himalaya he revealed himself and said that he had the power of causing rain. When the Elder wished to test his claim, the *deva* sang a

song, raised his hands and rain began to fall in an area of three *yojanas*.[52]

The same *Nikāya* states other class of gods, namely, *Satullapakāyikā*. They visited the Buddha and asked him several questions on different topics.[53] According to Buddhaghoṣa,[54] in a previous birth they were a ship's crew on a trading line. When the ship was once overwhelmed by the stormy sea, one of them sat like a *yogi* and thought of the good deeds he had done before starting on the voyage which would ensure him a happy rebirth. Requested by the others, he divided them into seven groups of one hundred each, and shouted to them the Five Precepts, assuring them that their *sīla* would bring them to a happy birth. As a result of following the precepts, they were reborn in Sakka's heaven, in different groups, each with his own *vimāna*. The name *Satullapā* was given to them because they shouted the precepts while they were divided in groups of one hundred (Sata-ullapa).

The *Samacitta* (*pariyāya*) *Sutta* of the *Aṅguttaranikāya*[55] speaks of the *Samacitta* class of *devas*. They have tranquil minds.

The *Majjhimanikāya*[56] mentions the following classes of gods.

1. *Parisuddhābhā*. Those who absorb the idea of untarnished brilliance are born among this class of gods. They belong to the plane of the third *jhāna*,[57] and their life-term is sixteen *kappas*.[58]

2. *Saṁkiliṭṭhābhā*. The persons who die after finishing meditation on impure light (tarnished brilliance) are born among Saṁkiliṭṭhābhā gods.

3. *Abhibhū*. This class of *devas* lives in the Rūpa-plane.[59] In the *Majjhimanikāya*, they are mentioned just before the Arūpa Brahmās. All the *Asaññasattā devā* are denoted by the word Abhibhū in the *Mūlapariyāya Sutta*.[60]

The *Suttanipāta*[61] mentions the following classes of gods :—

1. *Pabbatā*. According to the *Suttanipāta Commentary*,[62] they were wise (*Paññabanto*). They are mentioned with the *Nārada* class of gods.

2. *Sayaṁpabhā*. The word '*Sayaṁpabhā*' is a generic name for all the *devas*.[63] Those who maintain their parents and

engage in harmless trades are born among these gods. They are generally identified with the *Ābhassara devas*.[64]

3. *Nārada*. They are mentioned with the Pabbatā.[65]

In the *Sumaṅgalavilāsinī*,[66] the *Varavāraṇā* gods are mentioned. They are longlived deities. One day, when they heard that the Buddha would be born, they began to make garlands for putting on him on the day of his birth. But, according to their computation, the time passed so quickly that they could not finish the garlands even on the day of his death. When they came to learn that the Buddha was about to die, they came with the unfinished garlands; but they did not find the Buddha within the *cakkavāḷa*. They, therefore, remained in the sky, singing the praise of the Buddha.

The *Visuddhimagga*[67] mentions the *Lokavyūha devas* who belong to the realm of sense. It is a rule that the beings (even those of hell) are reborn in the Brahma-world after the destruction of the universe. According to some, the denizens of the hells would not be reborn in the Brahma-world because they had no *jhāna* practice. They would perish at the appearance of the seventh sun. When the *Lokavyūha devas* heard this, they, out of compassion, announced—being dressed in red garments and assuming very ugly forms—that as the world would perish after a hundred thousand years, the people should develop pity, sympathy and equanimity, support their parents, respect the seniors of the family, do meritorious deeds and love each other. The people followed their advice and attained *jhāna*. As a result, they were reborn in the Brahma-world.

The *Bhavya* class of gods is mentioned in the *Saṅkhapāla Jātaka*.[68]

It may be said that some subordinate gods among the *Cātummahārājika devas* attend the preaching of the *Mahāsamaya Sutta*.[69] They are 1. Māyā, 2. Kuṭeṇḍu, 3. Viṭeṇḍu, 4. Viṭu, 5. Viṭucca, 6. Candana, 7. Kāmaseṭṭha, 8. Kinnaghaṇḍu and 9. Nighaṇḍu.

Besides mentioning different classes of gods, Pali literature speaks of some individual gods, of which a detailed description is given below.

1. *Veṇhu* is the Pali form of *Viṣṇu*. He was present, with his retinue, at the preaching of the *Mahāsamaya* Sutta.[70] A

devaputta named Veṇḍu, also called Veṇhu,[71] visited the Buddha and asked him a question.[72]

2. *Varuṇa* is the name of a Vedic god. He is spoken of as the king of the gods and the companion of Sakka, Pajāpati and Īsāna. The *Tāvatiṁsa* gods were asked to look upon the banner of Varuṇa[73] for dispelling their fears when they were in battle against the Asuras. In the *Tevijja Sutta*[74], Varuṇa is mentioned with Indra, Soma, Īsāna, Pajāpati, Yama and Mahiddhi, as the gods invoked by the Brāhmaṇas. In the *Jayaddisa Jātaka*,[75] he is mentioned with Soma, Brahmā, and the lords of day and night. They are invoked by a king for saving the life of a prince from the clutches of an ogre.[76] In another place, Varuṇa is mentioned with Indra.[77] He is described also as one of the chief Yakkhas.[78] His followers are Vāruṇā,[79] and female attendants Vāruṇī who live in dread of him.[80]

3. *Soma* is offered sacrifices and generally mentioned with Varuṇa, Pajāpati and Yama.[81] He is called a Yakkha chief in the *Āṭānāṭiya Sutta*.[82] In later literature,[83] he is regarded as the Moon-god who founded the lunar dynasty.

4. *Kumāra*. His other name is Skanda, the Pali equivalent of which is Khanda, mentioned with Siva in the *Udāna Commentary*.[84]

5. Siva is mentioned sometimes as a *devaputta*[85] and sometimes as an individual god.[86] He visited the Buddha and uttered several verses on the benefit of consorting only with the good.[87] Buddhaghoṣa does not comment on the name in this context. However, he refers to the worship of the Sivilinga in the *Samantapāsādika*.[88] According to the *Cūlavaṁsa, Candadhara* is another name of the god Siva.[89]

6. *Yama* is the god of death.[90] His messengers are birth, old age, illness, punishment for crime and death. They are sent to the human world as a warning to abstain from ill and follow good. When beings die, they are led to him and he judges them according to their deeds. He questions them as to whether they have seen his messengers. When they give a negative answer, the *niryapālas* take them and throw them into different hells.[91]

The *Mahāsamaya Sutta*[92] mentions two Yamas (*duve yamā*). The *Dīghanikāya* Commentary[93] explains it as "*dve Yamaka-*

devatā". Buddhaghoṣa[94] speaks of four Yamas elsewhere (*na c'esa eko va hoti, catusu pana dvāresu cattāro janā honti*) at the four gates (of the *Nirayas*). He is also spoken of as *Vemānikapetarāja*, who sometimes enjoys all the pleasures of heaven in a celestial mansion surrounded by Kapparukkhas and experiences the fruits of his *kamma*.

Although the *Nirayas* are mentioned as Yama's abode[95] (*Yamakkhaya, Yamanivesana, Yamasādana*, etc.), all *saṁsāra* is regarded as subject to Yama's rule because escape from *saṁsāra* is escape from Yama's influence. In this sense Yama is called Vesāyī.[96] He is sometimes mentioned[97] with Indra, Varuṇa, Soma, Pajāpati, etc., as a god to whom sacrifices are offered. The *Aṅguttaranikāya*[98] says that once Yama longed to be born as a human being and to sit at the feet of a *Tathāgata*.

The weapon Yama holds is *Nayanāyudha*, one of the four most powerful weapons in the world. It seems to be comparable to Siva's third eye. Aṭ a glance to this "weapon" many thousands of Kumbhaṇḍas are shattered to bits.[99]

7. *Pajāpati* is a king of the gods; but we do not know what heaven he rules. Although the name is borrowed from Brāhmaṇical literature, his character was changed. He is mentioned with Brahmā.[100] He is also mentioned with Sakka, Varuṇa, Īsāna,[101] and Soma.[102] According to Buddhaghoṣa,[103] among the gods he is like Sakka in looks and enjoys the same life-span; but in the assembly of the gods he occupies the second seat. The *Āṭānāṭiya Sutta*[104] mentions him among the Mahāyakkhas, and refers to him as being invoked by the followers of the Buddha in times of danger.

8. *Īsāna*. He is one of the chief gods. The *Tevijja Sutta*[105] mentions him with Indra, Soma, Varuṇa, Pajāpati and Brahmā, as being invoked by the Brāhmaṇas. When the gods were fighting the Asuras, Īsāna led a *deva* host. Indra tells the *devas* that if, during the struggle, they are afraid, they should look at the crest of his own banner or at that of Pajāpati, Varuṇa or Īsāna, and their fear would disappear.[106]

He is equal to Indra in beauty and longevity.[107] In the assembly of the gods, Īsāna gets the fourth seat, next to Varuṇa.

9. *Jātaveda* is the god of fire. The *Jātakas*[108] contain

references to his worship. He is also called Aggideva. He is probably identical with the Vedic Agni. In the *Bhuridatta Jātaka,*[109] when a king named Mujalinda asked the Brāhmaṇas how to reach heaven, he was told that Aggideva is the Brāhmaṇadevatā *par excellence* and that he should be offered fresh ghee. He is called Aggi-Bhagavā. In the *Asātamanta Jātaka,*[110] it is said that on one birth day of a son, a fire (*Jātaggi*) is kindled; when the son comes of age and wishes to renounce the householder's life, this fire is taken to forest and homage is paid to Aggi-Bhagavā. But in the *Naṅguṭṭha Jātaka,*[111] the Bodhisatta refused to worship the fire-god because the latter has no power to protect his offerings. In the *Santhava Jātaka,*[112] the Bodhisatta, being a votary of the deity, wanted to make an offering of milk mixed with ghee; but when the flames blazed forth and burnt his hut, he lost his faith in the deity. The *Bhūridatta Jātaka*[113] speaks of the fire-god as Vessanara.

10. *Dhātā.* In the previous birth, he gave gifts to the Brāhmaṇas and was born in the deva-world.[114]

11. *Vidhātā.* He is offered sacrifices by the people for obtaining happiness.[115]

12. *Kāma* (Padyumna) is the god of desire.[116]

13. *Dhamma* is the god of righteousness who, in a previous birth, was the Bodhisatta and was born in the world of desire (*kāmaloka*). The sages and Brāhmaṇas praise him while gods and men worship him. He is everywhere, far and near. He is mighty and has boundless glory. All virtues are united in his form. The *Dhamma Jātaka*[117] says that he, being adorned with celestial dress in the midst of a multitude of nymphs, appeared before men, poising in the air with the chariot, and told them to fulfil the duty of service to mother and father and the threefold course of right (right doing, right saying, right thinking) and not to take the life of living creatures and other ten paths of evil doing. In the Milindapañha,[118] he is called a Yakkha.

14. *Adhamma* is one of the Kāmāvacara gods. In the previous birth he was Devadatta. He had a vehicle named *Adhammayāna.* On fast days, he appeared to men and admonished them to lead evil lives. He plunged headlong in

to hell[119] at the end of a discussion in mid-air between himself and Dhamma (the Bodhisatta).

15. *Vessavaṇa* is one of the four regent gods and rules the northern quarter (Uttarakuru).[120] His followers are the Yakkhas,[121] the numbering ten thousand crores. The god Kuvera is called Vessavaṇa[122] and he is so called according to the name of his kingdom Visāṇā. He is the god of wealth, and his city is said to enjoy all prosperity.[123] He had nine treasures.[124] Yakkha Puṇṇaka is his minister[125] The name of this god is found in the list of epico-purāṇic gods. His messengers are Tatolā, Tattolā, Tatotalā, Ojasi, Tejasi, Tatojasi Sūra, Rāja, Ariṭṭha and Nemi.[126] He has a lotus-lake called Dharaṇī. His sons are called Inda.[127] He has faith in the Buddha.[128] He becomes *sotāpanna* and his life-term is ninety thousand years.[129]

In the previous birth, when he was a Brāhmaṇa called Kuvera, he owned a sugarcane farm where he worked seven mills. He gave the produce of one mill in charity, and when his profits increased he gave alms for twenty thousand years. As a result of this, he was reborn in the Cātummahārājika-world.[130]

He is the spokesman[131] because "he was intimate with the Buddha, expert in conversation, well-trained."[132] He rides the Nārīvāhana,[133] which is twelve *yojanas* in length, its seat being of coral. He travels through the air and worships the Thera. He also works as the informer of the Buddha regarding the Thera's success in life.[134] When he was yet a *puthūjjana*, he used his *Gadāyudha*.[135] Vessavaṇa attends the meeting of the gods.[136] He seems to have been worshipped by those who desire children.[137] At the time of earthquake he quieted the fears of terrified people.[138]

As Vesssavaṇa is Sakka's intimate friend,[139] he accompanied the latter when he showed Moggallāna round *Vejayanta-pāsāda*.[140] He has power to grant any of the Yakkhas special privileges, such as the right of devouring anyone entering a particular pond, etc.[141] As he is the lord of the Yakkhas, they fear him greatly. If he is angry and looks but once, one thousand Yakkhas are broken up and scattered "like parched peas hopping about on a hot plate."[143]

Vessavaṇa is the holder of an office so that Sakka chose another Vessavaṇa when the existing Vessavaṇa died. It is the duty of Vessavaṇa to order the Yakkhas for choosing their special abodes.[143] The Yakkhiṇīs fetch water from Anotaṭṭa for the use of Vessavaṇa. The new Vessavaṇa sent word to all trees and shrubs, bushes and plants, bidding the tree-fairies choose the abode that liked them best.

Vessavaṇa's wife was Bhuñjatī.[144] They had five daughters —Latā, Sajjā, Pavarā, Acchimatī, and Sutā who were appointed to dance before Sakka.[145] Vessavaṇa enjoys great luxuries.[146] Ascetics[147] are sometimes favoured by Vessavaṇa.

16. *Dhataraṭṭha* is one of the four Regent gods who rules the eastern quarter with his followers, the Gandhabhas.[148] His sons are numerous and are called Inda.[149] He has a daughter named Sirī.[150] He was present at the preaching of the *Mahāsamaya*[151] and the *Āṭānāṭiya*[152] *Suttas.*

17. *Virūpakkha* is one of the *Cātummahārājikadevas* who rules the western quarter and becomes the lord of the Nāgas,[153] and as such he is waited on by the Nāgas regularly and, any question of dispute arising among them is referred to him for solution.[154] In the assembly of the *devas* he sits facing east.[155] Goddess Kālakaṇṇī is his daughter.[156]

18. *Virūḷha* is also named as Virūḷhaka. He is one of the Regent gods who rules the southern quarter, and, in the assembly of the *devas,* sits facing north.[157] His followers are the Kumbhaṇḍas.[158]

19. *Pajjuna* is the god of rain and the king of storm-clouds. He causes rains to fall. Whenever rains are wanted, he is prayed to. Sometimes Sakka commands him to pour down rains on earth.[159] He is also influenced by the exercise of *saccakiriyā* (protestation of truth).[160] When he comes, he is dressed in one cloud as an under garment, and another cloud as an outer garment and chants the rain-song. He appears in the east with thunder and lightning and causes rain.[161] The *Saṁyuttanikāya Commentary*[162] says that he is Vassavalāhaka and dwells in the Cātummahārājika-world. He is also mentioned among the Mahāyakkhas who are invoked in times of need.[163] The *Saṁyuttanikāya*[164] mentions his daughters, Kokanadā and Culla-Kokanadā who came to worship the

Buddha. Buddhaghoṣa is silent about them. He was present at the preaching of the *Mahāsamaya Sutta*.[165]

20. *Sakka*. Its Sanskrit form (Śakra) is not found as a name in pre-Buddhistic literature. It occurs many times in the Vedas as an adjective qualifying gods (usually Indra, the king of the gods) and is explained as meaning "able, capable". In Pali literature, the word 'Sakka' is used as a rank or position of the king of the Tāvatiṁsa gods and not as a personal name. He who comes in the *Tāvatiṁsa* to rule over it will be called Sakka. As the universe consists of many *cakkavāḷas*[166] and there is *Tāvatiṁsa-devaloka* in each *cakkavāḷa* and each *Tāvatiṁsa* is ruled by a Sakka, the number of Sakkas (i.e., the kings of the *Tāvatiṁsadevalokas*) is many. Besides, in each *cakkavāḷa*, we come in contact with many Sakkas within a world-cycle (i.e. the life-term of a single world-system or *cakkavāḷa*). As for example, the *Aṅguttaranikāya*[167] states that the Buddha, the Exalted One, became Sakka, king of the gods, for thirty-six times. The *Mandhātā Jātaka*[168] tells a story that king Mandhātā went to the *Tāvatiṁsa-devaloka*, where he was received by the then Sakka and given a half share to rule over the Tāvatiṁsa gods for a life-term of 36 Sakkas. The *Sādhīna Jātaka*[169] says that as Sadhina, the king of Mithila, kept fast-day vows, he was given half the share of *Tāvatiṁsa* and ruled there as a co-ruler for 700 heavenly years. It is said in the *Sudhābhojana Jātaka*[170] that a wealthy man of Vārāṇasī was reborn as Sakka because he gave away his wealth. It is interesting to note, in this connection, that sometimes Sakka sent nymphs to the earth for destroying the virtue of man because the meritorious people may down his position as Sakka by their virtuous power. The *Alambusā Jātaka*[171] says that Alambusā, a lovely nymph, was sent to destroy the virtue of Isisiṅga who was dwelling in the Himālaya region with all his senses mortified. Thus it is found that whereas Indra being called Śakra in Brāhmaṇical literature is one person and the ruler of all the *devas*, Sakka, in Pali literature, is not one and does not rule over all the *devas* of different heavenly worlds.

The *Saṁyuttanikāya*[172] says that one can acquire Sakkahood (i.e., the position of Sakka) if he observes the seven vows (*vatapadāni*) on earth—to maintain his parents, to revere his elders, to utter no slander, to be free from avarice, to give donations generously (*sakkaccaṁ*) and in open-handed liberality and kindness, to speak the truth, and to be free from anger.

A Brāhmaṇa named Magha acquired the position of Sakka by having observed these seven life-long habits, because of which Sakka came to be known as Maghavā. Thus it is found that Maghavā is not the personal name of any particular Sakka, but a title of all Sakkas, because the Sakka who was the real Magha is identified with the Bodhisatta,[173] while the Buddha says[174] that Sakka who visited him, and whose conversation is recorded in the Sakkapañha *Sutta*, was also known as Maghavā,

Apart from this, Sakka has also other titles. He is called Purindada[175] because he was a generous giver in the former births. He is Vāsava[176] because when he was a human being in his previous birth, he gave away dwelling-places (*āvasattham adāsi*). According to the *Dīghanikāya*,[177] he is so called because he is chief of the Vasu class of gods (*Vasūnaṁ seṭṭho*). Buddhaghoṣa[178] calls him Vasudevatā. Sakka can think of one thousand matters in a moment, for which he is called Sahassakkha (Thousand-eyed).[179] He is Sujampati because he married the Asura maiden Sujā.[180] Sometimes he is addressed as Kosiya.[181] Although he is a god of high position, he is spoken of as Yakkha.[182] He is Vatrabhū[183] because he slayed Vatra, the Asura chief. In the *Vidhurapaṇḍita Jātaka*, he is called Gandhabbarāja[184] and in the *Sudhābhojana Jātaka*, Mahinda.[185] The *Therīgāthā Commentary*[186] describes Sakka as Amarinda because he is the king of gods.

Sakka is always spoken of as *devānaṁ indo* (king of the gods) because he governs the *devas* of the Tāvatiṁsa-heaven.[187] Although the word *inda* is a synonym of 'king', it is applied to Sakka as a title. It is the Pali equivalent of Vedic Indra. Sakka and Inda may belong to different conceptions because a few statements about Inda in the *Nikāyas*[188] belong to Vedic mythology whereas Sakka belongs to Buddhist mythology, The later texts, particularly the *Jātaka Commentaries*, mention Inda frequently as identical with Sakka. The scholiast says, "Sakko ti Indo".[189] In the *Ayakūṭa*[190] and *Jayaddīsa*[191] *Jātakas*, though both the names of Sakka and Inda are mentioned, they are not different persons. C.E. Godage identifies Inda with Sakka and describes him as a tutelary god of the Kosiya clan for which he gained the epithet 'Kosiya.'[192]

In the *Dīgha*[193] and *Majjhima Nikāyas*,[194] Inda[194a] is described as seated in the company of Pajāpati and other gods in the Assembly Hall, Sudhammā. His two companions listened to the admonition of Gopaka and became disciples of the Buddha. For this, they surpassed Inda and his other companions in glory. The *Jayaddīsa Jātaka*[195] says that Sakka or Inda visits the earth in disguise. The *Dhammapadaṭṭhakathā*[196] mentions him as a giver of punishment to guilty people with his thunderbolt, the Indavajira,[197] because of which he is called Vajirahattha.[198]

In the *Āṭānāṭiya Sutta*,[199] Inda is mentioned with Soma and Varuṇa as a Yakkha, to whom appeal is made by the disciples of the Buddha when needs protection.

Inda is called Tidivapuravara[200] because he rules the Tāvatiṁsa kingdom.

The *Cūlavaṁsa*[201] mentions *Pākasāsana*, a name for Indra.

The name 'Inda' is also applied to the sons of four great kings of the four quarters.[202]

As said above,[203] Sakka was the king of the Tāvatiṁsa-heaven.[204] He dwelt in the Vejayanta-palace,[205] and having ascended the Paṇḍukambalasilāsana (throne made of yellow stone),[206] he ruled over the Tāvatiṁsa gods. His white umbrella, with its golden wreath, is five *yojanas* in circumference and he is accompanied by a glorious array of twenty-five millions heavenly nymphs.[207] Sometimes Sakka amused himself in the One-Lotus pleasure grove (*Ekapuṇḍarīka uyyāna*),[208] being equipped and provided with five hundred musical instruments.[209] His chief conveyance is the marvellous elephant Erāvaṇa,[210] but he went to war in the *Vejayantaratha*.

Sakka had to fight the Asuras and defended his kingdom from the Asura attack.[211] He went to battle in his chariot Vejayanta[212] and defeated the Asura chief. The gods fought against the Asuras under the banner and order of Sakka.[213] The *Saṁyuttanikaya*[214] mentions Pajāpati, Varuṇa and Īsāna as having been associated with Sakka in supreme command. He said that if the gods did not look to the crest of his banner, they might look up at that of Pajāpati, Varuṇa and

Īsāna. This trio are invoked in the *Tevijja Sutta.*[215] However, Sakka is not an absolute monarch. He is compared with a chieftain of the Kosala clan. On ordinary peaceful occasions, Sakka consulted the gods in the *Sudhammā, Sabhā*[216] rather than issued his commands to them. But Sakka surpassed them in ten things—length of life, beauty, happiness, renown, power, sight, hearing, smelling, taste and touch.[217]

Twenty-five *Suttas* of the *Saṁyuttanikāya*[218] describe Sakka's character. In the first and second *Suttas,* Sakka praises energy (*viriya*). In the third, he denounces timidity. In the fourth he shows forbearance to his enemy.[219] In the fifth he advocates the conquest of anger by kindness, and in the sixth, kindness to animals, while in the seventh he denounces trickery even towards enemies. In the ninth, he preaches courtesy and honour to the wise. In the eleventh, it is said that he acquired his position as Sakka by observing seven life-long vows.[220] Twelfth and thirteenth Suttas repeat this and explain his titles. In the fourteenth *Sutta,* Sakka explains how new gods, who outshine the old ones, do so because they observe the Buddha's teachings. In the fifteenth, he says that the dwelling place of the Arahants is most beautiful. In the sixteenth *Sutta,* Sakka praises gifts to the Order.[221] In the seventeenth, he praises the Buddha, but is told by Sahampati that wrong attributes were selected for the praise. In eighteenth to twentieth, he says that though the gods of the *Cātummahārājika* and *Tāvatiṁsa* worship him, he himself worships good men and arahants. Of the Suttas, Nos. XXI-II and XXIV-XXV describe him as denouncing anger and No. XXIII as abhorring deceit.

Sakka listened, in heaven, to Moggallāna's exposition of the simplest duties of a good layman.[222]

Sakka was present at the death of the Buddha and uttered, in verse, a simple lament very different from the thoughtful verses ascribed to Brahmā.[223]

These show that Sakka was regarded by the early Buddhists as a god of high character, kind and just, but not free from lust, ill-will and stupidity.[224] He is also subject to birth,[225] old age,[226] death, sorrow and woes. He exhibits anxiety and laments[227] like ordinary beings. He is timid and fearful and often runs away in fear.[228]

Sakka is always helpful to good men when they are in distress. When Cakkhupāla became blind, Sakka led him by the hand and took him to Sāvatthi.[229] He loved to test the goodness of men and to see whether their faith was genuine. He tested the leper Suppabuddha.[230] The *Jātakas*[231] speak of Sakka as providing holy men with hermitages, etc.

Sakka was a righteous ruler and often punished unrighteous people. The *Vighāsa* and *Somadatta Jātakas* state that Sakka frightened the ascetics who did not do their duties. It is found in the *Aṅguttaranikāya*[232] that Sakka punished a *deva* called Supatittha because he failed to keep the *rukkhadhamma*.

Sakka is the guardian of moral law in the world. When *dhamma* is destroyed and people become unrighteous, Sakka comes down to the earth to save it by frightening them so that they may do good instead of evil. The *Mahākaṇha Jātaka*[233] says that Sakka, having changed Mātali into a black hound and himself into a forester, came to the kingdom of Usīnara and the dog barked, terrifying the people and devouring all the unrighteous persons. He was always on the side of the good against the wicked and helped the former to realise their goal. Instances of such activities of Sakka are found in the *Ambacora, Ayakūṭa, Udaya. Kaccāni, Kāma, Kāmanīta, Kumbha, Keḷisīla, Kharaputta, Culladhanuggah, Dhajaviheṭha, Biḷārikosiya, Maṇicora, Vaka, Sarabhaṅga* and *Sudhābhojana Jātakas*. Sakka patronised good men and invited some such persons to his heaven, his charioteer Mātali being sent to fetch them. Note the cases of Guttila, Mandhātā, Sādhīna, and Nimi in the *Jātakas*.

Sakka protected the religion of the Buddha in Ceylon.[234] Being entrusted by the dying Buddha with the care of Vijaya and his successors, Sakka transferred the charge to the god Uppalavaṇṇa. Sakka placed the right collar-bone of the Buddha Cūḷāmaṇi-cetiya. He supplied building materials for the Mahāthūpa. He gave orders to Vissakamma to decorate the whole of Ceylon at the time of the enshrining of the relic in the Mahāthūpa. When Sonuttara brought the relics from the Nāga-world, Sakka provided the throne and golden casket for them and was himself present at the festival, blowing his conch-shell.

Though Buddhism is not a sectarian religion like Vaiṣṇavism, Śaivism, etc., Sakka's devotion to the Buddha and his doctrine reminds us of sectarianism. When the Bodhisatta cut off his hair and threw it into the sky, Sakka took it and deposited it in the Cūḷāmaṇi-cetiya.[235] He was present near the Bodhi-tree and blowed his Vijayuttara-saṅkha, when Māra attacked Gotama.[236] Sakka sang the praise of the Buddha when the latter accepted Bimbisāra's invitation to dine in his palace.[237] Sakka built a pavilion for the Buddha when he performed his *Yamakapāṭihāriya* at the foot of the Gaṇḍamba. He also gave orders to the wind-gods, the sun-god and the rain-god to uproot the pavilions of the heretics and cause discomfort to them.[238] When the Buddha, after performing the Twin Miracle, returned to Saṅkassa from the *Tāvatiṁsa*, Sakka invited Vissakamma to make three ladders (*tīṇi sopānāni*)—of gold, of silver, and of jewel respectively for the Buddha and his retinue, and he himself held the bowl and the robe.[239]

Several times, Sakka, out of his devotion to the Buddha, helped him in his work. When the Buddha went to the city of Vesāli in order to rid it of its plagues, Sakka was present at his side for driving away the evil spirits, thus making the Buddha's task easier.[240] Sakka, with the aid of Vissakamma, provided the Buddha and his monks with pavilions (*Kūṭāgāra*) in which they might travel by air to meet Culla Subhaddā at Uggapura.[241] The *Maccha Jātaka*[242] says that when the ponds at Jetavana were dry, Sakka caused rains for filling them up so that the Buddha might bathe. He protected the Buddha from the insults of those who came to question. The story of Ciñcāmāṇavikā speaks of Sakka as a protector of the Buddha from her charges.

When the Buddha was suffering from illness, Sakka carried the vessel of his excrement.[243] He did the same for other holy man like Sāriputta.[244] Sakka waited on the Buddha when he was in Gayāsisa for the conversion of the *Tebhātika* jaṭilas.[245] As said above, he was present at the Buddha's death and lamented in a verse which is different from the verse ascribed to Brahmā.[246] When the Buddha's relics were being distributed by Doṇa, Sakka saw Doṇa hide the Buddha's right tooth in his turban. He took the relic from Doṇa and deposited it in the Cūḷāmaṇi-cetiya because he thought that Doṇa was incapable of rendering adequate honour to the relic.[247] When Ajātasattu was preparing to deposit his share of the relics, Sakka gave orders to Vissakamma to set up a Vāḷasaṅghāṭayanta for protecting them.[248]

Besides, Sakka proved himself a true devotee of the Buddha by protecting the latter's followers. He came to rescue of the four seven-year-old novices—Saṅkicca, Paṇḍita, Sopāka and Revata—when they were made to go hungry by a Brāhmaṇa and his wife.[249] In the case of Paṇḍita-sāmaṇera, Sakka sent the Four Regent Gods to drive away the birds, made the Moon-deity shroud the moon, and himself stood guard at the door of Paṇḍita's cell, lest he should be dirturbed.[250] He feels delight when a monk achieves his ambition and honours him.[251] He helped not only monks and nuns, but also eminent laymen, such as Jotika. He built for him a palace of wondrous splendour, and provided it with every luxury.[252]

Sakka visited the Buddha several times. The *Sakkapañha Sutta* says that he went to see the Buddha at Vediyagiri in Ambasaṇḍā and asked a series of questions. Pañcasikha was sent by him with his *vīṇā*[253] to play and sing to the Buddha and to get permission for Sakka to visit him and put questions to him. As Sakka led pure life for a long time, the Buddha permitted him to put questions to him on any subject. It was not the first time that Sakka approached the Buddha for the purpose.[254] He went to him at the Saḷalaghara in Sāvatthi, but finding him in meditation, with Bhuñjatī, wife of Vessavaṇa, waiting on him, left the place with a request to Bhuñjatī to greet the Buddha in his name. He says[255] that he became a *sotāpanna* and earned for himself the right to be reborn eventually in the Akaniṭṭha-world, whence he would pass entirely away. The visit to the Buddha had a special object. Having seen the signs that his life was drawing to an end, Sakka was frightened and went to the Buddha for seeking his help.[256] It is said[257] that Sakka died in his old age as he sat listening to the Buddha, and was reborn as a new and young Sakka.

Sakka became an *uddhaṁ-sota*, treading the path of the *Anāgāmins*. As a result, he would live in *Avihā* for one thousand *kappas*, in *Atappā* for two thousand, and in *Sudassana* for four thousand, and would end in the Akaniṭṭhā-world, after having enjoyed life in the Brahma-worlds for thirty-one thousand *kappas*.[258]

The *Cūlataṇhāsaṅkhaya Sutta*[259] gives an account of another interview of Sakka with the Buddha. Here the former accepted the latter's answer regarding the extirpation of cravings. Moggallāna visited Sakka and asked questions to discover whether he understood the Buddha's teaching. But, instead of giving answer to it, Sakka showed Moggallāna the glories of his Vejayanta palace. When Moggallāna frightened him by a display of *iddhi*-power, Sakka repeated to him, word for word, the Buddha's answer. Moggallāna was satisfied and departed and Sakka told his handmaidens that Moggallāna was a "fellow of his" in the higher life, meaning probably that he himself is a *sotāpanna* and therefore a kinsman of the *arahant*.

Sakka has to deal with disputes arising among the *devas* themselves.[260] The lesser gods consulted Sakka for their difficulties and problems. For example, the *Khadiraṅgāra Jātaka*[261] states that the deity of Anāthapiṇḍika's fourth gateway, who incurred the displeasure of Anāthapiṇḍika by advising him to refrain from too much generosity towards the Buddha and his monks, consulted Sakka.

Sakka undertook to keep the fast and, having found obstacles in the world of gods, went into a garden in the world of men, where he sat in a pleasant spot and performed the duties of an ascetic.[262]

He claimed that his virtue is superior to other three kings—Varuṇa, the Nāga king Supaṇṇa and king Dhanñajaya—because he left behind various kinds of heavenly glory, all immediate sources of happiness, and came to the world of mankind in order to maintain his virtue. "Having abandoned all sport and pleasure, he utters no falsehood, he is averse to all outward pomp and carnal desire."[263]

When a person observes moral precepts, Sakka understands it as his throne is heated, and he tries to fulfil the man's desire.[264] He answers the prayers of good and barren women and grants them boon of sons.[264a] He granted boons to various persons. The *Mahāsuka Jātaka*[265] states that Sakka visited a parrot that clung to the dead stump of a tree through gratitude, and granted him the boon that the tree should once again become fruitful. The *Kanha Jātaka*,[266] says that Kaṇha was given four boons. In the *Akitti Jātaka*,[267] Akitti is granted several boons. When Sivi became blind, he was given two eyes of Truth, Absolute and Perfect (*Saccaparamita-cakkhuni*) by Sakka. It is said that Sakka has not the power of restoring sight; it was only due to the efficacy of Sivi's virtue.[268] Just before he had given the boon to Sīlavatī, Sakka took her to heaven, coming in the guise of an aged Brāhmaṇa to the palace, and kept her there for seven days. She was not only given the boon of two sons, one wise and ugly and the other foolish and handsome, but also a piece of *Kusa*-grass, a heavenly robe, a piece of sandal wood, the flower of the Pāricchattaka-tree and Kokanada-lute. All this went into the possession of her son Kusa, and later, Sakka offered him the Verocana-jewel.[269] He granted Phusatī, mother of Vessantara, ten boons[270] and to Vessantara eight.[271]

Sakka helped the Bodhisattas on several occasions in the attainment of his perfections, e.g., in his births as king Sivi,[272] Temiya,[273] Nimi,[274] and Vessantara[275] and in the birth as a hare.[27] The *Sasa Jātaka*[277] says that Sakka paints the picture of a hare in the moon to commemorate the Bodhisatta's sacrifice.

Sometimes Sakka comes down to earth for saving a family to which he belonged in previous birth from unrighteousness. The *Biḷārikosiya Jātaka*[278] says that Sakka comes on such occasion with Canda, Suriya, Pañcasikha and Mātali.

Before a boon is offered, Sakka tests the virtue of a person. The *Mahāsuka Jātaka*[278a] says that Sakka tested the virtue of a parrot king of the Himālaya by his supernatural power and when he found that the king was contented even with the dust as his food, he came to him in the guise of a goose, and preceded by Sujā in the shape of an Asura nymph, to offer a boon.

Sakka could perform miracles. When he was escaping with Sīlavatī, he caused a house to appear close at hand, with its door open and a bundle of sticks laid out ready.[279] He can cause the earth to rise up,[280] and sometimes he makes rain.[281]

Sakka's charioteer—Mātali is Sakka's chariot-driver (*saṅghāhaka*). In a previous birth, he was born in a rich family and gave away his wealth, on account of which he was reborn as Sakka's chariot-driver.[282] He was a constant companion of Sakka and accompanied the latter everywhere. He was more a confident than a servant.[283] He drove the Vejayantaratha which was drawn by one thousand Sindhava horses.[284] In the war against the Asuras, he accompanied Sakka and drove his chariot when he fled with his bride Sujātā.[285] He accompanied Sakka on his journeys to the world of men, changing his form variously, e.g., to a fish in the *Culladhanuggaha Jātaka*,[286] a Brāhmaṇa in the *Biḷārikosiya*[287] and *Sudhābhojana Jātakas*, and a big black dog in the *Mahākaṇda Jātaka*.[289] Sakka sent Mātali, on several occasions, to fetch to the Tāvatiṁsa human beings like Guttila, Nimi, Makhādeva and Sādhīna, and he proved himself an excellent guide, pointing out to the visitors the palaces of interest on the way.[290]

Mātali accompanied the Buddha also. When the latter descended from the Tāvatiṁsa after preaching there the Abhidhamma, Mātali followed him on his left and offered him celestial scents, garlands and flowers.[291] Mātali had a son named Sikhaṇḍi with whom Suriyavaccasā, daughter of Timbaru, was in love; but later she transferred her affections to Pañcasikha.[292]

Mātali is described as the son of Suriya both in the *Biḷārikosiya* [293] and the *Sudhābhojana Jātakas*.[294]

During several lives, Ānanda is said to have been Mātali.[295] So also was Mahākassapa.[296] Mātali was present at the preaching of the Mahāsamaya Sutta,[297] wherein he was described as a Gandhabba chief. In the *Āṭānāṭiya Sutta*,[298] he is mentioned among the chief Yakkhas to be invoked by the followers of the Buddha in time of need.

Sakka's family. Sakka had four wives—(1) Sudhammā, (2) Cittā, (3) Nandā and (4) Sujātā. When Sakka was Magha in the previous birth, then also he had four wives. As they did meritorious deeds in the previous births, they were reborn in heaven and became the mates of Sakka. When Magha and his friends built their hall, Nandā, one of Magha's wives, built a pond in the ground. Owing to this meritorious act, the *Nandāpokkharaṇi*[299] came into existence in the *Tāvatiṁsa* under her *name.*[300]

Sujā was not only Magha's wife, but also his maternal cousin. She shared his throne and spent her time in adoring herself, while Magha's other wives helped him in his good acts. When Magha was born as Sakka and looked for Sujā, he found that she was born as a crane in a mountain cave. He went to her and carried her to the Tāvatiṁsa to show her how her companions were born there for their good deeds. Then he exhorted her to keep to the five precepts. She followed the advice, eating only such fish as had died a natural death. After this life, she was born as the daughter of a potter of Vārāṇasī. Sakka filled a cart with treasures disguised as cucumbers and drove it there (Vārāṇasī) and declared that these would be given to a woman who kept the five precepts. When Sujā claimed them because she kept them, Sakka revealed his identity and gave them to her.

After this life, she was born as the daughter of Vepacitti, king of the Asuras, a bitter enemy of Sakka. As she was very beautiful, Vepacitti granted Sujā the boon of choosing her own husband. Sakka came to the assembly in the guise of an aged Asura, where she was to choose her husband. Owing to their previous association, Sujā threw the garland round the neck of the aged Asura. At this the others exclaimed that he was old enough to be her grandfather. But Sakka took Sujā up into the air and declared his identity. When the Asuras ran after them Mātali drove the Vejayantaratha to the Tāvatiṁsa, where Sujā was installed as Sakka's chief consort at the head of twenty-five million apsarases. She asked for a boon that she should be allowed to accompany Sakka wherever he went. Sakka granted it.[301]

Cittā. In the previous birth, she was one of the four wives of Magha. When Magha and his companions erected a hall, Cittā had a flower-garden wherein she grew every kind of flowering tree, shrub and creeper. As a result, she was born after death in the Tāvatiṁsa as Sakka's consort, and the Cittalatāvana came into being for her pleasure.[302]

Nandā. In the previous birth, she was also one of the four

wives of Magha. As she built a pond, she was reborn as the mate of Sakka, and the *Nandāpokkharaṇī* came into existence on account of her merit.[303]

Sudhammā.[304] She has been described earlier in connection with the Sudhammā-Sabhā.

Sakka also married five daughters of Vessavaṇa. They are Latā, Sajjā, Pavarā, Acchimatī and Sutā. Of these, Latā, in her previous birth, was good and holy, and after death she was born as a daughter of Vessavaṇa. A dispute arose among the daughters of Vessavaṇa as to who was the most skilled in dancing and singing and a contest was held on the banks of the Anotaṭṭa, in which Latā won. When Sutā asked Latā how she acquired her talents, the latter gave an account of her good deeds as a human being.[305]

Daughters of Sakka. Sakka had four daughters, Āsā, Saddhā, Siri and Harī. They are of golden forms, dressed in golden robe, look bright and glow like flames.[306] Once they came to sport in the Anotaṭṭa and while resting on the Manosilātala after sports, they saw Nārada coming towards them with a Pāricchattaka flower in his hand and wanted the flower. Nārada agreed to give it to one of them whom they would choose to be their queen. Being asked to choose the queen, Nārada advised them to go to Sakka who, in his turn, sent them to the ascetic Macchariya-Kosiya in the Himālaya. Sakka sent a cup of ambrosia to the ascetic and told them that she would be the best who would have a share of ambrosia from Kosiya. Hirī received the share of Kosiya's meal. This story is found in the *Sudhābhojana Jataka*.[307]

Asā. She is the goddess of hope. She has no comrade. She fulfils the hope of one who pleases her. She is beautiful, her teeth being white. She is adorned with rings of gold and spangled bracelets. She wears a radiant robe and a sprig on her head.

Siri. She is the goddess of glory. She looks like a morning star. She confers bliss on persons and fulfils one's desire at her will. A man cannot succeed in his endeavours without her favour even if he is skilful, virtuous and wise. On the other hand, she may favour slothful, greedy, lowborn and ugly people. Therefore she is recognised as false and dull.

Saddhā. She is the goddess of faith.

Hirī. She is the goddess of modesty and shyness. She is beautiful like the dawn. She does not crave for anything. When Mātali brought Hirī and the ascetic Kosiya to the Tāvatiṁsa, Sakka gave Hirī to the ascetic Kosiya as his chief consort.

Sons of Sakka. *Susīma* is one of the thousand sons of Sakka. He was a general of the *devas* in their fight with the Asuras; but he was lazy, and Sakka admonished him.[308]

Suvīra. Once when the Asuras marched against the *devas*, Suvīra was asked by Sakka to fight with them. He agreed to fight, but thrice showed his laziness in the matter. Therefore Sakka admonished him.[309]

Vajirahattha. He was a conqueror of the Asuras.[310] According to Buddhaghoṣa,[311] he is identical with Indra.

Indaka. In the previous birth, he offered a spoonful of food to Anuruddha. As a result, he was born in the Tāvatiṁsa as a *deva* of great power and majesty. He surpassed the other gods in ten qualities.[312] He is called Yakkha,[313] But the *Petavatthu Commentary*[314] explains it as *devaputto*.

21. *Vissakamma, Vissukamma*. He is the same as Viśvakarman of the Brāhmaṇical literature. The *Suruci Jātaka*[315] identifies Vissakamma with Ānanda in his previous birth. According to the *Dhammapada Commentary*,[316] the architect who helped Magha and his companions in their good deeds on earth was reborn as Vissakamma in the *Tāvatiṁsa-devaloka*.

Vissakamma is the chief architect, designer and decorator[317] among the *devas*. Sakka asks for his services whenever necessary. Thus, at the command of Sakka, he built one palace called Dhamma for Mahāsudassana[318] and another for Mahāpanāda.[319] He built some hermitages for the Bodhisatta in various births, e.g., as Sumedha,[320] Kuḍḍālapaṇḍita,[321] Hatthipāla,[322] Ayoghara,[323] Jotipāla,[324] Sutosoma,[325] Temiya[326] and Vessantara.[327] He also built the hermitages for Dukūlaka and Pārikā.[328]

Sakka sent Vissakamma to adorn Temiya on the day he left the kingdom.[329] He sent him in the guise of a shampooer also on the day when the Buddha renounced the world to bathe him and clothe him in his royal ornaments.[330] Once when Vissakamma acted on Sakka's orders he took the form of *Pañcacūḷāgāmadāraka* and went with Aśoka to fetch the relics for his *cetiyas* which lay buried in such a way that no one could find them.[331]

22. *Naḷakāra.* He was the Bodhisatta who became a god in the Tāvatiṁsa. In his previous birth he was a farmer in Vārāṇasī. One day, while going to his fields, he saw a Pacceka Buddha, took him home, fed him, and with his son, built for him a hut with reed walls on the banks of the Ganges, and looked after him in the rains and gave him robes to wear. When Sumedhā, queen of Suruci, prayed for a son, Sakka requested Naḷakāra to be born in her womb. At Sakka's request he was born to her.[332]

23. *Soṇadinna.* In the time of Kassapa Buddha Soṇadinna was a householder who built hermitages for holy men providing them with all necessaries. As a result, he obtained seven golden mansions.[333] On the way to the Tāvatiṁsa for visiting Sakka, king Nemi saw the mansions of Soṇadinna.

24. *Mahāsena.* He lived in the Ketumatī palace to the east of the Vejayanta. He was born in the world of men as Nāgasena at the request of Sakka and of the members of the Order,[334] led by Assagutta.

25. *Santusita.* He is the king of the *devas* of the Tusita-world.[335] It was the name of the Bodhisatta when he was in the Tusita,[336] and also that of his successor.[337] Santusita appears with a yak's tail whisk at important festivals.[338]

26. *Suyāma.* He is a *devaputta* and the king of the Yāma devas.[339] The *Suttanipātta Commentary*[340] says that Sirimā, the courtesan, was reborn, after death, as the wife of Suyāma. He accompanied the Buddha, holding a yak's-tail fan (vālavījana) when the latter descended from the *deva*-world to the earth at Saṅkassa.[341]

27. *Sunimmita.* He is a *devaputta* and king of the Nimmānarati-world.[342] Being born among the *Nimmānaratī-devas* Visākhā became his wife.[343]

28. *Vasavatti.* He is a *devaputta* and king of the Paranimmitavasavatti-world.[344] In his previous birth, he was virtuous and practised generosity, on account of which he surpassed the *devas* of his world in ten things.[345] The *Commentary*[346] says that though Māra rules over a part of this world, he is regarded as a recalcitrant vassal.

29. *Gods of the Brahma-world.*[347]

A. *Pacceka Brahma.*[348] The texts mention two classes of Pacceka Brahmā.

1. Suddhavāsa and 2. Subrahmā

B. *Mahā Brahmā.*

1. *Tudu.* In the previous birth he was a thera and the teacher of Culla Kokālika and became *Anāgāmīnh.* As a result, he was born in the Brahma-world.[349]

2. *Baka.* He thought that this world[350] was permanent and free from decay and death. The Buddha went to the Brahma-world and pointed out his error. But, being influenced by Māra, he refused to acknowledge his error, so that the Buddha, by his magical power, prevented Baka from disappearing from sight, while he himself vanished. Besides he told him four incidents connected with his previous birth as Kesava.[351] Once he was born in a noble family and became an ascetic under the name of Kesava. On one occasion, he turned a river into the desert by his supernatural power in order to rescue the members of a caravan. On another occasion, he found a village attacked by dacoits whom he drove away by showing them the vision of an approaching police party, with himself at the head. On the third occasion, when the Nāga of the river, seeing some people floating down the river in boats, making merry, singing and drinking, appeared before them, threatening destruction, Kesava, assuming the form of a Garuḍa, frightened the Nāga. The *Kesava Jātaka* contains another incident, according to which, after having developed the fourth *jhāna*, he was born in the Vehapphala-world. Thence he descended to the Subhakiṇha-world. Next he came down to the Ābhassara-world with a span of life of only a single *kappa.*[352]

3. *Ghaṭikāra.* In the previous birth, at the time of Kassapa Buddha, he was a potter of Vehaliṅga. He was a follower of the Buddha and looked after his blind parents. As result of his great faith in the Buddha, no rain fell on his house when it remained open for three months.[353] The *Naḷapāna Jātaka*[354] says that due to his faith no rain will fall on the site of his house as long as this *kappa* lasts. He converted Jotipāla, a young Brāhmaṇa of his time. He could not renounce the world as

he was the only support of his parents. He returned the gifts of five hundred cart-loads of husked rice given by Kiki, king of Vārāṇasī, saying that he had plenty for himself.[355]

Owing to his good deeds, he was born, after death, as a Mahābrahmā in the Avihā Brahma-world and became an *anāgāmī*.[356]

The *Saṁyuttanikāya*[357] says that besides Jotipāla, Ghaṭikāra had several other friends in Vehaliṅga, viz., Upaka, Phalagaṇḍa, Pukkusāti, Bhaddiya, Khaṇḍadeva, Bāhuraggi and Piṅgiya of whom he spoke at the time of his interview with the Buddha sometime after the Enlightenment. They listened to the Buddha's teaching and were reborn in the Avihā-world. On that occasion, Ghaṭikāra was addressed as Bhaggava by the Buddha. Formerly he had friendship with the Buddha too.

In other places,[358] it is found that Ghaṭikāra provided the Buddha with the eight requisities of a monk, when the Buddha decided to lead the life of a bhikkhu. Ghaṭikāra built *Dussathūpa* in the Brahma-world enshrining the garments worn by the Buddha at the time of his Renunciation. It was built of gems and was twelve *yojanas* in height.[359] Bhaddaji carried it on his out-stretched palm and showed it to the multitudes.[360]

4. *Nārada Mahābrahma.* The *Mahānārada Massapa Jātaka*[361] mentions him as belonging to the Kassapa-gotta. He came to the earth for helping Rujā to convince her father, Aṅgati, of the truth as declared by her. He frightened Aṅgati by revealing to him the horrors of hell.

5. *Hārita Mahābrahmā.* He was one of the chief Brahmās.[362] He was present at the preaching of the *Mahāsamaya Sutta* being the head of one hundred thousand other Brahmās.[363]

6. *Sahampati Mahābrahmā.* He was so called[364] because during the time of Kassapa Buddha, he was a monk named Sahaka, who, having practised the five *indriyas* (*saddhā*, etc.), was reborn in the Brahma-world. According to the *Suttanipāta*[365] *Commentary* he was an Anāgāmī-Brahmā born in the Suddhāvāsa Brahma-world, where he passed a whole *kappa* because he developed the first *jhāna* as a monk. The *Buddhavaṁsa Commentary*[366] says that his name should be *Sahakapati*.

Brahmā Sahampati may be identified with Brahmā Sayambhū of the Brāhmaṇical literature.[367] But, he is inferior to the Buddha. The *Saṁyuatanikāya*[368] says that Sahampati requested the Buddha to preach the *Dhamma* because all the Buddhas of the past had no other teacher than the *Dhamma* discovered by them.[369] It is interesting to note that this time the Buddha was hesitating as to whether he should preach the *Dhamma* until Sahampati requested. Buddhaghosa[370] says that his hesitation was not for his indolence, but because he wished Sahampati to make him this request. It may be assumed that as Sahampati was, at this time, the most senior of the Brahmās (*jeṭṭha-Mahābrahmā*),[371] the Buddha thought that if Sahampati requested him, the people would pay more attention to the *Dhamma*.

However, Sahampati appeared before the Buddha for several times. When Kokālika died and was reborn in Padumaniraya, Sahampati announced the fact to the Buddha.[372] He spoke of a series of verses praising the life and practices of the monks and of the results thereof, at Andhakavinda, when the Buddha sat under the open sky during the night and when the god was raining.[373] He again visited the Buddha with Sakka who uttered a verse in praise of the Buddha. Sahampati uttered another verse, exhorting the Buddha to preach the Doctrine, as there were those who would understand.[374] He uttered also a verse immediately after the death of the Buddha.[375]

Sahampati held over the Buddha's head a white parasol, three *yojanas* in diameter, when the Buddha attained Enlightenment.[376] A chain of jewels (*ratanadāma*) as large as Sineru was offered to the Buddha by him.[377] Sahampati waited upon Alindakavāsī-Mahāphussadeva when he attained arahantship.[378]

Sahampati was compassionate. He appeared before a Brāhmaṇī, mother of Thera Brahmadeva, and exhorted her to give her offerings to Brahmadeva instead of Brahmā.[379]

7. *Sanaṅkumāra Mahābrahmā*. In the previous birth, he practised *jhāna* while he was yet a boy with his hair tied in five knots (*pañcacūḷakakumārakāle*). As a result, after death, he

was reborn in the Brahma-world. He is so called because he liked the guise of a youth which he continued.[380] According to Rhys Davids,[381] the legend of Sanaṅkumāra is the Indian counterpart of the European legend of Sir Galahad.

In the *Janavasabha Sutta*,[382] Janavasabha speaks to the Buddha that Sanaṅkumāra attended the assembly of the *Devas*, presided over by Sakka and the Four Regent Gods. From his radiance, the *devas* of the assembly knew Sanaṅkumāra's presence and sat in their places with clasped hands waiting for him to choose his seat. Sanaṅkumāra sat cross-legged in the form of Pañcasikha,[383] above the assembly in the air. He expressed his delight that Sakka and all the *Tāvatiṁsadevas* should honour and follow the Buddha. His voice bore all the eight characteristics of a Brahmā's.[384] Sanaṅkumāra created thirty-three shapes of himself, each sitting on the side of a *Tāvatiṁsadeva*, and spoke to the *devas* of the advantages of taking refuge in the Buddha, the *Dhamma* and the *Saṅgha*. At his speech each *deva* imagined that only the shape sitting on his own side spoke and the others were silent. Then, sitting on Sakka's throne, he addressed the whole assembly on the four ways of *iddhi*; on the three avenues leading to Bliss; on the four *satipaṭṭhānas*; and the seven *samādhiparikkhārā*. He declared in the assembly that more than twenty-four lakhs of Magadhan disciples had been born in the *deva*-worlds as they had followed the teachings of the Buddha. In reply to a question put by Vessavaṇa, Sanaṅkumāra says that there had been Buddhas in the past and would be in the future.

The *Nikāyas*[385] describe Sanaṅkumāra as the author of a famous verse which runs as follows:

Khattiyo seṭṭho jane tasmiṁ ye gottapaṭisārino Vijjācaraṇa-sampanno so seṭṭho devamānuse ti.

But, in one place,[386] the verse is attributed to the Buddha. Sanaṅkumāra was a devout follower of the Buddha whom he visited on the banks of the Sappinī, and the above verse was uttered on this occasion.[387] He was present at the preaching of the *Mahāsamaya Sutta*.[388]

8. *Tissa Mahābrahmā*.[389] He was the Tissa mentioned as being present at the Mahāsamaya.[390]

The Devaputtas. The number of personal gods is limited. Most of them hold particular offices. Besides, mention of many sons of gods are found in literature;[391] but the names and offices of them are not known. The *Devaputta* Sutta of the *Saṁyuttanikāya*[392] mentions the following names of *devaputtas* who came to the Buddha for solving questions. In this connection it is found that some of them held offices.

1. *Kassapa.* One night he came to the Buddha and uttered several stanzas, admonishing monks for training themselves in their task laying stress on the practice of *jhāna.*[393]

2. *Kassapa* (2). He is another *devaputta.*

3. *Magha.*

4. *Magadha.*

5. *Dāmali.* He visited the Buddha at Jetavana and told him that an arahant had to work hard for nothing. The Buddha pointed out that there was nothing left for an arahant to do.

6. *Kāmada.* Having visited the Buddha he told him that the path of Aryan disciples was hard to follow and their goal hard to win.

7. *Pañcālacaṇḍa.* When he visited the Buddha at Jetavana, the latter said that one who was mindful and self-possessed knew the way to *Nibbāna.* The *Aṭānāṭiya Sutta*[394] mentions Pañcālacaṇḍa as a Mahāyakkha who is to be invoked by the Buddha's followers in time of danger.

8. *Tāyana.* He visited the Buddha at Sāvatthi and uttered certain verses in the hearing of the monks, stressing on the necessity of following the recluse's calling with energy and sincerity.

9. *Candimā.* He dwells in a *vimāna* called Canda, the moon,[395] which he controls. The moon cannot move in the sky without the permission of Candimā. Its movement can be stopped at his will.[396] Hence he is regarded as the Moon-god. The *Dīghanikāya*[397] mentions other *devas* who dwell in the moon. Candimā was worshipped for getting children.[398] He was present at the preaching of the *Mahāsamaya Sutta.*[399] The *Vibhaṅga Commentary*[400] says that Candimā is one of the *Cātummahārājika-devas* because he lives in their world. As Sakka enjoyed a particular status, Candimā is also associated

with a position or post which may be occupied after death by any one doing good work. For example, the *Biḷārikosiya Jātaka*[401] says that a wealthy man, having once given alms became the Moon-god. The *Sudhābhojana Jātaka*[402] says that Moggallāna was also reborn as Candamā. The *Sasa Jātaka*[403] describes that when the Bodhisatta, in his birth as hare, proved his unwillingness to stop to give alms, Sakka painted the figure of a hare on the moon, which sign would be seen throughout this *kappa*. In the previous birth, Candimā's father was the Bodhisatta who, after death, was reborn in the Tāvatiṁsa as Sakka, and by his request the Moon god came down on earth with him including Suriya, Mātali and Pañcasikha to bring back their family tradition of giving alms, which had been broken by a member of the family.[404]

When the Moon god was seized by the Asura Rāhu, he took refuge in the Buddha and uttered the verse:

Namo te buddha vīr atthu vippamutto si sabbadhi
Sambādhapaṭippanno smi tassa me saraṇaṁ bhavāti

"Adoration to thee, great Buddha. Thou art free from all impurities. I am distressed. Become thou a refuge to me." The Buddha addressed. Rāhu in the verse:

Tathāgatam arahantaṁ Candimā saraṇaṁ gato
Rāhu Candaṁ Pamuñcassu buddhā lokānukampakā ti

"In the arahant Tathāgato the moon-god has taken refuge. Rāhu! Release thou the moon. The Buddhas are merciful to the world." At this the Asura Rāhu released the moon-god, went to the place of the Asura chief, Vepacitti, and stood in great terror on one side. When the Asura chief wanted to know the cause of his terror, Rāhu replied in verse:

Sattadhā me phale muddhā jīvanto na sukhaṁ labhe
buddhagāthābhihito mhi no ce muñceyya .candiman ti

"If I do not release the moon, my head would be split up into seven pieces; and were I to live, I would have no enjoyment[405]...."

10. *Suriya.* As we have said above,[406] he is one of the *Cātummahārājika-devas* because he dwells in their world. He is regarded as the sun-god.[407] In a previous birth he gave away his wealth and, as a result, was born in heaven as Suriya.[408]

For the same reason, his father was born in heaven as Canda.[409] As mentioned above,[410] Suriya came down on earth with Sakka, Candimā, Mātali and Pañcasikha to bring back his family tradition of giving away wealth, which had been broken by a member of his family. He was seized by the Asura Rāhu like Canda and in the same way took refuge in the Buddha and was released from the fear of Rāhu.[411] Both Suriya and Candimā are subservient to Sakka who sometimes stopped their journey.[412]

The *Dīghanikāya*[413] mentions Suriya as Ādicca. According to Buddhaghoṣa, he was Aditi's son (*Aditiyā-putto*).[414] The *Suttanipāta*[415] states that Ādicca was also the gotta-name of the Sākyans. The *Vimānavatthu Commentary*[416] says that Adicca, (the sun) belonged to the Gotama-gotta and, as the Buddha also belonged to the same gotta, he became the friend of Adicca, so that he was always spoken of as Ādiccabandhu.[417] The same context explains that the Buddha is born in the same *ariyā jāti* and is the descendant of the Sun or the Sun in the Buddha's *orasa-putta* (breast-born son) in as much as he is the disciple of the Buddha. The *Saṁyuttanikāya*[418] states that the Buddha speaks of the sun as *mama pajā*. According to the *Majjhimanikāya Commentary*,[419] Ādicca is described as *tapataṁ mukhaṁ* (chief of heat producing things).

11. *Candimasa.* He is probably identical with Candimā.

12. *Veṇḍu.*[420]

13. *Dīghalaṭṭhi.*

14. *Nandana.* He visited the Buddha at Sāvatthi and asked him questions regarding virtue, wisdom, etc.

15. *Candana.* He is a vassal of the four Regent gods.[421] According to Buddhaghoṣa,[422] he was an *upāsaka* in the time of Kassapa Buddha and offered the four requisites to the Buddha and the monks. As a result of his pious acts, he became a deva. He is mentioned as one of the chief Yakkhas to whom prayers were offered by the followers of the Buddha in time of need.[423] He paid a visit to Mahāmoggallāna.[424] The *Saṁyuttanikāya*[425] records the conversation between Candana and the Buddha. He went to Nigrodhārāma for meeting Lomasakiṅgiya and putting questions to him regarding the True Saint. He

also recited to him stanzas learnt when the Buddha preached the *Buddhekaratta Sutta* in the Tāvatiṁsa.[426]

16. *Suddatta.*

17. *Subrahmā.*[427]

18. *Kakudha.* He visited the Buddha at the Añjanavana in Sāketa and asked him whether he experienced feelings of pleasure and sorrow. Kakudha uttered praises to the Buddha when he was satisfied with the reply of the Buddha that he was free from the said feelings. Sometimes he was addressed as a Yakkha.[428]

19. *Uttara.*

20. *Anāthapiṇḍika.*

21. *Siva.*[429]

22. *Khema.* He visited the Buddha at Jetavana and uttered several verses on the desirability of leading good life.

23. *Serī.* In a previous birth, he was a king and a great giver of gifts.

24. *Ghaṭikāra.*[430]

25. *Jantu.* He appeared before a number of monks in a forest-lodge on the slopes of the Himalaya and reminded them of their duties.

26. *Rohita.* In a previous birth, he was a sage called Rohitassa, a Bhojaputta of great psychic power, who crossed in one stride western ocean and the *eastern.* With such strides he travelled one hundred years for reaching the end of the world where there was no birth, old age, death, etc., but failed. He visited the Buddha and asked some questions.

27. *Nanda.*

28. *Nandivisála.* He visited the Buddha and conversed with him on the nature of the body and its riddance.[431]

29. *Susima.* When Ananda utters high praise of Sāriputta, Susīma confirms all that Ananda has said.

30. *Nānātitthiya.*

Besides, some other *devaputtas* are mentioned also in the texts.

31. *Gopaka.* In a previous birth he was a Sakyan maid of Kapilavatthu named Gopikā (Gopī) and led a virtuous life. As a result, she was born as a devaputta in the Tāvatiṁsa. The *Sakkapañha Sutta*[432] attributes a series of verses to Gopaka.

32. *Ghosa. Ghosaka.* In the previous birth he was born as a dog in a herdsman's house, where he had to accompany the herdsman on a visit to a Pacceka Buddha who took meals in his house. When the herdsman was unable to go himself, he would send the dog to summon the Pacceka Buddha. One day, when the Pacceka Buddha went elsewhere, the dog died of a broken heart. As a result, he was reborn in the Tāvatiṁsa as the god Ghosa or Ghosaka. He was later reborn as Ghosakaseṭṭhi.[433]

33. *Java, Javana.* Rujā said that she could see Java making a garland ready for her birth in the Tāvatiṁsa.[434]

34. *Aṅkura.* He was a *devaputta* of the Tāvatiṁsa who was present when the Buddha preached the *Abhidhamma* there.[435]

35. *Anekavaṇṇa.* He excelled even Sakka in majesty by virtue of his good deeds. Sakka fled in shame when Anekavaṇṇa appeared in the streets of the Tāvatiṁsa.[436]

In the previous birth, he was a monk under Sumedha Buddha, but later he was disheartened and left the Order. When the Buddha died, he repented for having lost his opportunity, and paid homage to the Buddha's shrine and observed the precepts.[437] He dwelt in the Anekavaṇṇavimāna.[438]

36. *Cūlaratha.* He excelled Sakka in glory.[439]

37. *Asama.* He visited the Buddha at Veluvana, in the company of Sahali, Nivika, Akoṭaka, Veṭambari and Māṇava-Gāmiya who were disciples of different teachers and, standing before the Buddha, uttered each the praises of his own teacher.[440] Of them, Mānavagāmiya sang the glories of the Buddha.[441]

38. *Mālabhāri, Mālābhāri.*

39. *Mahāratha.* He dwells in the Tāvatiṁsa. Owing to his good deeds, he excelled Sakka himself in Majesty.

40. *Gopāla.* He was a *devaputta* of the Tāvatiṁsa. Moggallāna preached to him during a visit to the Tāvatiṁsa and he became a *sotāpanna.*[442]

The *Sirikālakaṇṇi Jātaka* mentions a son of Virūpakkha who is described as *devaputta* under the name of *Deva* and brother of Kālakaṇṇī.[443]

Tutelary gods. They are generally described as the guardian god of kings on earth. The *Cullakāliṅga Jātaka*[444] mentions two kinds of tutelary deities. The one for conqueror appears in the shape of a white bull and the other for the defeated appears in the shape of a black bull. The *Cūlavaṁsa*[445] mentions Uppalavaṇṇa as the guardian god of Laṅkā and its people. This guardianship was given to him by Sakka. Seeing Vijaya and his followers in Ceylon, he sprinkled water on them and wound a sacred thread about their hands for protection.[446] Uppalavaṇṇa is identified with Viṣṇu, though they are distinct gods according to later mythology. Somewhere about A.D. 790, a shrine was erected to Uppalavaṇṇa in Devanagara (modern Dondra) in South Ceylon, which was later plundered by the Portuguese. A sacrifice was offered there for his victory by king Vīrabāhu, and Parakkamabāhu II rebuilt the shrine.

Tree-deities. Sometimes the Bodhisatta came to life in the form of tree-deities. He came once in the form of a divinity of a *tinduka* tree. Every year he received an offering worth a thousand pieces of money from a king of Northern Pañcāla. When the whole kingdom was going to ruin for his unrighteous rule, the divinity of the *tinduka* tree came to give him good advice.[447] The people worshipped the Tree-deities for obtaining children.[448] The following two tree divinities are known from Pali works.

1. *Sumanadeva.* His daughter, Kāḷi was married to Dīghataphala (a Yakkha resident in a palm tree outside Rājagaha). He offered the treasures lying buried within range of the shadow of his tree to Kāḷviḷaṅgiya's wife because she, disguised as a man, brought him the news of the birth of a son to Kāḷi.[449]

2. *Samiddhisumana.* As a *deva* he lived in the rājāyatana-tree standing at the gate of Jetavana. When he was an inhabitant in Nagadīpa, he saw some Pacceka Buddhas taking their meals and provided them with *rājāyatana*-branches with which to clean their bowls. The *rājāyatana*-tree was held as parasol over the Buddha's head on his journey to Ceylon. But it was left behind in Kalyāṇi for the Nāgas to worship.[450] Samiddhisumana accompanied the Buddha for a visit to Ceylon.

Certain goddesses of gardens are found in the Jātaka.[451] The Banyan Park is also worshipped.[452]

The *Meṇḍaka Jātaka*[453] mentions the worship of a hill. In connection with this, certain guardian deities of hills are mentioned. They are—

1. *Sumana.* Pali literature mentions two deities under this name. He is regarded as a guardian deity (Mahā-Sumana-Deva) of Samantakūṭa.[454]

2. *Sudassana.* He was a *deva* king of the Sudassanapabbata. As he was a heretic, Piyadassi Buddha visited him, refuted his views, and converted him with his ninety crores of followers.[455]

GODDESSES

Goddesses are rarely mentioned in Pali literature. It may be noted that most of the daughters of the gods belong to the *Tāvatiṁsa-devaloka* which they occupy for their meritorious deeds on earth. The *Jātakas*[456] state that they sometimes fall in love with men.

1. *Lakkhī. Lakkhī* is the Pali equivalent of Sanskrit *Lakṣmī.* She is also called Sirī in Pali (Sanskrit Śrī).[457] Sometimes both the names Sirī and Lakkhī are found mentioned together.[458] However to the Buddhists, Sirī-Lakkhī is regarded as the goddess of beauty and fortune. The *Abhidhānappadīpikā* [59] says that Sirī-Lakkhī is a synonym of the goddess of beauty and property. The commentary on the *Sumaṅgala Jātaka*[460] describes her as the goddess of *parivāra-sampatti* (family property) and *paññā* (wisdom). In the *Sālikedāra Jātaka*,[461] she is regarded as the goddess of wisdom and virtue. The *Dhajaviheṭha*[462] and *Sirī-Kālakaṇṇi*[463] *Jātakas* regarded her as the goddess of fortune, luck and wisdom. It is stated in the *Sarabhaṅga Jātaka*[464] that the persons who are wise are favoured by *Lakkhī.* The Commentary on the *Jātakas*[465] says that Sirī is identified with Lakkhī who is described as equal to *bhuripaññā* (very wise).

The *Paññā* and *Puñña* are co-related. When a man observes the precepts of a meritorious saint, he gets *paññā* (wisdom) and thereby he earns *puñña* by performing virtuous deeds.[466] The king, who is pure in deed, word and thought, filled with kindness, calm and awe, and free from anger and fear, he gets wisdom which is described as *Sirī-Lakkhī* in the *Sumaṅgala*

Jātaka.[467] When a man is favoured by Lakkhī, he will get great praise from her in this world and, after death, will reach heaven.[468] Thus it is found that Lakkhī was the goddess of wisdom like Sarasvatī, the goddess of learning, wisdom, etc., of the Brāhmaṇical literature.

The *Dhammapadaṭṭhakathā*[469] mentions *rajja-sirī dāyikā-devatā* which may be regarded as a name of Lakkhī, the goddess of kingdom and property.

The *Cūlavaṁsa*[470] mentions Vīralakkhī, the goddess who gives success to the hero in the battle.

In the *Sirī-Kālakaṇṇī Jātaka,*[471] Sirī is described as the daughter of Dhataraṭṭha, one of the four kings of the *Cātum-mahārājika-devaloka.* She comes down to earth through the air with raiment and ointment of golden hue and ornament of golden brightness diffusing yellow light. She presides over the course of conduct[472] and, being asked by the merchant Suci-parivāra (pure household), describes her conduct. She loves and lives with him who has done his duty even in cold, heat, wind, thirst and hunger, and in the fear of snake and poisonous fly.[473] She acts as his friend always wherever he is—living or dead, who is kind enough, without harsh word or curse to his friend or enemy, better, like or worse, helper or foe.[474] She favours him who is gentle (without anger), friendly, righteous, liberal, guileless, honest, upright, winning, bland and meek in high place.[475] As this conduct gives lordship over mankind she is called *Issariyadāyikā.*[476]

In the *Tesakuṇa Jātaka,*[477] Sirī-Lakkhī says that she loves the man who is energetic, bold and free from jealousy. He can get the treasure of bliss if he is earnest.[478] When these merits lie in a king, he is regarded as an ideal ruler by the gods, the Gandhabbas, angels, men and spirits.[479]

In the *Sirī Jātaka,*[480] the Buddha says,

Yaṁ ussukā saṁgharanti alakkhikā bahuṁ dhanaṁ
sippavanto asippā ca Lakkhi vā tāni bhuñjati

What great wealth the unlucky person (not favoured by Lakkhī) gathers by striving, the lucky person (favoured by Lakkhī) enjoys that whether he is skilled or unskilled.[481] The lucky persons get their wealth from a treasury[482] which contains of all such good things as fine looks, voice, figure, sovereignty with all its pomps, lordship and kingdom, imperial bliss, the crown of heaven, all human happiness, the joys of heaven *nibbāna*, true ties of friendship, wisdom's liberty, firm self-control, analytical knowledge or understanding training by which perfection is attained by the Sāvaka or Hīnayāna monks, salvation and *Paccekabodhibuddhabhūmi*, i.e., the position whence one gets supreme knowledge.

The Buddha explains that the favour of luck or Lakkhī is nothing but the result of the merit earned by a person in previous births through virtuous deeds and this enables a person to obtain treasures.[483] Thus 'earned merit' is regarded as the goddess Lakkhī. In this sense, she may also be considered as supreme deity because *nibbāna*, the final goal of the Buddhist doctrine, can be available only by earned merit.

Goddess Lakkhī lives in four objects—a fowl, a gem, a club, and a wife.[484] Golden colour is a lucky mark and a divine hue.[485] The Buddha says that the luck belonging to one person does not go to another. But, in his previous birth, he saw that the luck belonging to those of small wit went to the wise.[486] In connection with this, he tells an old-world tale in the *Sirī Jātaka*.[487] A stick-gatherer heard a quarrel among the fowls. In the course of the quarrel, one fowl boasted, "Anybody who kills me, and eats my flesh roasted on coals, gets a thousand coins in the morning." The other fowl said, "Anybody who eats my fleshy parts will become king; if he eats my outside, he will become the commander-in-chief or the chief queen, according as he is a man or a woman; in case he eats my bones, he will get the post of royal treasurer, if he be a householder, or will become the king's favourite if he is a holy man." Having heard this, a man killed the latter fowl and his wife cooked it. But, unfortunately, they could not eat it. When they went to bathe by putting the meat on the bank of the Ganges, the water washed it away. It floated in the river and came in sight of an elephant trainer. He took it and ate the fleshy parts of the fowl; his wife ate the exterior part of it. As a result, the elephant trainer became king within three days and his wife became queen.

Goddess, Lakkhi appears also in the earliest Buddhist

sculptures seated on a lotus between two elephants that pour water over her.[488]

Although, as shown above,[489] the goddess Lakkhī is treated as Sarasvati in Pali literature, the *Culavaṁsa*[490] mentions a Buddhist king who established a *Sarasvatīṁaṇḍapa* (the temple of the goddess Sarasvatī) in Ceylon. This shows that the goddess Sarasvati was a separate deity.

In the *Mahāummagga Jātaka*,[491] the Buddha refutes the Brāhmaṇical idea that Lakkhī and Sarasvatī cannot live together, i.e. they cannot favour one man at a time. He explains that a man cannot be favoured by Lakkhī (the goddess of wealth) unless and until he is favoured by Sarasvatī (the goddess of wisdom). He says that one cannot preserve wealth if he is not wise.

2. *Maṇimekhalā*. She is the goddess of ocean. She was commanded by the Cātummahārājikas to protect virtuous people who might suffer from shipwreck. In order to protect any virtuous man, she took station upon the sea. She is radiant. The *Saṅkha Jātaka*[492] says that when Saṅkha, a Brāhmaṇa of Vārāṇasī, was suffering from shipwreck, she offered him food, drink, rest and vehicles, because the Brāhmaṇa made a gift of shoes and a sunshade to the Paccekabuddha. At his request, the goddess 'caused a ship to appear, made of the seven precious things; in length it was eight hundred cubits, in width six hundred cubits, twenty fathoms in depth; it had three masts made of sapphire, cordage of gold, silver sails, and of gold were also the oars and the rudders.' The deity filled the vessel with seven precious things and guided the ship to the city of Molinī, the dwelling place of the Brāhmaṇa.

3. *Caṇḍī*. It is a name of the Mother Goddess in Brāhmaṇical literature. In Buddhist literature, this name is given to the goddess Kālakaṇṇī, daughter of Virūpakkha. Due to her bad temper[493] she is so called Kāli. She was also addressed as Kāli in the *Siri Kālakaṇṇī Jātaka*.[494] At another place, she is referred to as Alakkhī.[495]

The *Tesakuṇa Jātaka*[496] says that the king who cannot forsake low association, falsehood, anger, scorn, jealousy and passion and becomes careless and unrighteous and does not repent his bad deed and learn not to do it again, he is overpowered by Alakkhī (Goddess of Misfortune).

The blue colour is regarded as an unlucky mark and the unlucky person is known from his blue raiments.[497] Good luck and ill luck can never mate each other.[498] If a fool wins some favour from Siri and becomes proud and vain, he will be deprived of her favour.[499] Goddess Alakkhī is identified with Kālakaṇṇī (Misfortune).[500] As we have seen above, she is the daughter of Virūpakkha, one of the four kings of the *Cātummahārājika-devaloka*.[501] She comes down to the earth through the air diffusing a blue light, with her blue raiment. ointment, and jewels.[502] She loves him who is hypocritical, wanton, morose, envious, greedy and treacherous. She loves also hate, slander, strife, libel and cruelty. She enjoys pleasure from a man who is foolish and is despised by his friends.[503]

One day dispute between Kālakaṇṇī and Siri (daughter of Dhataraṭṭha) was made as to their precedence in bathing in the Anotatta. When the Four Regent Gods and Sakka referred them, for right judgement, to Suciparivāra (pure household), the Bodhisatta who was born as a merchant (seṭṭhi) of Vārāṇasī, declared that Sirī would bathe first because she is higher than Kālakaṇṇī.

4. *Bahusodarī*. She is a daughter of the gods who dwelt on the Gandhamādana.[504]

5. *Bīrāṇī*. She had a palace in the Cātummahārājika-world. Her mansion was 12 *yojanas* in height having nine storeys and one thonsand rooms. It was ornamented in great magnificence, with pinnacles of jewels and gold, having a park and lake covered with lilies and surrounded with trees worthy of the palace and she was attended by a thousand nymphs. In the time of Kassapa Buddha she was a slave in a Brāhmaṇa's house. When the Brāhmaṇa invited eight monks for feeding them daily at his house, his wife and daughters refused to feed them; but their slave agreed to carry out the work conscientiously and with great devotion. As a result, she was born in the heaven.[505]

6. *Yasuttarā*. A devatā of the Tāvatiṁsa. In the previous birth she was a resident of Vārāṇasī. Once she spān two

robes and washed them and offered them to the Buddha. At this the Buddha preached to her and she became *sotāpanna*. After death she was born in the Tāvatiṁsa and was loved much by Sakka. Due to the power of her merit, she owned a mervellous elephant.[506]

7. *Jālinī*. She is a goddess of the Tāvatiṁsa-world. Anuruddha was formerly her husband. When Jālinī saw her husband becoming old and feeble, she appeared before him in Kosala and told him to take rebirth among the gods. In reply to her request, Anuruddha told her that there would be no rebirth for him.[507]

8. *Lājā*. In the previous birth she was the watcher of a paddy-field in Rājagaha and poured some of the parched rice into the bowl of Mahā Kassapa with devotion. As a result, she was reborn in the Tāvatiṁsa.[508]

Mention of the umbrella-goddess is found in the *Jātaka*.[509] The Bodhisatta was born as a son of Kāsīrāja and was told to be king; but he was unwilling to accept kingship because once he had been cast into the *Ussada* hell for wrong committed as a king. Then the umbrella goddess told him that, if he wished to escape from becoming a king, he should pretend to be a cripple and to show no signs of intelligence.

Notes

CHAPTER IV

1. Cf. *Dīghanikāya*, Vol. I, pp. 211-223.
2. Vol. I, pp. 144-45.
3. See above.
4. E.g., *Vis.*, Vol. I, p. 48. When the *Mahāsamaya Sutta* (*Dīg.*, Vol.II, pp. 253-62) was preached at Mahāvana in Kapilavatthu, the gods of the ten thousand world-systems came to visit the Buddha and the monks. Of them, four gods of the Suddhāvāsa Brahma-world eulogised the Buddha in verse. The *Devatā Saṁyutta* (*Saṁ.*, Vol. I, pp.1-45) and the *Devatā Sutta* of the *Aṅguttaranikāya* (Vol. III, pp. 329-44; Vol. IV, pp. 27-40) refer to visits paid to the Buddha by various deities.
5. *Khud. Com.*, p. 123.
6. See above.
7. For details see above.
8. See below.
9. See below.
10. E.g., See *Jāt.*, Vol. IV, p. 11.
11. *Ibid.*, p. 38.
12. *Ibid.*, Vol. VI, p. 512.
13. See below.
14. Those who are reborn in heaven owing to their good deeds on earth are generally entitled to dwell in *Vimānas* (mansions).
15. *Jāt.*, Vol. III, p. 58.
16. See above.
17. *Dīg.*, Vol. III, pp. 139-40.
18. *Aṅg.*, Vol. III, p. 333.
19. *Khud. Com.*, pp. 120—22.
20. *Dīg.*, Vol. II, p. 108.
21. See above.
22. *Dham. Com.*, Vol. 1, p. 173.
23. *Dīg. Com.*, Vol. II, pp. 427f.
24. *Dīg.*, Vol. II, pp. 253-262.
25. *Dīg.*, *Com.*, Vol. II, p. 690.
26. Ibid., p. 689.
27. Ibid., pp. 690, 562.
28. *Vibh. Com.*, p. 519.

29. *Dīg.*, Vol. I, p. 19; Vol. III, p. 31; *Vibh. Com.*, p. 498.
30. *Dīg.*, *Com.* Vol. I, pp. 19-20.
31. *Aṅg. Com.*, (SHB) Vol. II, p. 544.
32. *mohassa anudahanatāya-mohahanavsena hi tesaṁ satisammoso* (*Vibh. Com.*, p. 498).
33. *Dīg. Com.*, Vol. II, p. 691.
34. Loc. cit.
35. Ibid., Vol. I, p. 144; *Aṅg. Com.*, PTS, Vol. III, p. 147; *Vibh. Com.*, p. 519.
36. *Vibh. Com.*, p. 498.
37. *Dīg.*, Vol I p. 20; Vol. III, p. 32.
38. *Dig. Com.*, Vol. I, p. 20-21.
39 *Maj.* Vol. I, p. 376.
40. *Dīg. Com.*, Vol. II, p. 691.
41. They are all Yakkhas.
42. Vol. IV, p. 119.
43. See p. 91.
44. *Aṅg.*, Vol. IV, pp. 265ff; ibid., p. 268, where the Buddha speaks of them to Visākhā.
45. *Aṅg.*, Vol. IV, pp. 265 ff.
46. Vol. III, pp. 254 ff; cf. *Mil.*, p. 191 (Ghanikā-cloud-spirits).
47. *Saṁ.*, Vol. III, p. 256
48. *Vibh. Com.*, p. 519.
49. Loc. cit.
50. *Saṁ.*, Vol. III, p. 256.
51. Loc. cit.
52. This is one of the causes of rains. The *Mahāsamaya Sutta* (*Dīg.*, Vol. II, p. 259) mentions another class of gods as Mandavalāhakā (fragile cloud-spirits).
53. *Saṁ.*, Vol. I, pp. 16-22.
54. See *Satullapakāyikavagga* in the *Saṁ. Com.*, Vol. I.
55. Vol. I, pp. 61ff.
56. Vol. III, pp. 102, 147.
57. *Vibh. Com.*, p. 520.
58. *Abhs.*, p. 23.
59. *Maj.*, Vol. I, p. 2, See *MS.*, Vol. I, p.5, note 6 (*Abhibhū. Maj. Com.*, Āluvihāra Series, Colombo, Vol. I, p. 35, says that this indicates the state of being without perception and hence advanced in contemplation).
60. Buddhaghosa explains the word by saying *abhibhavīti Abhibhū; kiṁ abhibhavīti ? Cattāro Khandhe, arūpino.* As these gods are beautiful and long-lived, they are considered to be eternal and identical with Brahmā (*Maj. Com.*, Āluvihāra Series, Colombo, Vol. I, p. 30)
61. Verses 404, 543.
62. Sut. Com., Vol. II, p. 435.

63. *Ibid.*, Vol. I. p. 379 (*ye te attano ābhāya andhakāraṁ vidhamitvā ālokakaraṇena Sayampabhāti laddhanāmā cha-kāmāvacaradevā*).
64. See above. ch. II.
65. *Sut. Com.*, Vol. I, p. 435 ; see also *Jāt.*, Vol. VI, pp. 568, 571.
66. Vol. II, pp. 576f.
67. See pp. 415-16.
68. *Jāt.*, Vol.V, p.171.
69. *Dīg.*, Vol. II, p. 258.
70. *Ibid.*, Vol.II, p. 259.
71. *See Anāthapiṇḍikavagga in Saṁ. Com.*, PTS, Vol. I, p. 110.
72. *Saṁ.*, Vol. I. p. 52. The *Cūlavaṁsa*, Vol. II, p. 152 mentions god Viṣṇu as Lotus-hued.
73. *Saṁ.*, Vol. I, p. 219.
74. *Dīg.*, Vol .I, p. 244.
75. *Jāt.*, Vol. V, p. 28; Vol. VI, p. 20.
76. Loc. cit.;
77. *Dīg.*, Vol. III, p. 204.
78. Loc. cit.
79. *Dīg.*, Vol. II, p. 259.
80. *Jāt.*, Vol. VI, pp. 500-01. At ibid., p. 586, Vāruṇī is explained as *Yakkhāviṭṭhā ikkhaṇikā* (fortune-tellers possessed by a Yakkha, the Yakkha being perhaps Varuṇa).
81. *Dig.*, Vol. I, p. 244; Vol. II, p. 259; at *Jāt.*, Vol. VI, p. 201, he is mentioned with Dhātā, Vidhātā, Sun, Moon and Kuvera.
82. *Dīg.*, Vol. III, p. 204.
83. E.g., *CV.*, ch. 62, verse 5; ch. 63, verse 14.
84. See p. 351.
85. *Saṁ.*, Vol. I, p.56.
86. *CV.*, ch. 93, verses, 9, 10.
87. *Saṁ.*, Vol. I, p. 56.
88. Vol. III, p. 626.
89. Ch. 74, verse 193.
90. See e.g., *Dham. Com.*, Vol. III, p. 337; *Yamassa santikaṁ-Maraṇasantikaṁ*.
91. *Maj.*, Vol. III, pp 179ff.
92. *Dīg.*, Vol. II, p. 259.
93. *Dīg. Com.*, Vol. II, p. 690.
94. *Aṅg. Com.*, (PTS.) Vol. II, p. 228.
95. E.g., *Jāt.*, Vol.II, p. 318; Vol. IV, p. 273 (*Vetaraṇīm Yamassa*); Vol. V, pp. 268, 274, 304. The *Vetaraṇī* is mentioned as forming the boundary of Yama's kindom [*Jāt.*, Vol. I, p. 21; Vol. III, p. 472. At Vol. IV, p. 405, Yama's abode is called *Ussadaniraya*. *Dham. Com.* Vol. I, p. 334 explains *Yamaloka* by *Catubbidhaṁ apāyalokoṁ*. Cf. *Pet. Com.*, p. 33 (*Yamaloko tipetaloka*); *ibid.*, p. 107 (*Yamavisayaṁpetalokaṁ*).
96. *Jāt.*, Vol. II, pp. 318.
97. E.g., Dīg., Vol. I, p. 244; at *Mil.*, p. 37, the list includes Kuvera, Suyāma and Santusita.

98. Vol. I, p. 142.
99. *Sut. Com.*, Vol. I, p. 225.
100. *Jāt.*, Vol. VI, pp. 568, 571; *Maj.*, Vol. I, pp. 140, 327, 329.
101. *Saṁ.*, Vol. I, p. 219; *Jāt.*, Vol. V, p. 28.
102. *Jāt.*, Vol. V, p. 28; *Dīg.*, Vol. II, p. 274; *Dīg. Com.*, Vol. III, p. 709.
103. *Saṁ. Com.*, Vol. I.
104. *Dīg.*, Vol. III, p. 204.
105. *Ibid.*, Vol. I, p. 244.
106. *Saṁ.*, Vol. I, p. 219.
107. *Saṁ. Com.*, Vol. I.
108. E.g., *Jāt.*, Vol. I, pp. 214, 494; Vol. III, p. 17; Vol. V, 452; Vol. VI, p. 201, etc.
109. *Ibid.*, Vol. VI, p. 202.
110. *Ibid.*, Vol. I, p. 285.
111. *Ibid.*, pp. 494-95, where it is said that the Bodhisatta, having received an ox as a gift, wishes to offer the flesh to Aggi-Bhagavā, but thinking that the deity will not relish a saltless meal, he goes away to fetch some salt. When he returns, he finds that the ox has been eaten up by the hunters. Then he says to the diety, "If thou, Aggi-Bhagavā, hast not the power to look after thine own, how canst thou guard me?" Thereafter he becomes a recluse.
112. *Ibid.*, Vol. II, pp. 43-5.
113. *Jāt.*, Vol. VI, p. 203.
114. *Ibid.*, pp. 201f.
115. Loc. cit.
116. E.B. Cowell, *Jāt.*, Vol. IV, p. 51 note.
117. *Jāt.*, Vol. IV, pp. 100-03.
118. See p. 212.
119. *Jāt.*, Vol. IV, pp. 100-03.
120. E.g., *Dīg.*, Vol. II, p. 207.
121. Loc. cit.,
122. *Dīg.*, Vol. III, p. 201; *Dīg.. Com..* Vol. III, p. 967; *Jāt.*, Vol. VI, p. 270 ; *Sut. Com.*, Vol. I, p. 369.
123. E.g., *Cv.*, Ch. 37, verse 106; ch. 39, verse 5; ch. 80, verse 5.
124. *Cv.*, ch. 37, verse 31; see Hopkins' *Epic Mythology*, pp. 142f.
125. *Jāt* , Vol. VI, pp. 307, 325.
126. *Dīg.*, Vol. III, p. 201.
127. Ibid., p. 202.
128. *Sut.*, p. 379.
129. *Aṅg. Com.*, (SHB), Vol. IV, p. 36.
130. *Dīg. Com.*, Vol. III, p. 966 ; *Sut, Com..* Vol. I, pp. 369ff; *Jāt.*, Vol. VI, p. 201.
131. In the *Āṭānātiya Sutta* (Dīg., Vol. III, p. 194), he recited the *Āṭānāṭiya* runs for the protection of the Buddha and his followers from the Yakkhas who had no faith in the Buddha.
132. *Dīg, Com.*, Vol. III, p. 962.
133. *Sut. Com.*, Vol. I, p. 370.

134. *Thera. Com.*, (SHB), Vol. I, pp. 46f.
135. *Sut. Com.*, Vol. I, p. 225.
136. *Dīg.*, Vol. II, p. 207.
137. *Thera. Com.*, (SHB), Vol. I, p. 409.
138. Ibid., p. 149.
139. *Maj. Com.*, Āluvihāra Series, Colombo, Vol. I, p. 476.
140. *Maj.*. Vol. I, p. 253.
141. See, e.g., *Dham. Com.*, Vol. III, p. 74; *Jāt.*, Vol. I, p. 128; Vol. III p. 325 (Makhādeva). Sometimes, e.g., in the case of Avaruddhaka (*Dham. Com.*, Vol. II, p. 237), a Yakkha had to serve Tessavaṇa for twelve years in order to obtain a particular boon (cf. *Jāt.*, Vol. II, pp. 16f.; three years in *Jāt.*, Vol. III, p. 502, Vessavaṇa sometimes employs the services of uncivilized human being (*paccantamilakk-havāsika*); *Dīg,. Com.*, Vol. III, pp. 865f.
142. *Jāt.*, Vol. II, p. 399; *Sut. Com.*, Vol. I. p. 225.
143. *Jāt.*, Vol. I, p. 328.
144. She was a devout follower of the Buddha (Dīg., Vol. II, pp. 270f.) Buddhaghosa says that she reached the second fruit of the path and found no pleasure in the luxuries of heaven (*Dīg. Com.*, Vol. III, p. 705).
145. *Vim.*, p. 4; *Vim. Com.*, p. 131.
146. See e.g., *Vim.*, IV, 3, 46 (*bhuniāmi Kūmakāmīrāiā Vessavano yathā*); cf. *Jāt.*, Vol. VI, p. 313.
147. "In one of the tortuous paths of the golden Mountain lives an ascetic , by name Jotirasa, who watches the sacred fire in a leaf-thatched hut, called *Kancanapatti* or Gold leaf, a favourite of Vessavaṇa; and Vesavaṇa bends him constantly four fruits from the tree. ......" (*Jāt.*, Vol. II, p. 399)
148. *See Sirī-Kālakaṇṇī Jataka.*
149. *Dīg.*, Vol. II, p. 257.
150. *Jāt.*, Vol. II, pp. 257-62.
151. *Dīg.*, Vol. II. pp. 253-62,
152. Ibid., Vol. III, pp. 194ff.
153. *Dīg.*, Vol. II, p. 258; Vol. III, p. 199.
154. E.g., *Jāt.*, Vol. VI, p. 168; cf. *Aṅg. Com.*, (PTS) Vol. I, pp. 253, 255.
155. *Dīg.*, Vol., II, pp. 207, 221,
156. *Jāt.*, Vol. III, p. 257.
157. *Dīg.*, Vol. II, pp. pp. 207, 221.
158. Ibid., Vol. III, p. 198.
159. *Jāt.*, Vol. I, pp. 329-332; when no rain fell in Kosala for many days, the Buddha, out of compassion for the living beings of the earth, wanted to cause rain. At this the yellow-stone of Sakka grew hot and summoned the king of the storm-clouds (Pajjuna) to pour down rain over the entire kingdom of Kosala.
160. Loc. cit.
161. Loc. cit.
162. *Sam. Com.*, Vol. I.

163. *Dīg.*, Vol. III, p. 205.
164. Vol. I, pp. 29f.
165. *Dīg.*, Vol. II, p. 260.
166. See above, Ch. I.
167. Vol. IV, p. 89 (*chattiṁsakkhattuṁ kho panāhaṁ. . . . . . Sakko ahosiṁ devānaṁ indo*); *Jāt.*, Vol. IV, p. 180, here it is said that the Buddha, in a previous birth, was Sakka who came in disguise to the kingdom of Usīnara to frighten the unrighteous people.
168. *Jāt.*, Vol. II, p. 312.
169. Ibid., Vol. IV, p. 357.
170. *Jāt.*, Vol. V, p.383 ; cf. Vol. IV, p. 63, where it is said that the Bodhisatta being born in a rich man's family of Varāṇasī gave away his wealth. As a result, he was reborn as Sakka ; also see *Jāt.*, Vol. I, pp. 349-54).
171. Ibid., Vol. V, p. 152.
172. Vol. I, pp. 228-31.
173. For a slightly different version, see *Dham. Com.*, Vol. I, pp. 264ff.
174. Loc. cit. The *Saṁyutta Commentary*, Vol. I, p. 267, says that Magha was not the Bodhisatta, but that his life was like that of a Bodhisatta (*Bodhisattacariyā viyassa cariyā ahosi*); this is supported by the story as given in the *Dīg. Com.*, Vol. III, pp. 710ff and *Dham. Com.* Vol. I, pp. 264ff, where no mention is found of the Bodhisatta; but in the *Jāt.*, Vol. I, pp. 201ff., it is found that the Bodhisatta fulfilled *Sattavatapadāni* and became Sakka, king of the *devas*.
175. *Saṁ.*, Vol. I, p. 230. The epithet Purandara (Destroyer of towns) was applied to Indra, the Vedic god.
176. Ibid., p. 229 ; cf *Dham. Com.*, Vol. I, p. 264.
177. Vol. II, p. 260.
178. *Dīg. Com.*, Vol. II, p. 690.
179. *Saṁ.*, Vol. I, p. 230.
180. Loc. cit.
181. *Dīg.*, Vol. II, p. 270 ; *Maj.*, Vol. I, p. 252.
182. *Maj.*, Vol. I, p. 252 ; cf. *Saṁ.*, Vol. I, p. 206 (*Sakkanāmako Yakkha*).
183. *Saṁ. Com.*, (PTS), Vol. I, p. 104 (*Vatranāmakam vā asuram abhibhavatī ti Vatrabhū*).
184. *Jāt.*, Vol. VI, p. 260.
185. Ibid., Vol. V, pp. 397, 411.
186. See pp. 112, 151.
187. E.g., *Aṅg.*, Vol. IV, p. 89; *Dīg.*, Vol. I, pp. 216f.; ibid. Vol., II, pp. 221, 275; *Saṁ.*, Vol. I, p. 219.
188. *Dīg.*, Vol. I, p. 244. Inda is mentioned here with Soma, Varuṇa, Isāna, Pajāpati, Brahmā, Mahiddi and Yama, as a god whom the Brāhmaṇas invoke and prey to, for union with Brahmā after death. Also see ibid., Vol. II, p. 274; *Sut.*, verse 310.
189. *Jāt.*, Vol. V. pp. 115, 411; Vol. p. 568. See *Dīg.*, Vol, II, p. 274, where Vāsava, i.e., Sakka is addressed by Gopaka as Indra.

190. *Jāt.*, Vol. III, p. 146 ; Vol. V, pp. 409-12.
191. Ibid., Vol. V, p. 33; Vol. VI, p. 127; the Tāvatiṁsa-gods are also described as *Sa-Indakā* in the *Vessantara Jātaka* (*ibid.*, Vol. VI, p. 568) and *sahindakā in* the *Nikāyas* (Dīg., Vol. II, pp. 208-212 *Saṁ.*, Vol. III, p. 90 (*sa-indakā devā sa-brahmakā sapajāpatikā*).
192. "Place of Indra in Early Buddhism", *University of Ceylon Review*, Vol. III, No. I, p. 53. (*MS.*, Vol. I, p. 308, note 1).
193. Vol. II; p. 274 (*Sa-Inda-devā sa-Pajāpatikā*); *ibid.*, p. 261 (Sa-Indadeve as Brahmake); *Sut.*, verse 1024 (*Brahmā vā Indo vā pi Sujampati*).
194. Vol. I, p. 140 (He is mentioned with Brahmā and Pajāpati); *Jāt.*, Vol. V, p. 411; Vol VI, p. 568; in Vol. IV, p. 568; he appears with Brahmā, Pajāpati, Soma, Yama and Vessavaṇa.
194a. He is called Vatrabhū (*Jāt.*, Vol. V, p. 153 ; *Saṁ.*; Vol. I, p. 47).
195. *Jāt.*, Vol. V, p. 33.
196. Vol. IV, pp. 105ff.
197. *Jāt.*, Vol. I, p. 354; for Saka's Vajirāvudha, see *Sut. Com.*, Vol. I, p. 225.
198. *Dīg.*, Vol. II, p. 259; *Dīg. Com.*, Vol. II, p. 689. When the thunderbolt strikes its victim, the sound of the bolt surpasses all other sounds by its intensity, volume and fearfulness (*Udāna Com.*, p. 67). It is not stopped by any obstruction and never misses its mark; it is *avirajjhanaka* (*Vibh. Com.*, p. 333).
199. *Dīg.*, Vol. III, p. 204.
200. Ibid., p. 176. He is also called Suravaratara (loc. cit.)
201. See Ch. 72, verse 186 ; *Abhidhānappadīpikā*, verse 20.
202. *Dīg.*, Vol. II, pp. 257 ; Vol. III, pp. 197-202.
203. See p. 30.
204. Loc. cit.
205. See above.
206. It stands under the *Pāricchattaka-Kovilāra* which is sixty *yojanas* long, fifty *yojanas* broad and fifteen *yojanas* deep. Sitting on it, Sakka, sinks as far as the middle of his body into the colour of the *jayasumana* flower (*Dīg. Com.*, Vol. II, p. 482; cf. *Jāt.*, Vol. V, p. 386). When the Buddha visited the Tāvatiṁsa-heaven for preaching to his mother, he occupied the Paṇḍukambalasilāsana. It becomes hot when Sakka's life comes towards its end; or his merit is exhausted; or when some mighty beings pray; or through the results of virtue in recluses of Brāhmaṇas or other beings, full or potency (*Jāt.*, Vol. IV, pp. 8f., 23, 323; Vol. III, p. 53; Vol. V, p. 92, etc.). It is mentioned that the Buddha occupied the seat on a subsequent visit to Tāvatiṁsa (ibid., Vol. II, p. 93). The seat was occupied also by the distinguished guests, such as Sādhīna (ibid., Vol. IV, p. 357). The throne is so called because it resembled a new blanket (*rattakambala*) *Mahāniddesa Commentary*, SHB, p. 313).
207. *Jāt.*, Vol. V, p. 386. Buddhaghoṣa says that Sakka's voice was sweet like the sound of a golden bell (*KS.* Vol. I, p. 302, note 2).
208. *Maj.*, Vol. I, p. 252 ; *MS*, Vol. I, p. 307, notes 2 and 3.

209. Loc. cit.

210. In the previous birth he was an elephant of a king of Magadha, who gave him to Magha and his companions for helping them in their good work on earth. When Magha and his companions were reborn in the Tāvatiṁsa, Erāvaṇa also was their companion in heaven. He was a *deva* like others because the *deva*-world was devoid of animals. However, when Magha and others went to a park to play, he assumed the form of an elephant, one hundred and fifty *yojanas* in size. He erected 33 heads (*kumbha*) for 33 gods, each being two or three quarter *yojanas* in girth. Each head had seven tusks, each of which was fifty *yojanas* long. Each tusk bore seven lotus plants, each plant seven flowers, each flower seven leaves, and on each leaf danced seven nymphs (*padumaccharā*). There was a special head called Sudassana for Sakka which was thirty *yojanas* around. Above it a canopy of twelve *yojanas* made of precious stones was also found. In the centre of it was a jewelled couch one *yojana* long, on which Sakka sat (*Dham. Com.*, Vol. I, pp. 273f.; also *Sut. Com.*, Vol. I, pp. 368f. (where there are a few slight variations).

Erāvaṇa is mentioned on many occasions. He is included among the *devas* who visited the Buddha to pay him homage (*Sut.*, verse 379). He was present at the preaching of the *Mahāsamaya Sutta* (*Dīg.*, Vol. II, p. 258) with the Nāgas. It is found in several places (e.g., *Maj. Com.*, Āluvihāra Series, Colombo, Vol. I, p. 472; *Dīg. Com.*, Vol. II, p. 688; also *Vim. Com.*, p. 15 and *KV*, Vol. II, p. 599) that Erāvaṇa is a *devaputta* and a Nāga only by birth (*Jātiyā*). The *Jātaka*, Vol. V, p. 137 describes Sakka as riding Erāvaṇa.

211. See above.

212. It is one hundred and fifty *yojanas* in length (*Dīg. Com* , Vol. II, p. 481 ; *Jāt.*, Vol. I, p. 202) and drawn by one thousand horses, with Matali as charioteer (*Saṁ.*, Vol. I, p. 224). It was sent to fetch destinguished human beings to Tāvatiṁsa, e.g., Nimi, Guttila and Sādhīna. It is described with its pole of gold and its framework overlaid with gilt representations of various animals and birds. When it travelled, the whole world was filled with the sounds of its wheels (*Jāt.*, Vol. V, pp. 408 f.).

213. *Jāt.*, Vol. I, p. 202.

214. Vol. I, p. 219.

215. *DB*, Vol. I, p. 310. It may be assumed that these three gods have the same power as that of Sakka.

216. See above.

217. *Aṅg.*, Vol. IV, p. 242; these are also attributed to the other rulers of the various deva-worlds.

218. Vol. I, pp. 216-240.

219. Here the enemy is his father-in-law, Vepacitta. In *Sutta* 22, a Yakkha is said to have come and sat on his throne, to anger him;

but Sakka, as he had a reputation for great forbearance, showed the Yakkha great honour and the latter vanished.

220. See also above.
221. Saṁ., Vol. I, p. 232.
222. *Saṁ.*, Vol. IV, pp. 269-80.
223. *DB*, Vol. II, p. 175.
224. *Aṅg*,, Vol. I, p. 144. In the story of Rohini, Sakka is seen as overpowered by beauty. He liked people to enjoy life and sent a heavenly dancer to amuse Mahāpanāda (*Sut. Com.*, Vol. II, pp. 400-01). When Sakka was rejoicing in his triumph over the Asuras, he saw a crane on a hill-top who wished to be able to eat fish without going down into the stream. Sakka immediately sent the stream, in full flood, to the hill top (*Jāt.*, Vol. III, p. 252).
225. *Aṅg.*, Vol. I, p. 144. It is said that Sunetta had thirty-six times (*chattiṁsakkhattaṁ*) been reborn as Sakka (*ibid.*, Vol. IV, p. 105).
226. *Jāt.*, Vol. II, p. 312. Sakka's life is given as lasting thirty million and sixty hundred thousand years.
227. *Saṁ.*, Vol. I, p. 219.
228. In the *Jātakas*, he is mentioned as being frightened of ascetics who practised severe penances, lest they should unseat him from his throne. See *Jāt.*, Vol. II, p. 394.
229. *Dham. Com.*, Vol. I, pp. 17f. The *Jātakas* contain many instances where Sakka rescued the good people in distress; cf. the cases of Dhammaddhaja, Guttila, Kaccāni, the Kinnarī Candā, Sambulā, Kusa, Mahājanaka's mother, Candakumāra's mother, and Mahosadha.
230. *Dham. Com.*, Vol. II, pp. 34f.; see also the story of the courtesan in the *Kurudhamma Jātaka* (*Jāt.*, Vol. II, p. 380).
231. Cf. the *Kuddālapaṇḍita, Hatthipāla, Ayoghara, Jotipāla,* (*Sarabhaṅga*), *Sutasoma, Dukūlaka, Pārikā and Vessantara Jātakas.*
232. Vol. III, pp. 370f.
233. *Jāt.*, Vol. IV, pp. 280-86. The *Keḷisīla Jātaka* (No. 202) says that when the Bodhisatta was born as Sakka, he, in the guise of an old man, came on the earth and frightened a bad king by physical torture and by showing his *Vajira*,
234. For details see MV., VII, 1ff.; XIII. 15; XVII. 9ff; XXVIII. 6ff; XXXI. 34, 75, 78.
235. *Jāt.*, Vol. 1, p. 65.
236. *Ibid.*, p. 72; Vijayuttara Saṅkha (conch-trumpet) is one hundred and twenty cubits in length (loc. cit.; *Bud. Com.*, p.287). Sakka also blew it on the occasion of the enshrinement of relics in the Mahāthūpa Mhv XXX. 74) and on the day of the coronation of Candakumāra (*Jāt*,, Vol. VI, p. 157).
237. *Vin.*, Vol. I, p. 38.
238. *Dham. Com.*, Vol. III, pp. 206, 208.
239. Ibid., p. 225; *Aṅg. Com.*, (PTS), Vol. I, p. 126.
240. *Dham. Com.*, Vol. III, p. 441.

241. Ibid., p. 470.
242. Vol. I, p. 330.
243. *Dham. Com.*, Vol. IV, pp. 269f.
244. Ibid., p. 164ff; *Dīg. Com.*, Vol. II, pp. 549f; *Jāt.*, Vol. I, p. 391.
245. *Vin.*, Vol. I, pp. 28f.
246. *Dīg.*, Vol. II, p. 157; also see *DB*, Vol. II, p. 176, note 1.
247. *Dīg. Com.*, Vol. II, p. 609.
248. Ibid., p. 613.
249. *Dham. Com.*, Vol. IV, pp. 176f.
250. Ibid., Vol. III, p. 143; cf. the story of Sukha, ibid., Vol. III, pp. 96f.
251. See, e.g., the story of Mahāphussa (*Sut. Com.*, Vol. I, pp. 55f).
252. *Dham. Com.*, Vol. IV, pp. 207f.
253. Sakka gave the Beluvapaṇḍuvīnā to Pañcasikha (*Sut. Com.*, Vol. II, pp. 393-94).
254. Dīg., Vol. II, p. 270.
255. Ibid., p, 286.
256. *Dīg. Com.*, Vol. III, p. 697. It is said that (*Dīg.*, Vol. II, p. 284) Sakka visited other Brāhmaṇas and recluses as well. They were pleased to see him and boasted that they had nothing to teach him; but he had to teach them what he knew.
257. *Dīg. Com.*, Vol. III, p. 732; cf. *Dham. Com.*, Vol. III, p. 270.
258. *Dīg. Com.*, Vol. III, p. 740.
259. *Maj.*, Vol. I, pp. 251ff. On an occasion, Sakka visited Uttara Thera on the Saṅkheyyaka mountain and listened to his sermon (*Aṅg.*, Vol, IV, pp. 163f.)
260. *Dīg. Com.*, Vol. III, p. 705,
261. *Jāt.*, Vol. I, p. 229.
262. Ibid., Vol. VI, pp. 257-58.
263. Loc. Cit.
264. E.g., see ibid., Vol. V, p. 279.
265. Ibid., Vol. III, p. 493.
266. Ibid., Vol. IV, p. 10.
267. Ibid., pp. 240f.
268. Ibid., pp. 410f.
269. *Jāt.*, Vol. V. pp. 280f., 310.
270. *Jāt.*, Vol, VI, pp. 481f.
271. Ibid., p. 572.
272. Ibid., No. 499.
273. Ibid., No. 538.
274. Ibid., No. 541,
275. Ibid., No. 547.
276. See Ibid., No. 316.
277. Loc. cit.
278. Ibid., No. 450.
278a Ibid., Vol. III, pp. 492ff.
279. *Jāt.*, Vol. V, p. 280.

280. E.B. Cowel, *Jāt.*, Vol. VI, p. 20.
281. *Jāt.*, pp. 301, 304.
282. Ibid., Vol. IV, p. 63.
283. See, e.g., the conversation reported in *Saṁ.*, Vol. I, pp. 221, 224, 234ff. ; and *Vim.*, IV, 9.
284. *Dham. Com.*, Vol. I, pp. 279f; *Jāt.*, Vol. I, pp. 202f.
285. Loc. cit.
286. *Jāt.*, No. 374.
287. Ibid., No. 450.
288. Ibid., No. 535.
289. Ibid. No. 469.
290. See *Guttila, Nimi, Makhādeva* and *Sādhīna Jātakas.*
291. *Dham. Com.*, Vol. III, pp. 225-26.
292. *Dīg.*, Vol. II, p, 268.
293. *Jāt.*, No. 450.
294. Ibid., No. 535.
295. See ibid., Vol. I, p. 206; Vol. IV, p. 186, Vol. V, p. 412; Vol. VI, p. 129.
296. Ibid., Vol, IV, p. 69.
297. *Dīg.*, Vol. II, p. 258.
228. Ibid., Vol. III, p. 204.
299. See above.
300. *Jāt.*, Vol. I, pp. 201, 204-05, *Dham. Com.*, Vol. I, pp. 269ff.
301. *Dham. Com.*, Vol. I, pp. 269, 271, 274f.; *Dīg. Com.*, Vol. III, pp. 716f. *Jāt.*, Vol. I, pp. 201; Vol. III, pp. 491f., where Sujā accompanies Sakka in his travels; in p. 494 she is called Sujātā.
302. *Dham. Com.*, Vol. I, pp. 269f.; *Jāt.*, Vol. I, pp. 201f.
303. Loc. cit.
304. See above.
305. *Vim.*, III, 4; *Vim. Com.*, pp. 131ff.
306. *Jāt.*, Vol. V, pp. 382-412.
307. Ibid., Vol. V. pp. 399-405.
308. *Sam.*, Vol. I, pp. 217-18.
309. Ibid., p. 216.
310. See *Dīg.*, Vol. II, p. 259.
311. *Dīg. Com.*, Vol. II, p. 689.
312. *Pet.*, pp. 27f; *Pet. Com.*, pp. 136-38; *Dham. Com.*, Vol. III, pp. 219-20; 80-1.
313. *Pet.*, p. 28, Verse 69.
314. See p. 139.
315. *Jāt.*, Vol. IV, p. 325.
316. Vol. I, p. 272. The *deva* who accompanied Sakka in the guise of a dog in the *Mahākaṇha Jātaka* was Mātali and not Vissakamma.
317. In Brāhmaṇical literature, Visvakarman is described as the architect of the gods (Hopkins, *Epic Mythology*, p. 201). He is the builder of Varuṇa's palace (ibid., p. 113) and of the divine assembly hall (ibid p. 113).

318. *Dīg.*, Vol. II, p. 180.
319. *Jāt.*, Vol. IV, p. 323; *Dīg., Com.*, Vol. III, p. 856.
320. *Jāt.*, Vol. I, p. 7 (Vissakamma here is addressed as a *devaputta*).
321. *Ibid.*, p. 314
322. Ibid., Vol. IV, p. 489.
323. Ibid., p. 499.
324. Ibid., Vol. V, p. 132.
325. Ibid., pp. 190-01.
326. Ibid., Vol. VI, pp. 29, 211.
327. Ibid., pp. 519f.
328. Ibid., p. 72.
329. Ibid., Vol. VI, p. 12.
330. Ibid., Vol. I, p. 60; *Bud. Com.*, p. 280; he also excavated ponds in which the prince might bathe (*Aṅg. Com.*, (PTS), Vol. pp. 126f.).
331. *Dīg. Com.*, Vol. II, p. 614.
332. *Jāt.*, Vol. IV, pp. 318-23.
333. Ibid., Vol. VI, p. 118.
334. Mil., pp. 6f.
335. *Dīg.*, Vol. I, p. 218; *Aṅg.*, Vol. IV, p. 243; *Sām.*, Vol. IV, p. 280.
336. *Bud. Com.*, p. 45; *Jāt.*, Vol. I, p. 48.
337. *Jāt.*, Vol. I, p. 81.
338. E.g., *MV*, XXXI, 78.
339. *Aṅg.*, Vol. IV, p. 242; *Dīg.*, Vol. I, p. 217.
340. Vol. I, p. 244.
341. *Dham. Com.*, Vol. III, p. 226; *Vis.*, p. 392; cf. *Bud. Com.*, p. 239; at ibid., p. 287 Suyāma appeared before the Buddha with *tigāvutāyataṁ saradasamayarajanikarasassirikaṁ dibbacāmaraṁ* for fanning him slowly when he enlightened; *Aṅg. Com.*, (PTS), Vol. I, p. 126; *Jāt.*, Vol. I, pp. 48, 53; *M.V.*, XXXI, 98.
342. *Jāt.*, Vol. I, p. 81; *Saṁ.*, Vol. IV. p. 280; *Aṅg.*, Vol. IV, p. 243.
343. *Vim. Com.*, p. 189.
344. *Dig.*, Vol. I, p. 219.
345. See above, Ch. II.
346. *Maj. Com.*, Āluvihāra series, Colombo, Vol. I, p.28.
347.
348.
349. *Saṁ.*, Vol. I, p. 149; *Aṅg.*, Vol. V, p. 171; *Jāt.*, Vol. IV, pp. 244-45; *Sut. Com.*, Vol. II, p. 476.
350. See note 4 of *MS.*, Vol. I, p. 388; 'According to *Maj. Com.*, "this" is a *Brahmaṭṭhāna*' (*MS.*, loc. cit., note 5).
351. *Maj.*, Vol. I, pp. 326-31.
352. See *Jāt.*, No. 346; ibid., Vol. III, pp. 358ff. (*Bakabrahma Jātaka*, No. 405).
353. *Mil.*, pp. 223f., cf. *Maj.*, Vol. II, p. 54 and see also note 1 of *MS*, Vol. II. p. 250.
354. *Jāt*, Vol. I, p. 172.
355. *Maj.*, Vol. II, pp. 46-54; *Bud.*, XXV, p. 41.

356. *Dham. Com.*, Vol. I, p. 380.
357. Vol. I, pp. 35f., 60.
358. *Jāt.*, Vol. I, p. 65; *Sut. Com.*, Vol. II, p. 382; *Vim. Com.*, p. 314. The begging bowl, provided by Ghaṭikāra, vanished when the Buddha was given a bowl of milk-rice by Sujātā (Jāt. Vol. I, p. 69).
359. *Dāṭhāvaṁsa*, verse, p. 35.
360. *M.* XXXI, II, MT. 562.
361. *Jāt.*, Vol. VI, pp. 220, 242ff.
362. See, e.g., *Dīg. Com.*, Vol. II, p. 693.
363. *Dīg.*, Vol. II, p. 261; *Dīg. Com.*, Vol. II, 693; cf. ibid., Vol. I, p. 40.
364. *Sam.*, Vol. V, p. 233.
365. Vol. II, p. 476.
366. See pp. 12, 29; *Maj. Com.*, PTS, Vol. II, p. 372.
367. Rhys Davids and Oldenberg, *Vin. Texts*, Vol. I, p. 86, note 1. It is difficult to believe that the Pali name of Brahmā Sahampati, the ruler of the Brahma-worlds (see Spence Hardy's *MB*, pp. 43, 56), is not connected with the Brahman Svayambhū of the Brāhmaṇical literature. Perhaps the Sanskrit equivalent of Sahampati might by Svayampati.
368. Vol. I, pp. 137f.
369. Ibid., Vol. I, pp. 139. See also ibid., Vol. V, pp. 167f., 185f, 232, where Sahampati gives an assurance to the Buddha regarding the four *Satipaṭṭhānas* and the five *indriyas*.
370. E.g., *Sam. Com.*, (PTS), Vol. 1, pp. 198f.
371. *Dīg. Com.*, Vol. II, 467. See also *Dīg.*, Vol. II, pp. 36f. and *DB*, Vol. II, p. 30, note 4.
372. *Sut.*, p. 125; cf. *Saṁ.*, Vol. I, p. 151; *Aṅg.*, Vol. V, p. 172.
373. *Saṁ.*, Vol. I, p. 154.
374. Ibid., p. 233.
375. Ibid., p. 158; *Dīg.*, Vol. II, p. 157.
376. *Bud. Com.*, p. 287. This incident was sculptured in the Relic chamber of the Mahāthūpa (*MV.* XXX. 74); cf. *Jāt.*, Vol. IV, p. 266. The *Aṅg. Com.*, PTS., Vol. I, p. 126 says that Mahābrahmā (not in name) hold the umbrella or parasol when the Buddha descended from the deva-world after performing Twin-miracles.
377. *Khud. Com.*, p. 171; *Vin. Com.*, Vol. I, p. 115; *Vis.*, Vol. I, p. 201.
378. *Vibh. Com.*, p. 352.
379. *Saṁ.*, Vol., I, pp. 140f.
380. *Maj. Com.*, Āluvihāra Series, Colombo, Vol. II, p. 584.
381. *DB*, Vol. II, p. 292, note 3; cf. Vol. I, p. 121, note 1 (Sanaṅkumāra means 'ever bachelor'. According to legend common to Brāhmaṇas and Buddhists there were five 'mind born' sons of Brahmā, who remained always pure and innocent, and Sanaṅkumāra was one of the five. See the passages quoted by Chalmers in the *JRAS.*, 1894, p. 344).
382. *Dīg.*, Vol. II, pp. 200-19.
383. Because all *devas* liked *Pañcasīkha* (*Dīg. Com*,, Vol. II, p. 640).

384. *Dīg.*, Vol II, pp. 211-14.
385. *Maj.*, Vol. I, p. 358 ; *Saṁ.*, Vol. I, p. 153 ; *Aṅg.*, Vol. V, p. 327. See *Chānd. Up.*, Ch. VII, (note 4 of p. 24 of MS, Vol. II).
386. *Saṁ.*, Vol. II, p. 284.
387. Ibid., Vol. I, p. 153.
388. *Dīg.*, Vol. II, p. 261.
389. *DB.*, Vol. II, p. 292, note 3.
390. *Dīg.*, Vol. II, p. 261; *Dīg. Com.*, Vol. II, p. 692.
391. E.g., *Jāt.*, Vol. VI, p. 484, where it is said that sixty thousand sons of the gods were destined to rebirth and descended on earth with the birth of the Buddha as Vessantara.
392. Vol. I, pp. 46-67.
393. Ibid., p. 46.
394. *Dīg.*, Vol. III, p. 205.
395. For its diameter see above.
396. *Dham. Com.*, Vol. II, pp. 143, 146; Vol. III, p. 97.
397. Vol. II, p. 259.
398, *Jāt.*, Vol. IV, p. 1.
399. *Dig.*, Vol. II, p. 259.
400. See p. 519.
401. *Jāt.*, Vol. IV, pp. 63, 69,
402. Ibid., Vol. V, pp. 386, 412.
403. Ibid., Vol. I, p. 172.
404. Ibid., Vol. IV. pp. 63, 69.
405. *Saṁ.*, Vol. I, p. 50.
406. *Vibh. Com.*, p. 519.
407. See *Ādityopasthāna Jātaka* No. 175.
408. *Jāt.*, Vol. IV, p. 63
409. See above.
410. See p. 133.
411. See above.
412. E.g., when he wished the Sāmaṇeras Paṇḍita and Sukha to be able to meditate undisturbed (*Dham, Com.*, Vol. II, p. 143; Vol. III, pp. 97, 208).
413. Vol. III, p. 196.
414. Loc. cit.; *Dīg. Com.*, Vol. III, p. 963.
415. Verse 423. According to Buddhagoṣa (*Vibh. Com.*, p. 466) Ādicca and Koṇḍañña were gotta-names of the Khattiyas.
416. See p. 116.
417. E.g., Dīg., Vol. III, p. 197; Sut., verse 1128.
418. Vol. I, p. 57.
419. Āluvihāra Series, Colombo, Vol. II, p. 783.
420. See above.
421. *Dīg.*, Vol. II, p. 258.
422. *Maj. Com.*, Āluvihāra Series, Colombo, Vol. II, p. 951.
423. *Dīg.*, Vol. III, p. 204.
424. *Saṁ.*, Vol. IV, p. 280.

425. *Loc. cit.*
426. *Maj.*, Vol. III, pp. 199f.
427. See above.
428. See *KS*, Vol. I, p. 262, note 1.
429. See above.
430. See above.
431. *Saṁ.*, Vol. I, pp. 63f.
432. *Dīg.*, Vol. II, pp, 263-89.
433. *Dham. Com.*, Vol., pp. 169-173, 187; *Dīg. Com.*, Vol. I, p. 317.
434. Jāt., Vol. VI, pp. 239f.
435. *Pet.*, p. 28; *Pet. Com.*, p. 137.
436. *Dham. Com.*, Vol. I, pp. 426-28.
437. *Vim.*, pp. 74-5, *Vim. Com.*, pp. 318ff.
438. *Vim.*, pp. 74-5.
439. *Dham. Com.*, Vol. I, p. 426.
440. *Saṁ.*, Vol. I, p. 65.
441. *Ibid.*, pp, 65, 67; *Mil.*, p. 242.
442. *Vim.*, V. 14 ; *Vim. Com.*, pp. 270ff.
443. *Jāt.*, Vol. III, p. 261.
444. Ibid., p. 5.
445. See Ch. 83, verse 49; see also *CV.*, trs. Vol. II, 152, note 3.
446. *M.*, VII. 5.
447. *Jāt.*, Vol. V, p. 99, The *Maj. Com.*, (PTS, Vol. II, p. 372, mentions Vanadevatā and Rukkhadevatā).
448. *Jāt.*, Vol. IV, p. 294.
449. *Maj. Com.*, Āluvihāra Series, Colombo, Vol. II, p. 813.
450. *MV.*, I, 52ff.
451. *Jāt.*, Vol. VI, p. 24.
452. Ibid., Vol. I, p. 127.
453. Ibid., Vol. IV, p. 194.
454. *MB*, I, 33; Samantakūṭa is a mountain peak in Ceylon where Mahāsumana Deva lived. It is said that when the Buddha visited the Island for the third time, he left on the mountain the mark of his foot prints (*M.*, I, 77). As a result of this, the mountain became a sacred place of pilgrimage. In later times many kings of Ceylon paid the shrine great honour.
455. *Bud. Com.*, pp. 209-10.
456. *Jāt.*, Vol. I, p. 110; Vol. II, pp. 39, 176.
457. E.g., Ibid, Vol. III, pp. 262, 443.
458. Loc. cit.; ibid., Vol. V, p. 112.
459. Cf. (*Atha*) *Lakkhī Sirī* (thiyaṁ)—verse 81; sompatti sampadā Lakkhī Sirī—verse 906.
460. *Jāt.*, Vol. III, p. 443.
461. Cf. *Sirī pi puññaṁ pi panna pi* (ibid., Vol. IV, pp. 281-82).
462. Cf. *lakkhī ti sirī paññā ti pi* (ibid., Vol. III, p. 306).
463. Cf. *ahaṁ Sirī ca Lakkhī ca, bhuripaññā ti maṁ vidū* (ibid., p. 262)

464. Ibid., Vol. V, p, 146, where it is said that the moral observants are wise, i.e., who are self-restrained in body, speech and mind and never tell a lie for serving their own work. Lakkhī does not forsake wise man who is grateful, tender, heart-winning, gracious, proves himself a good and steadfast friend, enjoys his own property with others and speaks smoothly, etc.
465. Loc. cit., ibid., Vol. III, p. 306.
466. *Jāt.*, Vol. III, p. 306.
467. Ibid., pp. 442-43.
468. Ibid., p. 306.
469. Vol. I, p. 17; Vol. II, p. 17.
470. Ch. 72, verses 101, 112; ibid., Ch. 76, verse 233.
471. Vol. III, pp. 257, 262; see *Jāt.*, Vol. V, p. 392, where *Siri*='glory', is regarded as the daughter of Sakka, king of the *Tāvatiṁsa-devaloka.*
472. *Jāt.*, Vol. III, p. 258.
473. Ibid., p. 262.
474. Ibid., pp. 262-63.
475. Ibid., p. 262; cf. ibid., p. 443 where it is said that the king possesses Lakkhī permanently if he is free from anger.
476. Ibid., p. 258.
477. Cf. *Uṭṭhānaviriye pose ram'āhaṁ anusuyyake* (ibid., Vol. V, p. 112).
478. Ibid.. Vol. V, p. 113; cf, ibid., Vol. III, p. 262.
479. Ibid., Vol. V, p. 113.
480. Ibid., Vol. II, p. 413.
481. See below.
482. Cf. *Esa devamanussānaṁ sabbakāmadado nidhi/yaṁ yad evābhipatthenti sabbaṁ etena labbhati Suvaṇṇatā, sussaratā susaṇṭhānasurūpatā / adhipaccaparivāro sabbaṁ etena labbhati // Padesarajjaṁ Issariyaṁ cakkavattisukhaṁ pi yaṁ l devarajjam pi dibbesu sabbaṁ etena labbhati // Mānusikā ca sampatti devbloke ca yā rati / yā ca nibbāna-sampatti sabbaṁ etena labbati / Mittasampadaṁ āgamma yoniso ve paynñjato/ Vijjāvimutti vasībhāvo sabhaṁ etena labbhati//paṭisambhidā vimokho ca yā ca sāvakapārami / paccekabodhibuddhabhūmi sabbaṁ etena labbhati// Evaṁ mahiddhiyā esā yadidaṁ puññasampadā / tasmā dhīrā pasaṁsanti paṇḍitā katapuññatan=ti. //*
483. *Jāt.*, Vol. II, p. 414.
484. Cf. *Kukkuṭamaṇayo daṇḍo thīyo ca puññalakkhaṇā uppajjanti apāpassa katapuññassa jantuno ti* (*ibid.*, p. 415).
485. Ibid., Vol. III, p. 261.
486. Ibid., Vol. II, p. 412.
487. Ibid., Vol. II, p. 411ff.
488. Cf. Rhys Davids, *Buddhist India,* p.217.
489. See p. 141.
490. Ch. 73, verse 86.
491. *Jāt.*, Vol. VI, pp. 356-62.
492. *Ibid.*, p, 135; Vol. IV, pp. 15-21.
493. *Ibid.*, Vol. III, p. 259.

494. Ibid., p. 264.
495. Ibid., Vol. IV, p. 378.
496. Ibid., Vol. V, pp.112-13.
497. Ibid., Vol. III, pp. 259-60.
498. Ibid., Vol. VI, p. 349.
499. Ibid., Vol. III, p. 263.
500. Cf. *ahaṁ Kālī alakkhikā Kālakaṇṇiti maṁ vidū* (ibid., p. 259).
501. Ibid., pp. 257, 259.
502. Ibid., p. 258.
503. Ibid., pp. 259-60.
504. Ibid., Vol. VI, p. 83.
505. Ibid., Vol. VI, pp. 117f.
506. *Vim.*, IV. 3; *Vim Com.*, pp. 181ff.
507. *Saṁ.*, Vol. I, p. 200.
508. *Dham. Com.*, Vol. III, pp. 6ff.
509. *Jāt.*, Vol. VI, p. 4.

CHAPTER V

The Buddha

The Buddha is not a proper name; it is a generic name or an appellative applied to a being who has attained Englighten-ment. Buddhist literature mentions many gods and Brahmās; but none of them is supreme. The Buddha is superior to all beings, human and divine, by his knowledge of the Truth (*Dhamma*). The difference between the gods and the Buddha lies in the fact that the gods rule over their respective worlds whereas the Buddha rules over the whole universe.

The Buddha is the embodiment of knowledge. He appears on earth when knowledge is necessary for human and divine life. He is not born in the early period of *kappa* when people live longer than one hundred thousand years because, during this period, they are not able to recognise the nature of old age and death, and therefore are not benefited by his preaching. He is born on earth when men live not less than one hundred years and not more than ten thousand.[1] As he comes in a suitable age for our welfare the Buddha may be regarded as an *avatāra*. The *Purāṇas*[2] mention the Buddha as one of the *avatāras* of Viṣṇu. The *Suttanipāta Commentary*[3] says that the Buddha is born in the *Vivaṭṭamānakappa*, but not in the *Saṁvaṭṭamānakappa*. According to the *Buddhavaṁsa Commentary*,[4] one Buddha is born in the *Sārakappa*; two in the *Maṇḍakappa*; three in the *Varakappa*; four in the *Sāramaṇḍa-kappa*; and five in the *Bhaddakappa*.

Even though the Buddhist doctrine is based upon the theory of *Kamma*, and a man gets rewards or his prayer is granted according to his meritorious deeds, there is a rule mentioned in the *Saṁyuttanikāya*[5] that those who take refuge unto the feet of the Buddha are released from danger. Thus the gods Canda and Suriya being seized by Rāhu prayed to the Buddha for protection and the latter cammanded Rāhu to release them. Rāhu, though he is a chief of the *asuras*, did so because he was afraid of the Buddha. This fact shows that the Buddha is not only a preacher of the Truth but also a supreme authority controlling the universe, who protects the good from danger.

The Buddha is found everywhere. He can travel throughout the universe. Once he reached the Tāvatiṁsa-heaven in three strides for preaching the *Abhidhamma* to the gods. The *Brahmanimantanika Sutta*[6] states that he went to the *Brahma-loka* for refuting the false views held by Baka, the great Brahmā, that the *Brahma-loka* is permanent.[7] Besides, he walked long distance in the air for alms.[8]

The Buddha can know anything of this universe by his supernatural insight.[9] The epithet 'world-knower' (*loka-vidū*) was applied to the Buddha Maitreya.[10] He can see everything my means of the radiance of his body. When he performs twin-miracles (*Yamakapāṭihāriya*), everybody can see each other.[11] The *ñāña* is one of his four illimitables. He uses one of the three ways for converting people, i.e., by exhibition of miraculous dowers (*iddhipāṭihāriya*), by reading their thoughts (*ādesanāpāṭhāriya*), or teaching them what is beneficial to them according to their character and temperament (*anusāsanīpāti-hāriya*), the last method being used frequently.[12] Sometimes he sends a ray of light from his Gandhakuṭi[13] to encourage a monk engaged in meditation and, appearing before him in this ray of light, preaches to him.[14]

A Buddha possesses ten powers consisting of perfect comprehension in the ten fields of knowledge.[15] He can digest the food of the *devas* or which contains the *ojā* put into by the *devas*.[16] The Buddha defeats Māra's forces and attains to supreme perfection in all knowledge and virtue at the foot of the Bodhi-tree.[17] When Vipassi, the Buddha, gained truth and was unwilling to teach if the people did not acknowledge his preaching (truth), one of the great Brahmas came to him and requested him to teach. At this request, he preached.[18] The *Commentary*[19] says that the Buddha has the power of love which is so great that no evil action can show its results in his presence. He loves man and prefers to accept the offer of food by poor men.[20]

The *Buddhavaṁsa Commentary*[21] says that the Buddha is immune from the following four dangers—'no misfortune can befall the four requisities intended for a Buddha; no one can encompass his death; no injury can befall any of his thirty-two Mahāpurisalakkhaṇā or eighty anuvyañjanā; nothing obstruct his sura.'

All these characteristics of the Buddha remind us of the Supreme god of Brāhmaṇical literature. But nowhere is the Buddha mentioned as the creator of the universe. Donald A. Mackenzie[22] says that Buddhism does not speak of a supreme personal god. Gods mentioned in the texts are "living creatures." They have no power over the universe and consequently their worship is not profitable. However, the Buddha like the Absolute of the *Upaniṣads*, possesses all the characteristics of the supreme god except one, i.e., the power of creation.

The texts mention two kinds of the Buddha—Pacceka Buddhas, i e., the Buddhas who attain to complete Enlightenment but do not preach the way of deliverance to the world; and Sammāsambuddhas, who are omniscient and teach *nibbāna*. The Commentaries mention four classes of the Buddhas[23]—(1) *Sabaññu-Buddha.* (2) *Pacceka-Buddha,* (3) *Catusacca-Buddha,*[24] and (4) *Suta-Buddha.*[25]

One of the main characteristics of the Buddha is that he can remember all those facts that happened many *kappas* ago. Gautama, the Buddha, when he heard by his heavenly ear, that the breathren of the *Saṅgha* were discussing on a subject, came to them and solved various questions. In this connection, he described the facts about six Buddhas before him. All these Buddhas including Gautama are *Sabaññu-Buddhas.* The six Buddhas are Vipassī, Sikkhi, Vessabhu, Kakusandha, Koṇāgamana, and Kassapa.[26] Their particulars are given in a table on next page.

Sl. No.	Name of the Buddhas	*Kappa* or aeon in which they are born.	Their Social rank	*Gotta*, family	Length of life at that epoch	Tree under which they became enlightened
1.	Vipassī	91st before the present.	Noble	Koṇḍañña	Year 80000	Pāṭali
2.	Sikhi	31st before the present.	-do-	-do-	„ 70000	Puṇḍarīka
3.	Vessabhu	-do-	-do-	-do-	„ 60000	Sāla
4.	Kakusandha	The present aeon	Brāhmaṇa	Kassapa	„ 40000	Sirīsa
5.	Koṇāgamana	-do-	-do-	-do-	„ 30000	Udumbara
6.	Kassapa	-do-	-do-	-do-	„ 20000	Nigrodha
7.	Gotama	-do-	Noble	Gotama	„ 100	Assattha

According to the *Buddhavaṁsa*, Dīpaṅkvara, Koṇḍañña, Maṅgala, Sumana, Revata, Sobhita, Anomadassī, Paduma, Nārada, Padumuttara, Sumedha, Sujāta, Piyadassī, Atthadassī Dhammadassī, Siddhattha, Tissa and Phussa[27] appeared in the world before Vipassi, and Taṇhaṅkara, Medhaṅkara and Saranaṅkara before Dīpaṅkvara.[28] The *Cakkavattiśihanāda Sutta*[29] says that Metteyya Buddha will be born in the world during the present *kappa*. Gautama prophesied the names of ten future Buddhas who met him.[30] They are Metteyya, Uttama, Rāma, Pasenadi Kosala, Abhibhū, Dīghasoṇī, Saṅkacca, Subha, Todeyya, Nāḷāgiripalabyya.

The Buddha is generally called Tathāgata.[31] He is usually addressed as *Bhagavā*. Gautama Buddha is addressed under various names, such as *Sakka*,[32] *Brahmā*,[33] *Mahāmuni*[34] and *Yakkha*.[35] The *Visuddhimagga*[36] speaks of nine epithets applied to Gautama.

Every Buddha has to pass a life of the Bodhisatta.[37] In their last birth, all the Bodhisattas dwell as *Devaputtas* in the Tusita-heaven. When a Bodhisatta's life comes to an end, the gods of the ten thousand worlds gather round him and request him to seek birth as a human being on the earth because he will become the Buddha.[38] Before entering into mother's womb the Bodhisatta in his last birth must first consider the continent in which he will be born.[39] Then he considers the family.[40] Next he thinks of his mother who would be wise and virtuous and she would die seven days after the Buddha's birth. Then he goes with the other *devas* to *Nandanavana* in the *Tusita*, where he announces his departure from their midst and falls from the *Tusita* while playing and enters into his mother's womb. He is conscious of his fall; but is not aware of *cuti-cittaṁ*, or dying thought. On the day of his conception, the Bodhisatta's mother dreams that the four regent gods 'raise her with her bed, and, having taken her to the Himālaya, bathe her in Lake Anotatta, robe her in divine clothes, anoint her with divine perfumes and deck her with heavenly flowers.' They lay her in a golden mansion with her head to the east. When she lies there the Bodhisatta in the form of a white elephant enters her womb through her right side. The earth trembles and the whole universe including the

Lokantarika hells where even moon and sun cannot shine, becomes resplendent.[41] Immediately the four regent gods go towards the four quarters to protect him and his mother. At the end of ten months, when the Bodhisatta is born, the *Suddhāvāsa-Brahmās* first receive the child in a golden net, and from them the four regent gods take him on an antelope-skin and present him to his mother. At his birth, two showers of water (hot and cold) fall from the sky and bathe the mother and the child. Just after his birth, he stands firmly on his feet, and takes seven steps to the north, while a white canopy is held over his head; he finds no one anywhere equal to him and announces his supermacy over the world by roaring the 'lion's roar'.[42] Seven days after birth, the Bodhisatta's mother dies because she must bear no other child. According to the commentaries,[43] the age of the Bodhisatta's mother at the time of his birth is between fifty and sixty.

The Buddha is recognised as a great man for his thirty-two marks. He is 'flat-footed', and does not toe or heal the ground in walking. On the soles of his feet apear signs of wheels with a thousand spokes with tyre and hub. He has long fingers and toes. His hands and feet are soft and look like a net. His ankles are like rounded shells and his legs are like an antelope's. He can touch and rub his knees with either hand standing and without bending. His male organ is concealed in a sheath. His complexion is like bronze or gold. His skin is so delicately smooth that no dust cleaves to his body. The small hairs on his body turn upward; they are blue-black like eye-paint, and are curling to the right. The front part of his body is like a lion's. There is no furrow between his shoulders. The height of his body is equal to the compass of his arms. His bust is rounded. His taste is supremely acute. He has forty teeth and his jaw is as a lion's. His tongue is very long. He has divine voice like that of the Karavīka bird. He has the eye lashes like those of a cow. A hairy mole appears between his eyebrows which is white and soft like cotton. His head is like a royal turban.

Some Buddhas see all the four omens.[44] On the night before the Enlightenment the Bodhisatta dreams five great dreams.[45] Other particulars of the Gautama Buddha are mentioned in the *Brahmāyu Sutta*[46] which are evidently characteristics of all the Buddhas.

However, the Bodhisatta, in previous births, was born on earth, for several times in different forms; but he never became less than a quail or more than an elephant. He is free from the eighteen inauspicious states. He is never born blind, deaf, insane, slobbery or crippled, or among savages, in the womb of a slave or as a heretic. He was born several times in the purgatories,[47] but is never born among the *petas* or the Kālakañjakas, neither in *Avīci* nor in the *lokantarika-nirayas* neither as Māra, nor in the worlds where there is no perception nor in the Suddhāvāsas, nor in the Arūpa-worlds, and nor ever in another *Cakkavāḷa*.[48]

The wisdom of a Bodhisatta is greater than that of a Pacceka Buddha.[49] But when he starts his career, he has to resolve before a Buddha to become a Buddha for the welfare and liberation of all creatures.

Notes

Chapter V

1. *Bud. Com.*, SHB, pp. 158f.
2. A.B. Keith and A.J. Carnoy, *The Mythology of All Races,* VI, p. 168.
3. Vol. I, p. 51.
4. SHB, pp. 158f.
5. Vol. I, pp. 50-51 ; cf. *MAR*, Vol. VI, p. 192.
6. *Maj.*, Vol. I, pp. 326ff.
7. *Brahma-loka* is not permanent.
8. *Thera. Com.*, SHB, Vol. I, p. 65.
9. T.O. Ling, *BME*, p. 96 (*Dīg.*, Vol. I, pp. 87, III, 150, 224 ; Vol. III, p. 77).
10. T.O. Ling, op. cit., p. 116. The epithet was applied to the arahant also according to the *Saṁ.*, Vol. I, p. 62; Vol. V, pp. 197, 343.
11. When the Bodhisatta fell from the Tusita heaven and entered the womb of queen Māyā, a very bright light appeared illuminating the deva, Brahma and the human worlds, etc. The light was so brilliant that the beings of one world could see the beings of another world (*Vis.*, Vol. I, p. 392; *Mil.*, p, 336; *SBE*, Vol. XXXVI, p. 220). The colour of the Buddha's skin becomes exceedingly bright during the night on which he attains Enlightenment, and the night when he dies (*Dīg.*, Vol. II, p. 134). The *Sut. Com.*, Vol. II, p. 525 says that no other light can shine where a Buddha is present.
12. *Bud. Com.*, SHB, p. 81. According to the Buddha's rivals, he possesses the power of fascination (*āvattanīmāyā*); but this is untrue, as sometimes (e.g., in the case of the Kosambi monks) he cannot compel even his own disciples to obey him. The *Sut. Com.*, Vol. I, p. 331, says that the beings who are converted only by a Buddha are called *buddha-veneyyā*. Some people are pleased by the Buddha's looks, others by his voice and words, yet others by his austerities, such as the wearing of simple robes, etc.; and finally, those whose standard of judgement is goodness reflect that he is without a peer (*Dham. Com.*, Vol. III, pp. 113f).
13. The dwelling place of the Buddha. It was a special apartment at the Jetavana monastery (*Jat.*, Vol. I, p. 92).
14. *Sut. Com.*, Vol. I, pp. 16, 265.

15. *Aṅg.*, Vol. V, pp. 33; *Maj.*, Vol. I, p. 69, etc. At *Saṁ.*, Vol. II, pp. 27f., ten similar powers are given as consisting of his knowledge of the *Paṭiccasamuppāda.* The powers of a disciple are distinct from those of a Buddha (*KV*, p. 228); they are seven (see, e.g., *Dīg.*, Vol. III, p. 283).
16. *Sut. Com.*, Vol. I, p. 154.
17. *Bud. Com.*, SHB, p. 248.
18. *Dīg.*, Vol. II, pp. 36-45.
19. *Sut. Com.*, Vol. II, p. 475.
20. *Dham. Com.*, Vol. II, p. 135.
21. See p. 248.
22. *Indian Legend*, p. 130 ; cf. *ERE*, Vol. IV, pp. 571-72.
23. For their practices regarding perfection, see *Aṅg. Com.*, SHB, Vol. I, p. 65.
24. They are all arahants.
25. They are all learned men.
26. *Dīg.*, Vol. II, p. 7.
27. The first twenty-four prophesied Gautama's appearance in the world.
28. The *Lalitavistara* mentions fifty-four Buddhas and the *Mahāvastu* more than a hundred.
29. *Dīg.*, Vol. III, pp. 76f.; see also *Anāgatavaṁsa* in *JPTS*, 1886, p. 37.
30. *JPTS*, loc. cit.
31. This term is explained at great length in the Commentaries; e.g., *Dīg. Com.*, Vol. I, pp. 59f.
32. *Sut.*, Verse, 345; perhaps the equivalent of 'Sākya'.
33. Ibid., p. 91; *Sut. Com.*, Vol. II, p. 418.
34. *Bud. Com.*, SHB., p. 38.
35. *KS*, Vol. I, p. 262.
36. See pp. 198ff (*Bhagavā arahaṁ sammāsambuddhas, vijjācaraṇasampanno, sugato, lokavidū, anuttaro, purisadammasārathī, sathā devamanussānam, Buddho Bhagavā.*
37. Those who seek to become Buddha are the Bodhisattas.
38. Except the Bodhisatta who later became Vipassi Buddha, all the other Bodhisattas leave *Tusita-devaloka*, before completing the full span of life there (*Dīg. Com.*, Vol. II, p. 427). The gods see five signs on each Bodhisatta and understand that their life in the Tusita has come to an end.
39. The Buddhas are born only in Jambudīpa.
40. They are born only in Brāhmaṇa or Khattiya families whichever is more esteemed during that period.
41. This was seen also when he issues from his mother's womb.
42. *Dīg.*, Vol. II, p. 15 (*Aggo'ham asmi lokassa, jeṭṭho'ham asmi lokassa, seṭṭho'ham asmi lokassa, ayam antimā jāti, natthi dāni punabbhavo*).
43. *Dīg. Com.*, Vol. II, p. 437; *Ud. Com.*, p. 278.
44. *Dīg Com.*, Vol. II, p. 457.

45. See *Aṅg.*, Vol. III, pp. 240 f.; *Jāt.*, Vol. I, p. 69.
46. *Maj.*, Vol. II, pp. 137ff.
47. *A.*, I. pp. 299ff.
48. *Sut. Com.*, Vol. I, pp. 50f.
49. *Jāt*, Vol. IV, p. 341.

CHAPTER VI

Spirits and Semi-Divine Beings

The word 'spirit' is generally applied to those who are dead on earth and are reborn in different worlds according to their merits or demerits earned through different deeds. They are classed as departed spirits and are called *devaputtas* or *Vimāna-devas* and *petas* when they are reborn in *devaloka* and *petaloka* respectively.

Besides, supernatural beings are regarded as spirits who are capable of being visible at their pleasure and are frequently conceived as good and hostile to mankind. They are divided into two categories, namely, (1) good and (2) evil. The evil spirits are troublesome and terrifying to human beings. They are Asuras, Yakkhas, Rakkhasas, Pisācas, Māras, etc. All these evil spirits are demons. But, the Yakkhas are sometimes regarded as semi-divine beings. The spirits who dwell in gardens, houses, hills, rivers, seas, trees, royal umbrellas, waters, etc., are generally treated as semi-divine beings. Of them, those who cause anxiety, fear, etc., to mankind, are grouped as demons or evil spirits.

As said above, four great kings of the Cātummahārājika-world are the guardian spirits or gods of the four quarters.[1] They rule over the Gandhabbas, Kumbhaṇḍas, Nāgas and Yakkhas. These are all spirits; but are regarded as lower gods. Besides, Supaṇṇas, Kinnaras, etc., are called spirits.

Departed spirits in Heaven. The departed spirits who receive heavenly mansions for their good deeds performed on earth called *Vimāna-devatā* (male or female deities). The *Vimānavatthu Commentary* mentions 90 mansions[2] which are situated in heaven (particularly in the *Tāvatiṁsa devaloka*).[3] The said mansions are movable. On several occasions the deities come pown on earth with their own mansions; but none can go to any region higher than his own one.[4] The Vimānas are different because their forms and comforts and pleasures provided therein are proportionate to the meritorious deeds to their nature and to the desire of the dwellers of the Vimānas. The Vimāna-devas have beautiful golden yellow complexion which emit rays of brilliance around them. They possess all types of wealth. They have beautiful gardens containing an abundance of sweet-scented flowers, plants, creepers, etc. Sweet sounds of dancing and music from the Vimānas enrapture the soul and regale the ears. The departed spirits in the Vimānas assume brilliant and dazzling human forms. The climate the inhabitants of the Vimānas enjoy is quite good for health and mind. But it is to be remembered that the pleasure in the celestial mansions is physical. It is not the deeper joy and is regarded as inferior to the nobler and purer bliss which is enjoyed by the bhikkhu.

Peta. The *Petaloka,* as mentioned above,[5] is situated above the animal kingdom. It is regarded as a kind of hell because the spirits of the dead suffer here from severe pain owing to their misdeeds done in previous births.[6] According to L. de La Vallée Poussin, though the *Petas* are found throughout the world of men, they dwell especially in the kingdom of Yama, which is divided into 36 provinces, situated 500 *yojanas* below Jambudīpa. Their life-term is 500 years, a day being equal to a human month.[7]

The *Āṭānāṭiya Sutta* describes the *petas* as "back-biters and murderous, brigands, crafty-minded rogues, thieves and cheats."[8] The *Petavatthu*[9] says that a woman who is mean-minded and miserly by her nature and who scolds or curses her husband when he gives away anything out of faith is reborn as a *peti* and has to subsist on dirt, filth, pus and blood. If a noble householder, especially who is rich and well-to-do, does not give away a portion of his wealth and if he spurns out the beggers from his door, he has to suffer in the *petaloka.*[10]

It is the duty of a householder to make their kinsmen who are reborn in the *petaloka*[11] free from the effects of sin. A recluse or an ascetic has to do the same duty. The householders perform *pubba-petabali,* a ceremony of offering (*dakkhiṇā*) for the benefit of the dead ancestors which establishes the bond of affection between the living and the dead.[12] Ancestor-worship is not mentioned in the

Buddhist literature. It is said that devout daughters or sons can afford relief to their deceased forefathers by their earned merit through gifts offered on behalf of themselves or their forefathers.[13] The *Piṭṭhadhītalikapetavatthu* says that sorrow, lamentation and weeping are not necessary for relieving the *petas* from the effects of sin; only gifts offered to the departed relatives, household deity or other gods, which help to acquire merit for the donor, are enough for the *petas* to be free from the effects of sin.

As there is no agriculture, no cattle-breeding, trade or commercial transaction in the *petaloka*,[14] the *petas* subsist on food which they get in their place of residence or which is offered to them by their friends, associates, and relatives. If a *peta*, for whose sake the offering is made, does not come to receive and enjoy it, another *peta* who expects such offering gets it and is profited. If no *peta* comes to receive it, the giver himself derives some benefits therefrom.[15]

The *petas* revisits their old homes, standing behind the wall of the homestead or where four crossroads meet.[16] They have human figure, voice, feelings and sentiment; but their condition of life is pitiable. The *Petavatthu* mentions some stories from which we know how the *petas* suffer in the *petaloka*.[17] He is not free from love and desire for companions of the other sex, whether male or female, enjoys fully the company of a lover of the other sex who is still in the world of living.

The *petas* are of different kinds.[18] Among them, the Vimāna-petas are more fortunate because they have some good to their credit which is mixed with a little evil. But, below them a large number of *petas* and *petīs* are found, who suffer intolerable miseries. When the offence of a *peta* is very serious, he has to suffer for thousands of years in hells.

Gandhabba. They dwell in the Cātummahārājika-world and are regarded as the lowest of all gods.[19] The *Dīghanikāya*[20] states that those who practise a little *sila* are reborn in the Gandhabba world. In the *Saṁyuttanikāya*,[21] they are described as dwelling in the fragrance of root wood, and sap-wood, and in their flowers and scents.

The *Aṅguttaranikāya*[22] states that the Gandhabbas are classed together with the *asuras* and the *nāgas*. But they are heavenly musicians who wait on Sakka. They are sometimes described as *vihaṅgamā* (going through the air).[23] In the *Āṭānāṭiya Sutta*,[24] they are mentioned among those who trouble monks and nuns in their meditations in solitude. It is often said that the Gandhabbas preside over conceptions, but this is due to an erroneous translation of the word *gandhabba* in certain passages.[25] The males among them form the masculine counterpart of the accharā, the nymphs. As mentioned above,[26] they are ruled by Dhataraṭṭha, king of the eastern quarter.[27]

Besides Dhataraṭṭha, other chieftains of the Gandhabba-world are[28] – (1) Panāda, (2) Opamañña, (3) Mātali,[29] (4) Cittasena, (5) Nala and (6) Janesabha. They were present at the preaching of the *Mahāsamaya Sutta*.[30] Some of them, e.g., Janesabha, Cittasena and Opamañña are mentioned in the *Āṭānāṭiya Sutta* [31] as Yakkha chieftains who are invoked by the Buddha's followers in times of need. Janesabha may be identical with the Yakkha named Janavasabha.

The Gandhabba called Pañcasikha was considered a favourite of the Buddha.[32] When Sakka visited the Buddha at the Indasālaguhā, he sent Pañcasikha in advance, for obtaining permission for the interview.[33] Having approached the Buddha, Pañcasikha played on his Beḷuvapaṇḍu-vīṇā and sang in praise of the Buddha, the Doctrine, the Arahants and Love. This is really a love-poem addressed to his beloved, Suriyavaccasā, daughter of the Gandhabba Timbarū. The Buddha praised his music and song and questioned him about the poem. Pañcasikha said that, when Suriyavaccasā was going with her father to dance before Sakka, he fell in love with her; but she favoured Sikhaṇḍi, son of Mātali. Pañcasikha composed a song and sang to her. Having heard this song, Suriyavaccasā was greatly pleased with the references in the song to the Sākyan sage of whom she heard when she went to the *Sudhammasabhā* and she consented to marry Pañcasikha. Sakka blessed the marriage.

The *devas* loved Pañcasikha and wished to resemble him.[34] Brahmā Sanaṅkumāra assumed the form of Pañcasikhas at the assembly of the gods of *Tāvatiṃsa*.[35] When Sakka spoke the Buddha's praises, Pañcasikha described to the Buddha the happenings in the assembly of the *devas*.[36]

Pañcasikha received the first report of good deeds done by human beings from the *Cātummahārājika-devas* and their ministers. He would pass them on to Mātali who, in his turn, presented them to Sakka.[37] When the Buddha descended from *Tāvatiṁsa*, Pañcasikha was present to honour him by song and music.[38] He was present with the Buddha on another occasion.[39] Buddhaghoṣa says[40] that Pañcasikha was once born as a human being. While yet a boy, he wore his hair in five knots[41] (*pañcacuḷaka-dārakakāle*). He became chief of those who tended the calves. He did public work together with other lads—repairing roads, digging well, building rest-houses, etc., and he dies while young. Next he was reborn in the Cātummahārājika-world. He was destined to enjoy ninety thousand years in the Cātummahārājika-world, where he wore on his person one hundred cart loads of ornaments and rubbed nine pots of perfume on his body. He put on red robes, and a chaplet of red gold on his head, round which his hair was arranged in five locks (*kuntalikehi*), which fell back just as in the case of a young boy (*pañcacūḷikadārakaparihāreṇ'eva*).

Pañcasikha is also regarded as an officer (like Sakka). The *Biḷārikosiya Jātaka*[42] says that Ānanda was once born as Pañcasikha who with Sakka and others made Bilārikosiya a generous man. Likewise, Anuruddha is identified with Pañcasikha in the *Sudhābhojana Jātaka*.[43]

Nymphs. The celestial nymphs inhabiting the heaven of Sakka are called *accharā*, the Pali equivalent of the Vedic *apsarases*. The *Accharā Sutta* of the *Saṁyuttanikāya*[44] says that they dwell in the Nandana, the celestial park in *Tāvatiṁsa*. It is free from sorrow because the gods of *Tāvatiṁsa* enjoy pleasure in the Nandana. The nymphs of it play the lute and awake the gods and goddesses in the morning and delight them by dancing and singing. The *Vimānavatthu*[45] mentions the names of such nymphs. They are—Nandā, Sunandā, Sokatiṇṇā, Alambusā, Missakesī, huṇḍarīka,[46] Enipassā, Suphassā and Subhaddā. According to a bhikkhu-god,[47] delight in Nandana is an illusion. He also says that the nymphs are fiends because they shut the door of salvation by offering deceptive delight. Sometimes Sakka sends them to earth for seducing the ascetics who by force of their virtue, threaten his suzerainty in heaven.[48] Once he sent the nymphs for aiding the Bodhisatta in a musical contest, by dancing to the tune of his lyre.[49]

Kumbhaṇḍa. They are so called because they have huge stomachs, and their genital organs are as big as pots.[50] They live in the south. Their king is Viruḷha.[51]

Nāga. They play a prominent part in Buddhism and are gifted with miraculous powers and strength. They are classed with other divinities,[52] with whom they are sometimes friendly, sometimes inimical, especially with the Garuḷas.[53] Though they are confused with snakes, they are believed to be able to assume human form at their will. They are represented as hooded snakes with three (sometimes seven) heads, or as snakes with human heads, or as human beings with the hood of a cobra.[54] They are divided into two groups—(1) *thalaja* and *jalaja.* Those who live beneath the surface of the earth are called *thalaja* and those who live in rivers as well as in the sea are called *jalaja-nāgas.*[55] The texts mention several Nāga dwellings, e.g., Mañjerika-bhavana under Sineru, Daddara-bhavana at the foot of Mount Daddara in the Himālaya, likewise, the Dhataraṭṭhanāga lived in the waters of the river Yamunā; and the Nābhasā Nāgā in lake Nabhasa; there were also the Nāgas of Vesāli, Tacchaka, and Payāga.[56] The *Vinaya*[57] mentions four royal families of the Nāgas (*Ahirājakulāni*)—Virūpakkha, Erāpathā, Chabyāputtā and Kaṇhagotamakā.

Sometimes the Nāgas fall in love with human beings. The *Bhūridatta Jātaka*[58] speaks of a *nāga* widow who married a human prince and bore some children. They were watery and delicate.

The Nāgas are passionate and easily angered. Their breath is poisonous, and their glancc deadly.[59] They are carnivorous.[60] Generally their diet is made of frogs.[61] When they are in the world of men, they sleep on ant-hills.[62] They dance when music is played, but they never dance if Garuḷa is near or if there are human dancers.[63]

The Nāgas were the followers of Buddha.[64] It is said that a Nāga king protected the Buddha from a heavy storm of rain by spreading his hood above his head like an umbrella.[65] They were sometimes worshipped by human beings and were offered sacrifices of milk, rice, fish, meat and strong drinks.[66]

They dwell in the Cātummahārājika-world and occupy its western quarter, with Virūpakkha as their king.[67] Their jewell is famous for its beauty and for its power of fulfilling the wishes to its possessor.[68]

The word *nāga* is often used as an epithet of the Buddha and the Arahants.[69] The Bodhisatta was born several times as king of the Nāgas, e.g., Atula, Bhūridatta, Mahādaddara, etc.

Supaṇṇa. They were mythical birds mentioned with the Nāgas, Kumbhaṇḍas, Yakkhas and *Cātummahārājika-devas*, and are mentioned among the guards of the *Tāvatiṁsa-devaloka.*[70] The *Vimānavatthu Commentary*[71] identifies them with the Garuḷas. In the *Jātaka*, Suppaṇṇa is given a name Karoṭi (a species of Garuḍa). The Supaṇṇas are so called because of their food and drinks which were called Karoṭi.[72] They live in the Simbali-grove[73] which is regarded as the special tree of the Garuḷa-world.[74] They are represented in art as winged men.[75] According to Buddhaghoṣa, their bodies were formed for quick flight. The Garuḷas[76] are huge in size, sometimes one hundred and fifty *yojanas* from wing to wing.[77] They can raise a storm by their wings and it is called the Garuḍa-wind.[78] The *Sussoṇḍī Jātaka*[79] says that this wind can plunge a whole city in darkness and cause houses to fall through its violence. The *Bhūridatta Jātaka*[80] says that a Garuḷa has such strength that he can carry off a whole banyan tree, tearing it up from its roots. They are often described as the eternal enemies of the Nāgas[81] and as living in those places where Nāgas are found.[82] It was regarded as the highest happiness of the Nāgas to be free from the attacks of the Garuḷas.[83] The plumage of a Garuḷa is so thick that a man can hide in it.[84] The Garuḷas can assume human form. Once two Garuḷa kings played dice with the kings of Vārāṇasī and having fallen in love with their queens, they took them to the Garuḷa city. One of the queens was Sussoṇḍī[85] and the other Kākāti.[86] But they were returned to their husbands. The *Paṇḍara Jātaka*[87] says that the Garuḷas learnt the Ālambāyana spell from the ascetic Karambiya. The Nāgas could not resist this spell and were caught by them.[88]

The Garuḷas led sometimes virtuous lives, keeping the fast and observing the precepts. The *Paṇḍara Jātaka*[89] mentions a Garuḷa king who was virtuous. The *Vidhurapaṇḍita Jātaka*[90] mentions a son of Vinatā who visited the park of Dhanañjaya Koravya and gave him a golden garland as a present after hearing Vidhurapaṇḍita's preaching. The Bodhisatta[91] and Sāriputta[92] were both on different occasions, born as Garuḷa kings.

Kinnara. Little birds with heads like men's are called Kinnara.[93] The feminine form of Kinnara is *kinnarā* or *kinnarī.* Generally, they are found on the mountains and on the banks of river.[94] They were devoted to the Buddha.[95] The Bodhisattas also are born as Kinnara.[96] The Kinnaras worshipped the gods in danger,[97] and fell in love with human being.[98]

Yakkha. They are generally described as *amanussā* (non-human beings) and are mentioned along with the Devas, Rakkhasas, Dānavas, Gandhabbas, Kinnaras and Mahoragas (Nāgas).[99] The *Aṅguttaranikāya*[100] mentions them as between manussā and *Gandhabbā* while the *Petavatthu Commentary*[101] places them immediately above the *petas* and says that the happier *petas* are called *yakkhas.* They are of many kinds—spirits, ogres, dryads, ghosts, spooks, etc.

In philosophy, the term *yakkha* is used for a *purisa* (soul).[102] Elsewhere[103] *yakkha* is explained by *satta, nara, māṇava, posa, puggala, jīva, jagu, jantu, indagu* and *manuja.* The term *yakkha*, like *nāga*, is also used as an appellative. It is applied to many gods, such as Sakka,[104] Kakuddha[105] and four regent gods.[106] The scholiast says in the *Jayaddisa Jātaka*[107] that the figure of hare in the moon is called *yakkha.*

Generally speaking, the Yakkhas are semi-divine beings, having a *deva's* supernormal powers by which they can influence the people and become partly helpful and partly harmful to them. Sometimes they are called *devatā*[108] or *devaputta.*[109] Some of the Yakkhas are called *rukkha-devatā*[110] (spirits of the trees) and others *bhumma-devatā*[111] (spirits of the earth). Yakkhas like Indakūṭa and Suciloma are mentioned as capable of putting intelligent questions on metaphysics and ethics. As all of the Yakkhas possess supernatural power, they can assume any shape at will and transfer themselves to any place.

The word *yakkha* is derived from the root *yaj*, to sacrifice, so that a Yakkha is understood as a being to whom sacrifice is offered.[112] Several direct references to sacrificial offerings to the Yakkha-demons are mentioned in the *Jātakas*.[113] They are benevolent to men and interested in the spiritual welfare of the human beings and resemble tutelary genii. Even though some of the Yakkhas do not believe in the Buddha and his teachings[114] and molest the followers of the Buddha in their woodland hunts.[115] The *Mahāsamaya Sutta*[116] mentions their presence at the preaching of it. The *Āṭānāṭiya Sutta*[117] speaks of Yakkha-worship, some of the Yakkha chieftains, e.g., Nighaṇḍu Puṇṇaka, Kāmaseṭṭha, Kinnaghaṇḍu, Koraṭiya, Gula, Cara, etc., are worshipped by the followers of the Buddha whenever necessary.

Some Yakkhas act as messengers from another world and save prospective sinners from committing evil.[118] The Yakkha Vajirapāṇi is represented as a kind of mentor, hovering in the air, and threatening to kill Ambaṭṭha if he does not reply to the Buddha's question.[119] In many cases the Yakkhas are regarded as "fallen angles" who come eagerly to listen to the word of the Buddha so that they may rise to a higher sphere of existence, e.g., Piyaṅkaramātā, Punabbasumātā, and even Vessavaṇa listened to the *Parāyaṇavagga* recited by Veḷukandakī Nandamātā.[120]

Vessavaṇa is their king[121] who settle the disputes between the devas.[122] The Yakkhasenāpati helps him in this respect, and his business is to preside over the courts during eight days of each month.[123] They are his servants and messengers and wait upon him in turn.[124] The female Yakkhas drew water for him.[125] The Yakkhas hold regular assemblies on Manosilātala on the Bhagalavatīpabbata.[126] They have to act as guardians and are liberal spenders of underground riches, hidden treasures, etc., with which they delight men.[127]

Sometimes the Yakkhiṇīs are married with human beings. For example, Kuveṇī, the Yakkha princess of Ceylon (Laṅkā), was married by Vijaya and two children were born to her.[128] Though the Yakkhas are invisible, they are killed by Vijaya with the help of Kuveṇī,[129] but their clothes are found fit for Vijaya and his followers to wear.[130] Cetiyā, who could make herself invisible and assume the form of a mare, lived with Puṇḍukābhaya for four years and gave him counsel in battle. When Paṇḍukābhaya held festivities, he had the Yakkha Cittarāja on the throne beside him.[131] The Yakkhas mentioned here are probably regarded as human beings.

The epithet *mahiddhika*[132] is frequently applied to the Yakkhas. Their appearance is striking as a result of their good deeds in the previous birth.[133] They enjoy all kinds of luxury,[134] and are called *kāmakāmī.* Those Yakkhas who performed bad deeds in the previous birth are possessed of odd qualities, i.e., they are shy, they fear palmyra leaf and iron. Their eyes are red and they neither wink nor cast a shadow.[135] They dwell in their self-created palaces anywhere in the air, in trees, etc. Most of them are *ākāsaṭṭha* (suspended in the air); but some of them, like the abode of Āḷavaka are *bhumaṭṭha* (lying on the ground) and are described as being fortified.[136] Sometimes whole cities, e.g., Āḷakamandā, were under the protection of Yakkhas.

The Yakkhas are of different grades. The highest among them are very nearly to the *devas* and have deva-powers, while the lowest resemble the *petas.* They are specially mentioned as being afraid of palm-leaves.[137]

The Yakkhas are evidently relics of an ancient demonology. They are regarded as the creatures of the wilds and the forests. Some of them have ethnological features.[138]

T.O. Ling[139] says that the *pisācas*, *yakkhas* and the *rakkhasas* are the most common demons of the Buddhist Pali canon and of the *Atharvaveda.* Though the Vedic Pisācas and Buddhist Yakkhas are of different origin, their characteristics overlap and the terms *pisāca*, *yakkha* and *rakkhasa* are interchangeable.

The *Jātakas*[140] refer to the Yakkhas as degraded to the state of red-eyed and hairy cannibal ogres who cast no shadow and possess horrific and uncanny qualities. They are represented as assuming disguises.[141] As they are more active during the night, they come out then in the guise of a waggoner and kill men and oxen for devouring their flesh. In the *Jātakas*,[142a] Yakkha is described as 'with seven tufts inspiring dread alarm.' They are carnivorous, but generally devour men rather than animals.[143] They also dwell in water. As said above,[144] they were granted special privileges, such as the right of devouring any one entering particular ponds.

The female Yakkha (Yakkhiṇī) is more fearful and evil-minded than the male. The Yakkhiṇīs used to entice ship-wrecked men, and then imprisoned and devoured their flesh and blood[145] and also the corpse.[146] They eat babies[147] and are full of spite and vengeance.[148] A hostile Yakkha devoured Buta Thera's elder brothers and sisters while he himself propitiated the Yakkha by making him a child's sponsor. The *Jātaka*[149] speaks of the Yakkhas whose custom in a forest is to put down poisoned food on the road for unwary travellers to eat; when the travellers died having eaten the food, the Yakkhas would come out and devour their flesh. A rival women is reborn as a female Yakkha who devour the woman's child.[150] Thus it is found that the Yakkhas are demons.

As mentioned above,[151] the word *pisāca* is one of the common terms for demons and it is not differentiated from Yakkha. The *Udāna*[152] says that the Yakkha, Ajakalāpa, also calls himself as a Pisāca. The Pisāca-demons haunted the residence of some monks and took possession of the monks and sapped their vitality.[153] The *Commentaries*[154] mention *Paṁsu-pisācaka* as a class of *pisāca* who are born in filth.

Asura. Those who are hostile to virtue and goodness are called Asuras. They are more exalted class of evil spirits than the commonplace demons, the *pisācas, yakkhas* and *rakkhasas*. They are usually described as in conflict with the *devas*.[155] The Asura-world is one of the four evil destinies (*apāyā*).[156] It is not pleasant to be reborn among the Asuras.

The Asuras were originally Devas because Sakka refers to them as the 'older Devas' in the *Saṁyuttanikāya*.[157] Elsewhere[158] the *asuras* are regarded as Vāsava's brethren who possess wondrous powers and great glory. The *Suttanipāta Commentary*[159] says that, when Sakka was born among the *asuras*, they received him cordially. Originally the *asuras* dwelt in *Tāvatiṁsa*, the kingdom of Sakka, together with the *devas* and are regarded as older *devas*. The older *devas* fell from deva-hood when they lost morality by attacking the *devas* and became *asuras*.[160] This reminds us of the Iranian tradition that the *devas* became demons. The *Milindapañha*[161] says that the *asuras* are called *dānava* because they are the descendants of Danu, the mother of the Asuras. Buddhaghoṣa[162] says that they are all descendants of an Asura maiden named Sujātā.

According to the *Saṁyutta Commentary*,[163] Sakka with his followers were born in the Asura-world (which later became *Tāvatiṁsa*), where the *asuras* prepared a drink called *gaṇḍapāna* for them. They did not drink it; but the *asuras* drank, became unconscious and were thrown to the bottom of Sineru. When they regained consciousness, they made a vow never to drink intoxicants (*surā*) again, because of which they are called *asuras*.

Elsewhere[164] *asura* is defined as *bibhaccha*, i.e., awful and vile, who used a drum called Āḷambara made of a crab's claw. It was left in *Tāvatiṁsa* when the *asuras* had to leave *devaloka*. Since then Sakka took possession of it,[165] its sound resembled a peal of thunder and was called *Āḷambara-megha* for this.

As mentioned above, the *asuras* attacked the *devas* first.[166] But, according to the *Kulāvaka Jātaka*, when Magha was born as Sakka, he did not like to share his kingdom with others, and having made the *asuras* drunken, expelled them to the bottom of Sineru, where the *Asurabhavana* developed. It is 10,000 *yojanas* in extent.[167] The Cittapāṭali tree grew there. When it blossomed, the *asuras* remembered that they were no longer in deva-world. To regain their kingdom, they climbed Sineru, "Like ants going up a pillar." Alarmed at this, Sakka went out to fight them in the ocean. But he was worsted in the fight and fled in his *Vejayantaratha*. When he knew that his chariot was hurting the *garuḷas*, he turned it back. At this, the *asuras* thought that Sakka obtained reinforcements and was turning towards them and they fled to the *Asurabhavana*. Thus Sakka triumphed over the *asuras* and set up 5 guards for keeping his kingdom free from the *asuras*.[168]

The *asuras* are of various classes. Of these, two are mentioned in the *Piṭakas*, the Kālakañjaka and the Dānaveghasa. They were present at the preaching of the *Mahāsamaya Sutta*.[169] The *Commentary*[170] describes the Dānaveghasā as archers (*dhanuggahaasurā*). Asura Sucitti belongs to this class.[171]

The Kālakañjakā are described as of a fearsome shape.[172] They resemble the *petas* not only in shape, but also sex-life, diet and longivity, and also intermarry with them.[173] They are the very lowest of the *asuras* groups, among whom Korakkhattiya was born after his death from epilepsy.[174] The Bodhisattas are never born among them because in this case they would have to suffer from excessive thirst which they cannot quench even by immersing themselves in the Ganges.[175]

The king of the *asuras* is called Asurinda,[176] Several Asura leaders mentioned in the texts are as follows.

1. *Vepacitti*.[177] He is Vemacitra or Vemacitrī in the Sanskrit texts.[178] He was present with Namuci (Māra) at the preaching of the *Mahāsamaya Sutta*.[179] The *Aṅguttara Commentary*[180] says that Vepacitti, Rahū and Pahārada were the chiefs among the *asuras*. Of them, Vepacitti was the highest (*sabbajeṭṭhaka*).[180a]

According to Buddhaghosa,[180b] Vepacitti's original name was Sambara. The *Saṁyuttanikāya*[181] says that, when Sambara refused the request of the sages for guarantee of safety, they cursed him and from that time he slept badly and was plagued by nightmares. Thus his mind was deranged (*cittaṁ vepati*), for which he was called Vepacitti ("crazy-nerve").

Sambara and Vepacitti may be of different origin. When Vepacitti was ill on account of a curse of sages, Sakka visited him and offered to cure him if he would teach him *Sambarimāyā* (magic art of Sambara). Vepacitti, after consulting the *asuras*, refused Sakka's offer and told him that Sambara, having practised magic, fell into purgatory, where he had to suffer for a century.[182] In this context, Buddhaghoṣa calls Sambara an Asurinda, and a juggler (*māyāvī*), who practised his māyā and had been roasted in hell for the past century.[183] This story contradicts Buddhaghoṣa's previous statement that Sambara and Vepacitti were identical.[184] Mrs. Rhys Davids[185] suggests that Sambara was the name of an office rather than that of a person. The *Mahāummaga Jātaka*[186] mentions Sambara as a chieftain of the *asuras* skilled in wiles. When the *asuras* were defeated in a fight with the *devas*, Vapacitti, the king of the *asuras*, was bound hand and foot and brought to Sakka in the Sudhammā-hall, where the Asura king reviled at Sakka with scurrilous words; but

Sakka remained silent.[187] On another occasion Vepacitti suggested that victory would be decided on one's excellence in speech. Accordingly, Sakka and Vepacitti both recited several verses. Vepacitti's verses belonged to the sphere of violence, while those of Sakka spoke of concord and harmony. As a result, both the *devas* and *asuras* declared victory in favour of Sakka.[188]

Once Sakka resolved that he should not betray even his enemy. Vepacitti read his thoughts and came up to him. When Sakka said to him "Stop, thou art my prisoner", Vepacitti reminded him of his resolve and was permitted to go free.[189]

Even though Sakka was engaged in fight with Vepacitti, there is a relationship between the two because Sakka married Sujā, the daughter of Vepacitti.[190] The *Kathāvatthu* says that other members of Vepacitti's family intermarried with the *devas*, and, according to the *commentary* on the *Kathāvatthu*, a troop of *asuras* belonging to the retinue of Vepacitti, was once rescued from the fourfold plane of misery and was taken up among the *devas*.[191]

2. *Rāhu.* He is spoken of as one of those possessing personality (*attabhāva*).[192] His physical constitution is vividly described in the *commentaries*.[193] He is said to be four thousand eight hundred *yojanas* in height. The breadth of his chest is one thousand two hundred *yojanas*. His forehead is fifty *yojanas* in breadth and head nine hundred *yojanas* in height. His hands and feet are two hundred *yojanas* in length, each finger-joint measuring fifty *yojanas*. The space between his two eye-brows measures fifty *yojanas*. His face is one hundred *yojanas*, nose three hundred *yojanas* and the depth of his mouth one hundred *yojanas*. As mentioned above,[194] the eclipses of the sun and moon are caused by Rāhu. He hides them in his mouth, and caresses their abodes with his hand, or with the lower part of his jaw, or with his tongue. Sometimes he takes them up and places them against his cheek; but he is unable to stop the course of the sun and moon, because they worship the Buddha. Whenever he attempts to do so, he has to meet with disaster.

Thus he is described as one of the four "stains" (*upakkilesā*) of the sun and the moon, preventing them from shining in all their glory.[195] He is described also as one of the five causes of lack of rain (*vassassa antarāya*). Sometimes he gathers water into his hands and spills it into the ocean. As a result, the rain is stopped.[196] The *Dīghanikāya Commentary*[197] says that when Rāhu steps into the ocean, the waters of even the deepest part reach only up to his knees.

The *Aṭṭhāna Jātaka*[198] says that it is impossible to bring Rāhu down from the sky.

Buddhaghoṣa[199] says that Rāhu did not visit the Buddha for a long time because he thought that he would fail to see him as he is so tall. But, one day, he went to the Buddha who being aware of Rāhu's thought contrived to make himself so tall that Rāhu had to crane his neck to see his face. At this Rāhu confessed his folly and became the Buddha's disciple.

Rāhu is called Rāhubhadda when he was present at the preaching of the *Mahāsamaya Sutta*.[200] He is also called Veroca, and the hundred sons of Bali were called after his name, he being their uncle.[201] Veroca may probably be identical with Verocana, the lord of the *asuras*, who went with Sakka to visit the Buddha during his siesta.[202] The texts mention *Rāhumukha* which is described as a kind of torture.[203] In this, the victim's mouth is forced open by a stake, and fire or spikes are sent through the orifice of the ear into the mouth, which becomes filled with blood.[204]

3. *Pahārāda*. The *Commentary*[205] says that he was one of the three leaders of the *asuras* who conceived an idea of visiting the Buddha on the day of Enlightenment.

4. *Māra*. In Pali literature Māra is generally regarded as the personification of evil spirit which takes different shapes and tries to destroy virtue and goodness. The commonest use of the word *māra* is in the sense of Death. He is so called because he destroys all those who seek to evade from this *saṁsāra* (world).

The texts mention 5 Māras—Khandha-Māra, Kilesa-Māra, Abhisaṅkhāra-Māra, Maccu-Māra and Devaputta-Māra.[206] Sometimes, Māra is spoken of as one, three,[207] or four.[208] When Māra is described as one, the reference is given generally either to the *kilesas* or death.[209] In the older books,[210] the term *Māra* is applied to the whole of the worldly existence, the five khandas or the realm of rebirth as opposed to *nibbāna*.

The *Kilesas* are the instruments of Death which enable Death to hold sway over the world.[211] They brought about all temptations which were regarded as the work of Death.

Maccu-Māra is identified with Sanskrit *Mṛtyu* (Death) which is always regarded as an evil or supreme ill.[212]

Devaputta-Māra is considered as the head of the Kāmāvacara-world.[213] He is mentioned also as the dweller of the *Vasavatti-devaloka* and is called Vasavatti because he rules all.[214]

People who delight in objects cognisant to the eye,[215] etc., and have attachment[216] are completely to go under Māra's sway. Those who are unrestrained in their senses, immoderate in their food, idle and weak[217] are overthrown by Māra.

The *Dhammapada* says that those who can restrain the mind and check its propensities and attain the Noble Eightfold path can be free from Māra.[218] In the *Saṁyuttanikāya*,[219] Vajirā tells Māra; "There is no *satta* here who can come under your control; there is no being but a mere heap of saṁkhāras (*suddhasaṅkhārapuñja*)."

When the Bodhisatta sat with firm resolve for becoming a Buddha, Devaputta-Māra attacked him with his forces which spread to a distance of twelve *yojanas* before the Bodhisatta, twelve behind, and nine each on the right and the left. The thousand-armed Māra came riding on his elephant, called Girimekhala, one hundred and fifty *yojanas* in height. His army assumed different fearsome forms and were armed with dreadful weapons. When Māra approached the Bodhisatta, the *devas*, *nāgas* and others who surrounded him fled in terror.[220] But the Bodhisatta remained there and called to his assistance the ten *pāramīs* which he practised to perfection.[221] As a result, Māra's ten-fold army fled. Seeing this Māra hurled his last weapon *Cakkāvudha* at the Buddha; but it stood over him like a canopy of flowers.[222] He challenged the Buddha to show that the seat on which he sat was his own and the followers of Māra shouted that it was Māra's. The Buddha found no witness and asked the earth to be a witness. The earth[223] roared in response and Māra and his followers fled away. Then the *devas* gathered round the Buddha and celebrated his victory. This account of the Buddha's victory over Māra is greatly elaborated in later chronicles and illustrated in countless Buddhist temples.

It is said that, when Māra attacked the Buddha, "old temptations" of the Buddha came upon him with renewed force.[224] Māra's army is divided into ten parts. The first of them consists of Lust; the second is Aversion; the third Hunger and Thurst; the fourth Craving; the fifth Sloth and Indolence; the sixth Cowardice; the seventh Doubt; the eighth Hypocrisy and Stupidity; the ninth Gains, Fame, Honour and Glory and the tenth is Lauding of oneself and the condemning of others.[225]

Even though Māra was defeated by the Buddha, he followed the latter for seven years, watching for transgression on his part. But all his processes of attack were in vain, and, he left Gotama "like a crow attacking a rock,"[226] and his lute slipped from his arm, which, according to the *Commentary*,[227] was picked up by Sakka and given to Pañcasikha.

Māra had three daughters who are represented as tempting the Buddha. They are *Taṇhā*, *Arati* and *Ragā*, and they are the personification of three of the ten forces in Māra's army. They assumed numerous forms of varying age and charm, full of blandishment; but they were overcome by the Buddha.[228]

As mentioned above, Māra was the spirit of Evil represented in various disguises for carrying out nefarious plans. All temptations due to lust, fear, greed, etc., were regarded as his activities.

Māra appeared before the Buddha on various occasions. Soon after the Buddha's first *vassa*, Māra approached him and asked him not to teach the monks anything regarding the highest emancipation because he was under Māra's control. The Buddha replied that he was free of all fetters, human and divine.[229] Māra upholds false views. On one occasion, when the Buddha said to Baka, the Brahmā, that the view which he held about the permanancy of his world was wrong, Māra appeared into a company of Brahmās and warned the Buddha.[230] On another occasion, Māra entered into the body of Vetambarī and made him utter heretical doctrines.[231] He appeared before the Buddha in the shape of an elephant, a cobra, and in various forms, beautiful and ugly,[232] and for causing feelings of fear and dread, he made the rocks of Gijjhakūṭa fall with a crash. He tempted the Buddha by suggesting that, as human life was long, there was no need for haste in living the good life.[233] Māra came in the guise of a bullock and broke the bowls of the monks. He made a great din so that the minds of the monks listening to the Buddha were distracted. When the Buddha went for alms to Pañcasālā, he entered into the bodies of the Brahmana householders. As a result, the Buddha had to return with empty bowl.[234] The *Vinaya Commentary*[235] states that the Buddha and his monks experienced difficulty in obtaining food at Verñja due to Māra's machinations. He interrupted the Buddha's sermon to the monks on *nibbāna*, coming in the guise of a peasant and asking whether they saw his oxen. He tempted the Buddha with the fascination of exercising power to rescue those who suffer from the cruelty of rulers. He also found opportunity to destroy the insight[236] which was earned by the disciples of the Buddha and disturbed them[237] when they were in meditation. It is said in the *Māratajjaniya Sutta* that Māra tried to upset the venerable Moggallāna by means of stomach ache.[238] In the *Mahāsamaya Sutta,*[239] Māra appeared as hostile to the whole assembly who gathered in honour of the Buddha. Once Māra approached the monks in the shape of a very old and holy Brāhmaṇa and asked them not to abandon the pleasures of this life. He tried to frighten Samiddhi who by the Buddha's help won arahantship.[240] He influenced Godhika to commit suicide[241] and tried to rouse fear in Rāhula in the guise of a huge elephant.[242] Māra is subdued when a disciple continue in meditation, or becomes fully enlightened.[243]

Māra assumed various forms and tempted bhikkhuṇīs, e.g., Āḷavikā, Kisāgotamī, Somā, Vijayā, Uppalavaṇṇā, Cālā, Upacālā, Sisupacālā, Selā, Vajirā and Khemā, often in lonely spots.[244] Māra's temptations were not only confined to monks and nuns, but also to lay men and women. He tried to lure them from the path of goodness.[245]

The *Majjhimanikāya Commentary*[246] says that Māradevaputta, having dogged the Buddha's footsteps for seven years, and finding no fault in him, came to him and worshipped him.

The *Māratajjaniya Sutta*[247] says that Moggallāna was once born as Mara under the name Dūsī; Kāḷā was his sister's name, and the Māra of the present age was his nephew. Dūsī is similar to Māra of Gotama's days because both are responsible for many acts of mischief. Māra-devaputta is described as a being of great power, with as strong bent for mischief, especially directed against holy men.

The Pali works mention also a class of Mārakāyikadevā.[248] They are so called because they are the followers of Māra and are credited by the *Pubbaseliyas* and *Aparaseliyas* with making arahants discharge seminal fluid, though neither the arahants nor the gods themselves were guilty of physical impurity. One of those gods once entered the bodies of five hundered women friends of Visākha, and made them drunk. As a result, these women commit gross improprieties before the Buddha.[249]

Māra bears many names, some of them being Kaṇha,[250] Adhīpati, Antaka,[251] Namuci[252] and Pamattabandhu.[253] Pāpimā[254] is his usual epithet; but other words like *anatthakāma, ahitakāma* and *ayogakkhemakāma*[255] are also used.

T.O. Ling says that Māra is 'demon' and identical with 'yakkha'.[256] He points out that the Pali works explicitly sometimes refer to Māra as Yakkha.[257] He argues that the name Kaṇha applied to Māra points to a connection between Māra and popular demonology because the *Dīghanikāya* regards Māra to be the ancient common name for a *pisāca.*[258] He also states that Windisch, L. De la Vallée Poussin, Oldenberg and Churles Eliot are of the view that the conception of Māra is developed entirely within the Buddhist circle.[259]

According to Windisch, the Māra legend originated from the Enlightenment of the Buddha when he addressed Māra, 'You are overcome, O Death.' He was sure that no new life and no dying for him and his adherents again would follow on death.[260] The experiences described in the *Māra Saṁyutta* is the root of the Māra legend rather than the crucial conflict with Mara which is hinted at in the *Padhāna Sutta* of the *Suttanipāta* because later works like the *Lalitavisṭara, Buddhacarita* and *Mahāvastu* contain the same conflict more elaborately, and state that the *Māra Saṁyutta* is an older legend, the *Padhāna Sutta* occupying an intermediate position.[261]

Notes

Chapter VI

1. See above, Ch. II.
2. For details, see B. C. Law, *HHBP*, pp. 36-85.
3. Most of the departed spirits are reborn in *Tāvatiṁsa*. In rare cases, the spirits go to the Nimmānarati—and Brahm-world. Only in one case Pāyāsi went to the *Cātummahārājika* world for his stinginess in making gifts. It is clear that the devotion with which the gift is made determines the place after his death.
4. Some Vimānas connected with the lower spirits in lower heavens (i.e. the spirits who are not sufficiently purified) are found on earth in the desert, sea, forest, etc. (cf. *Vimāna* of king Pāyāsi and some stories of the *Petavatthu*).
5. See p. 11.
6. *BCS*, Preface, p. VIII; *Jāt.*, Vol. VI, pp. 595.
7. *ERE*, Vol. IV, p. 134 (*KV*, XX.3).
8. *Dīg.*, Vol. III, pp. 197-98; *Jat.*, Vol. V, pp. 1-3.
9. See pp. 7f.
10. *BCS*, p. 26. The *Kiṁchanda Jātaka* (*Jāt.*, Vol. V, p. 2) speaks of a Spirit who, in a phantom palace, enjoys heavenly pleasure at night and suffers from severe pain during day because he earns merit by virtuous deeds performed at night but is a back-biter and bribe-taker, and issuer of unrighteous judgements during day. At the approach of dawn he has to assume a form as big as a palm tree, eighty cubits high, and his whole body is ablaze. He has only one finger on each hand, his nails are as big as spades, and with these nails he tears out the flesh on his back and eats it. Cf. *Jāt.*, Vol. I, p. 110; *ibid.*, Vol. IV, p. 2.
11. *Aṅg.*, Vol. III, p. 43.
12. *Dīg.*, Vol. III, p. 66; *Aṅg.*, Vol. III, p. 43 (*dāyajjaṁ paṭipajjati atha vā pana petānaṁ Kālakatānaṁ* (*dakkhiṇam*) *anuppadassati*). It is said that the parents, in the spirit of Brahmanical faith, normally desire to have sons in the expection that they will make offerings to them when they become *petas* (*loc. cit.*; *BCS*, p. 15).
13. *BCS*, p. 104. According to the Buddhists, liberality should be made discriminately. Gifts to the bhikkhu and the Buddhist *Saṅgha* produce the highest merit and which has the power to alleviate the suffering of the *petas* and *petīs*. The *Tirokuḍḍa-petavatthu* speaks

of Bimbisara as a giver of sumptuous dinners to the whole *Saṅgha* who acquired merits by which he relieved his relatives of their suffering in the *Petaloka*. B.C. Law says that it is sectarian narrowness of the Buddhists (*BCS*, p. 106). In the *Patavatthu*, p. 28, the god Aṅkura said to Indra that those who are really worthy of honour should be given gifts that would bear a rich fruit, "just as the seeds do when they are sown in a suitable soil."

14. *BCS*, p. 28.
15. *Aṅg.*, Vol. V, pp. 269ff.
16. *BCS*, p. 27; at pp. 105-06, B.C. Law says that food, drinks, clothes, etc. are not interchanged hand to hand between the giver and a *peta*. Only the merits produced from a gift are transferred to the spirits from which they meet their needs and become free from miseries.
17. For details, see B.C. Law, *BCS*, pp. 43-103. In rare cases, it is said that a *peta* was of extraordinary height and had some limbs of an unusual form on account of his deeds done upon earth (*ibid.*, p. 107).
18. Ibid., p. 108.
19. *Dīg.*, Vol. II, p. 212.
20. Ibid., pp. 212, 271-74.
21. *Vol.* III, pp. 250 f.
22. *Vol.* IV, pp. 200, 204, 207.
23. Ibid., Vol. II, p. 39.
24. *Dīg.*, Vol. III, pp. 203, 204.
25. Cf. *mātāpitaro ca sannipatitā honti, mātā ca utunī hoti, gandhabbo ca paccupaṭṭhito hoti* (*Maj.* Vol. I, pp. 157, 265f.) According to the commentaries, *gandhabba* means *tatrūpakasatta-tasmim okāse nibbattanako satto*, i.e., a being who is fit and ready to be born of parents. (*Maj. Com.*, Aluvihara, Series, Colombo, Vol. I, pp. 481f).
26. See ch. II.
27. *Dīg.*, Vol. II, p. 257.
28. Loc. cit., p. 258.
29. See above, pp. 119f.
30. *Dīg.*, Vol. II, p. 258.
31. Ibid., Vol. III, p. 204.
32. *Dīg. Com.*, Vol. III, p. 699.
33. See *Dīg.* Vol. II, pp. 263ff.
34. *Dīg. Com.*, Vol. II, p. 640.
35. Loc. cit.
36. *Dīg.*, Vol. II, p. 220.
37. *Dīg. Com.*, Vol. II, p. 650.
38. *Dham. Com.*, Vol. III, p. 225; *Vis.* p. 392.
39. E.g., MV, XXX. 75; XXXI. 82.
40. *Dīg. Com.*, Vol. II, p. 647.

41. It was a custom in Ceylon to tie young boys' hair round their heads in several knots. According to Buddhaghosa (*Dīg. Com.*, Vol. I, p. 296), one way of insulting a man was to shave his head, leaving him five locks of hair (*garahāyā ti pañcasikhāmuṇḍakaraṇaṁ*). See also *Jāt.*, Vol. VI, p. 496, where it is said that a traitor tied his hair in five knots which is regarded as a sign of disgrace.
42. *Jāt.*, Vol. IV, p. 69.
43. *Ibid.*, Vol. V, p. 412.
44. Vol. I, p. 33.
45. See p. 16.
46. For Apsaras see Monier Williams, *Skt Eng. Dict.* s.v.
47. He was a bhikkhu in the previous birth who died while meditating. When he was reborn in the *Tāvatiṁsa-devaloka,* the nymphs of that world received him as their lord (*Saṁ.*, Vol. I, p. 33).
48. E.g., see *Jāt.*, Vol. V, p. 152.
49. Ibid., Vol. II, p. 253.
50. *Dīg. Com.*, Vol. III p. 964.
51. Dīg. Vol. II, p. 257. According to the *Vidhurapaṇḍita Jātaka,* Kumbhīra is one of the chiefs of the Kumbhaṇḍas (*Jāt.*, Vol. VI, p. 272).
52. *Dīg.*, loc. cit.
53. Ibid., Vol. I, p. 54; *Saṁ.*, Vol. III, p. 240, Vol. V, pp. 47, 63.
54. *PED*, s.v.
55. See, e.g., *Jāt* , Vol. VI, p. 160.
56. *Dīg.*, Vol. II, p. 258.
57. Vol. II, p. 109.
58. *Jāt.*, Vol. VI, p. 160.
59. Loc. cit., p. 164.
60. Ibid., Vol. III, p. 361.
61. Ibid., Vol. VI, p. 169.
62. Ibid., p. 170.
63. Ibid., p. 191.
64. *MV*, XXXI, 27f.; *Mbv.*, pp. 153f.
65. *MB*, p. 182.
66. *Jāt.*, Vol. I, pp. 497f.
67. *Dīg.*, Vol. III, pp. 199.
68. *Jāt.*, Vol. VI, pp. 179-80.
69. *MN,* p. 201.
70. See above.
71. See p. 9.
72. *tesaṁ karoṭi nāma pānabhojanaṁ* (*Jāt.*, Vol. I. p. 204).
73. *Jāt.*, Vol. III, p. 397.
74. *Vis.*, Vol. I, p. 206.
75. See Fergusson, *Tree and Serpent Worship*, pl. XXVI. 1; XXVIII. 1, etc.; also Gründwedel : Buddhistiche Kunst, pp. 47-50.
76. *Dham. Com.*, Vol. III, p. 135.
77. *Jāt.*, Vol. III, p. 397.

78. *Jāt.*, Vol. V, p. 77.
79. Ibid., Vol. III, p. 188.
80. Ibid., Vol. IV, p. 177.
81. Ibid.,V ol. II, p. 13; Vol. III, p. 103.
82. Ibid., Vol. III, p, 187.
83. Ibid., Vol., IV p, 463.
84. E.g,, Naṭakuvera could hide in the plumage of Garuḷa (*ibid.*, Vol. III, p. 91).
85. Ibid., p. 187.
86. Ibid., Vol. III, p. 91.
87. Ibid., Vol, VI, pp. 175f.
88. *Jāt.*, Vol. VI, pp. 178, 184. The Garuḷas did not know how to seize the Nāgas effectively before they learnt the Ālambāyana spell because the Nāgas swallowed large stones so as to be of great weight. As a result, the Garuḷas died of exhaustion in trying to carry them.
89. Loc. cit.
90. Ibid., Vol. VI, pp. 261f.
91. Ibid., Vol. III, p. 187.
92. Ibid,, p. 400.
93. *Jāt.*, Vol. IV, pp. 106, 254, 438; Vol. V, pp. 47, 456; *Mil.*, p. 267.
94. *Jāt.*, Vol. IV, pp. 262ff.; *Thera. Com.*, *SHB.*, Vol. I, p. 179.
95. *Thera Com.*, *SHB.* Loc. cit., *AP.*, Vol. I, p. 165.
96. *Jāt.*, Vol. IV, pp. 282ff.
97. Loc. cit.,
98. Ibid., Vol VI, p. 422.
99. E.g., *ibid.*, Vol. V, p. 420.
100. Vol. II, p. 38.
101. See pp. 45, 55.
102. *Sut.*, Verse 478 (*ettāvatā Yakkhassa suddhi*); verse 875 (*ettāvat' aggaṁ no vadanti h' ekā, Yakkhassa suddhiṁ idha paṇḍitāse*).
103. *MN*, p. 282.
104. *Maj.*, Vol. I, p. 252; *Vim. Com.*, p. 333.
105. *Saṁ.*, Vol. I, p. 54.
106. *Vim. Com.*, loc. cit.
107. *Jāt.*, Vol. V, p. 33.
108. *E.g.*, *Saṁ.*, Vol. I, p. 205.
109. E.g., *Pet. Com.*, pp. 113, 139.
110. Ibid., p. 5, *Jāt.* Vol. III, pp. 309, 345.
111. *Pet. Com.*, pp. 5, 55.
112. See *PED*, under 'Yakkha'. *Yajanti tattha baliṁ upaharantī ṭi yakkhā (Vim., Com.*, p. 224), or *pūjanīyabhāvato Yakkho, ti vuccati* (*ibid.*, p. 333).
113. *Jāt.*, Vol. III, p. 146; Vol. II, p. 149.
114. *Dīg.*, Vol. III, p. 194f.
115. *Ud.*, IV, 4.
116. *Dīg.*, Vol. II, p. 256.

117. *Ibid.*, Vol. III, pp. 204f.
118. See e.g., *Pet.* pp. 45-56.
119. *Dīg.*, Vol. I, 95. The commentary of this *Nikāya* (Vol. I, p. 264) states that he is not an ordinary *Yakkha* but *Sakka* himself.
120. *Aṅg.*, Vol. IV, p. 63.
121. See above, *Dīg.*, Vol. II, p. 257.
122. *Jāt.*, Vol. VI, p. 270.
123. *Sut. Com.*, Vol. I, p. 197.
124. *Dīg.*, Vol. II, p. 207; Vol. III, p. 202.
125. E.g., *Jāt.*, Vol. IV, p. 492. The commentary *(Dīg. Com.*, Vol. II, p. 370) mentions Yakkhadāsī who have to dance and sing to the *devas* during the night. They drink a cup of toddy (*surā*) early in the morning and go off into a deep sleep, from which they rise in the evening ready for their duties.
126. Loc. cit.; cf. Dīg., Vol. III, p. 201 and *Dīg. Com.*, Vol. III, p. 967.
127. E.g , *Pet. Com.*, pp. 145, 274. They were the seven Yakkhas who guarded the wealth of Yotiyaseṭṭhi (*Dham. Com.*, Vol. IV, pp. 208f.).
128. Cf. *Vin.*, Vol. III, p. 37; Vol. IV. p. 20. Sexual intercourse with a Yakkha is forbidden.
129. *MV*, VII. 36.
130. *Ibid.*, p. 38.
131. *Ibid.*, 87.
132. *Pet.*, II. 9; *Jāt.*, Vol. VI, p. 118.
133. *Pet.*, I.2, 9; II. 11, IV. 3, etc.
134 *Ibid.*, p. 4.
135. *Jāt.*, Vol. IV, p. 492; Vol. V, p. 34; Vol. VI, pp. 336-37; these characteristics are not found in all Yakkhas.
136. *Sut. Com.*, Vol. I, p. 222.
137. *Jāt.*, Vol. IV, p. 492.
138. See Stede : *Gespenstergescichisten des pet avatthu* V, 39ff.
139. *BME*, pp. 15-16.
140. *Jāt.*, Vol. I, p. 103; cf. *Dīg.*, Vol. II, pp. 344-45 and *Jāt.*, Vol. V, p. 34; T.O. Ling, *op. cit.*, pp. 16-17.
141. See *Jāt.*, Vol. I, p. 129: Vol. VI, p. 303; Vol. IV, p. 491.
142. *Ibid.*, Vol. V, p. 91.
143. T.O. Ling, *op. cit.*, p. 16.
144. See p. 104 and see *Jāt.*, No. 6.
145. *Jāt.*, Vol. IV. p. 549; Vol. V, p. 34; Vol. II, pp. 15ff. and p. 128.
146. *Jāt.*, Vol. I, p. 265.
147. *Ibid.*, Vol. V, p. 21; Vol. VI, p. 336.
148. *Dham. Com.*, Vol. I, p. 47; Vol. II, pp. 35f.
149. *Jāt.*, Vol. III, p. 200; T.O. Ling, *op. cit.*, p. 17.
150. *Jāt.*, Vol. V, p. 21; T.O. Ling, *op. cit.*, p. 17.
151. See p. 203.
152. See p. 5; see also *Jāt.*, Vol. V, p. 420; *Itv.*, pp. 57f; *Saṁ.*, Vol. IV, p. 154, etc. (T.O. Ling, *op. cit.*, p. 28 note 3).

153. *Vin.*, Vol. I, p. 149 (T.O. Ling, op. cit., p. 17).
154. *Maj. Com.*, Aluvihāra series, Colombo, Vol. II, p. 173, 610-11, 921; *Aṅg. Com.*, *SHB*, Vol. I, p. 438; *Ud. Com.*, p. 247.
155. *Aṅg.*, Vol. II, p. 91.
156. E.g., *Itv.*, p. 92; *Jāt.*, Vol. VI, p. 595; *ibid.*, Vol. V, p. 186; pet p. 66.
157. Vol. I, p. 222. The *Sut. Com.*, Vol. II, p. 484 explains them as *Pubbadevā*.
158. *Jāt.*, Vol. V, p. 139.
159. Verse 484-5.
160. In the *devāsurasaṅgāma*, the *devas* first attack the *asuras* from which it may be said that the *asuras* and *devas* are separate classes of beings dwelling in the same Tāvatiṁsa-heaven. It is more accurate to say that the *asuras* were older *devas* and they had common origin with the *devas*, because if they were of different origin and the *asuras* belong to evil destinies (*apāya*), they could not dwell in the same heaven. It is probable that the new gods found asura—qualities among the older *devas* and attacked them for removing them from *devaloka*.
161. See p. 153: *Abhidhānappadīpikā*, p. 14. T.O. Ling says that the *asuras* of later Indian mythology may be fallen gods and all the demons, i.e., the Yakkhas, Rakkhasas, Pisācas, etc., have become Asuras in later literature (*BME*, p. 25). E.W. Hopking says that the Asuras 'included all the sinful demons' in the Epics (*Epic Mythology*, p. 46).
162. This cannot be Sujātā, Vepacitti's daughter, whom Sakka married (*Jāt.*, Vol. I, pp. 205-6).
163. *Saṁ. Com.*, PTS, Vol. I, p. 338.
164. *Aṅg. Com.*, SHB, Vol. II, p. 526.
165. *Jāt.*, Vol. II, p. 344.
166. For details about *Devāsurasaṅgāma*, see *Saṁ.*, Vol. I, pp. 216ff.
167. *Sut. Com.*, Vol. II, p. 485; elsewhere at, the same page, it is given as 100,000 *yojanas*.
168. See above.
169. *Dīg.*, Vol. II, p. 259.
170. *Dīg.*, *Com.*, Vol. II, p. 689.
171. *Dīg.*, Vol. II, p. 259.
172. *Dīg. Com.*, Vol. III, pp. 789, 820.
173. KV, p. 360.
174. *Dīg.*, Vol. III, pp. 7f.; *Jāt.*, Vol. I, p. 389.
175. *Vibh. Com*, p. 5.
176. Sakka was also called Asurinda and Asurādhipa; see e.g., *Jāt.*, Vol. I, p. 66; Vol. V, p. 245, where it is said that he was called Asurādhīpa from the time he conquered the *asuras*.
177. *Saṁ.*, Vol. I, p. 222; Vol. IV, pp. 201ff.; *Jāt.*, Vol. I, p. 205.
178. E.g., *Dvy.*, pp. 126-148; *Mtu.*, Vol. III, pp. 138, 254.
179. *Dīg.*, Vol. II, p. 259.
180. E.g., *Aṅg. Com.*, SHB, Vol. II, p. 758.

180a. *Saṁ. Com.*, PTS, Vol. I, p. 342.
180b. *KS.*, Vol. I, p. 293, note 1.
181. *Saṁ.*, Vol. I, p. 227.
182. *Ibid.*, p. 239.
183. *Ibid.*, pp. 237-38, *Saṁ. Com.*, PTS, Vol. I, p. 355.
184. *KS.*, Vol. I, p. 306, note.
185. *Ibid.*, Vol. I, p. 305, note. 4.
186. *Jāt.*, Vol. V, pp. 452, 454.
187. *Saṁ.*, Vol. I, pp. 221f; cf. Vol. IV, p. 201; according to which his bondage caused him no inconvenience so long as he remained with the Devas; but the moment he desired to rejoin the Asuras, he felt himself bound. Vepacitti's capture is also referred to in the *Theragāthā*, verse 749. Sakka said to Mātali that he won twofold victory because he defeated Vepacitti in battle and did not revile him.
188. *Saṁ.*, Vol. I, pp. 222ff.
189. *Ibid.*, p. 225.
190. *Dham. Com.*, Vol. I, pp. 278 f.; cf. *Jāt.*, Vol. I, pp. 205f.
191. See *Points of Controversy*, p. 211.
192. *Aṅg.*, Vol. II, p. 17.
193. E.g., *Aṅg. Com.*, SHB, Vol. II, p. 474; *Dīg. Com.*, Vol. II, pp. 487f.; *Maj. Com.*, Āluvihāra series, Colombo, Vol. II, p. 790.
194. See pp. 133ff.
195. *Aṅg.*, Vol. II, p. 53; *Vin.*, Vol. II, pp. 295; cf. *Jāt.*, Vol. III, p. 365.
196. *Aṅg.*, Vol. III, p. 243.
197. Vol. II, p. 488.
198. *Jāt.*, Vol. III, p. 477.
199. *Dīg. Com.*, Vol. II. p. 285; *Maj. Com.*, Āluvihāra Series, Colombo, Vol. II, pp. 790f.
200. *Dīg.*, Vol. II, p. 259.
201. *Dīg. Com.*, Vol. II, p. 689.
202. *Saṁ.*, Vol. I, pp. 225f.
203. E.g., *Maj.*, Vol. I, p. 87; Vol. III, p. 164; *ND.*, p. 154; *MIL.*, pp. 197, 358.
204. *Aṅg. Com.*, SHB, Vol. I, p. 293.
205. *Ibid.*, Vol. II, p. 758.
206. *Thera. Com.*, SHB,, Vol. II, pp. 16, 46; *Vis.*, Vol. I, p. 211.
207. *Dīg. Com.*, Vol. II, p. 659; Vol. III, pp. 846, 858; *CN. Com.*, p. 47; *Sut. Com.*, Vol. II, p. 508; *Maj. Com.*, Āluvihāra Series, Colombo, Vol. II, p. 619.
208. *MN.*, p. 129; *Sut. Com.*, Vol I, p. 201; *ITV. Com.*, p. 136.
209. *ITV. Com.*, pp. 197-98; *Ud. Com.*, p. 325; *Net. Com.*, pp. 86, 235; *Thera. Com.*, Vol. II, p. 70.
210. *CN.* No. 506; *Saṁ.*, Vol. III, pp. 74, 189, 195, 198; Vol. IV, pp. 91, 202; *Sut. Com.*, Vol. II, p. 506.
211. See *e.g.*, *Aṅg.*, Vol. IV, p. 228.
212. *BME*, pp. 56-57.

213. *Ang.*, Vol. II, p. 17.
214. *Sut. Com.*, Vol. I, p. 44; *Maj. Com.*, Āluvihāra Series, Colombo, Vol. I, p. 28; *Jinālankāra Ṭīkā*, p. 217.
215. *Saṁ.*, Vol. IV, p. 91.
216. Ibid., Vol. III, p. 73.
217. *Dham.*, *Yamaka*, verse 8.
218. *Ibid.*, *Yamaka*, verses 7, 40.
219. Vol. I, p. 135.
220. The *Mārasaṁyutta* (Saṁ., Vol. I, pp. 103ff) says that the approach of Māra is recognised only by the Buddha, even though others are present.
221. *Jāt.*, Vol. I, pp. 71ff., *Bud. Com.*, pp. 239f.; cf. *Maj. Com.*, Āluvihāra Series, Colombo, Vol. I, p. 384.
222. This is mentioned in very late accounts and especially in Sinhalese books.
223. Here earth is personified, she is probably *Bhummadevatā.*
224. See Article on Buddha in the *ERE.*
225. See the first part of the *Padhāna Sutta.*
226. *Sut.*, verse, pp, 446.; cf. *Saṁ.*, Vol. I, p. 122; *Sut. Com.*, Vol. II, 391f.
227. *Sut. Com.*, Vol. II, pp. 393f.
228. *Saṁ.*, Vol. I, pp. 124f.; *Dham. Com.*, Vol. III, pp. 195f.
229. Vol. I, p. 22.
230. For details, see *BME*, pp. 101-02.
231. *Saṁ.*, Vol. I, P. 67; *Dham. Com.*, Vol. IV, p. 141.
232. *Saṁ.*, Vol. I, pp. 103ff.
233. E.g. *Dīg.*, Vol. III, p. 58.
234. *Dham. Com.*, Vol. III, pp. 257f.
235. Vol. I, pp. 178f.
236. *BME*, p. 52.
237. Loc. cit.
238. Loc. cit.
239. *Dīg.*, Vol. II, p. 261.
240. *Dīg.*, *Com.*, Vol. III, p. 864.
241. *Saṁ.*, Vol. I, p. 122.
242. *Dham.*, Vol. IV, pp. 69f.
243. *BME*; p. 53.
244. *Saṁ*,, Vol. I, pp. 129-34; *Therī*, verses 57-59.
245. *Sut. Com.*, Vol. p. 44; see also *Jāt.*, Vol. I, pp. 231f.
246. Āluvihāra Series, Colomba, Vol. I, p. 533. But the *Mahāvamsa*, XXXI, 85, says that Māra obstructed good work even after the Buddha's death.
247. *Maj.*, Vol. I, p. 333.
248. *KV*, pp. 164 f.; *Dham. Com.*, Vol. III, p. 102.
249. Loc. cit.
250. *BME*, pp. 98, 104-05.
251. Ibid., p. 57.

252. *Ibid.*, p. 65.
253. *MN*, Vol. II, pp. 489, 328; another name of Māra was Pajāpati.
254. *BME*, p. 56.
255. E.g. *Maj.*, Vol. I, p. 118.
256. For details, see *BME*, pp. 44-45.
257. Ibid., p. 46, Māra is called 'great Yakkha' in the *Mahāvastu.*
258. Loc. cit., (*Dīg.*, Vol. I, p. 93).
259. *BME.*, pp. 46-47. E.W. Hopkins identifies Kāma, the god of desire or love, with death (*māra*) and adds that this identification is Buddhistic (*ibid.*, p. 47).
260. Ibid., p. 47.
261. Ibid., p. 48.

CHAPTER VII

Links Between Early and Later Buddhist Mythology

Buddhist mythology changed its character with the modification of Buddhism through the ages. To find out some connections between early and later Buddhist mythology, we have to know the general history of Buddhism. This religion reveals itself in the following forms in different periods—(1) Early Hīnayāna (c. 450 to 350 B.C.); (2) Later Hīnayāna (c. 350 to 100 B.C.); (3) Early Mahāyāna (c. 100 B.C. to 700 A.D.); and (4) Later Mahāyāna, i.e. Vajrayāna (700 to 1300 A.D.).

History of Buddhism. In the beginning, there were two *yānas*, viz., Sāvaka-yāna and Paccekabuddha-yāna. The former says that the Sāvakas attain *nibbana* (status of an Arahant) but cannot obtain *bodhi* (enlightenment, status of the Buddha). On the other hand, the Pacceka Buddhas attain Buddhahood, but cannot preach the way of deliverance to the world. These two *yānas* were regarded as Hīnayāna after the development of Mahāyāna, the principal difference between the two being that the Hīnayānists preach Arahanthood as the highest emancipated state and Buddhahood not to be attained by every being, while the Mahāyānists are of the opinion that every individual is pure in origin and can acquire Buddhahood and help others in getting emancipation.

The Mahāyānists claim that the Buddha was regarded as supramundane (*lakottara*) and had been deified from the advent of Mahāyānism (i.e. during Kālāśoka's reign, c. 386 B.C.) when the Mahāsaṅghika sect sprang up from Hīnayāna. N. Dutta[1] says that some Mahāyānic traces in regard to the conception of the Bodhisattva, the Pāramitā practices, and the goal of Buddhahood are found in the doctrines of the Mahāsaṅghikas and

Sarvāstivādins,[2] and their offshoots. The Mahāyāna incorporates the conception of countless Buddhas and Boddhisattvas, advocates the worship of images of gods, demi gods and goddesses and recommends the use of *mantras* for attaining emancipation.

In its later phases, i.e., between the 7th and the 13th century A.D., Mahāyāna Buddhism lost its high ideals of universal love for all mankind and of salvation of all, and yielded to gross superstitions and esoteric and immoral principles (*mantra, maṇḍala, dhāraṇī, mudrā*, etc.) of Tantrism and people thought that these were the easiest means for attaining emancipation. Of these, *mantra* was regarded as the simplest means, and Mahāyāna at this stage was divided into Mantrayāna and Pāramitāyāna. Mantrayāna is the initial stage of Tantric Buddhism. During this period, *mantra, dhāraṇī, mudrā, maṇḍala*, etc. were emphasised to make people believe in magic, sorcery, charms, etc., which were applied to gods, demigods, ghosts, goblins, demons, fiends, etc. When men and women regarded themselves as manifestations of *Upāya* (*Karuṇā*, universal compassion) and *Prajñā* (*Śūnyatā*, perfect knowledge) and thought that liberation or highest truth would come into light on the combination of *Upāya* (male) and *prajñā* (female) 'like that of water and milk' and on the immersion of duality in a state of non-duality, the full-fledged Tantrism (Vajrayāna) originated. At this stage, the Yoga or sexo-yogic practices were added to the elements of Mantrayāna.

Vajrayāna attaches much importance to the worship of various gods and goddesses. It considers everything as *vajra* (void or *śūnyatā*). A god is meditated on as *vajra*, nature of the self and the *dharmas*. The image of the god, the *mantras*, the process and articles of worship, the worshipper himself, etc., are all supposed to be *vajra*.

The ultimate reality in Vajrayāna is identified with the conception of a Lord Supreme (*Bhagavat*) as Vajrasattva, sometimes also called Vajradhara. He is the Supreme God, because he is the non-dual state of *śūnyatā* and *Karuṇā*. Those who realise Vajrasattva become Vajrasattvas.

Upāya (male) and *Prajñā* (female) emanate from Vajrasattva who is one and non-dual. This monotheistic idea of Vajrayāna resembles the Buddha's supremacy in early mythology. But with the evolution of the conception of Vajrasattva, the monotheistic god turns into a new and expanded pantheon of gods and goddesses in Vajrayāna. Vajrasattva is the Ādi-Buddha (the primal Enlightened one) who possesses five kinds of knowledge, conceived as his five attributes, from which five kinds of meditation (*dhyānas*) proceed. From these, five deities known as the five Dhyāni-Buddhas or Tathāgatas emanate. They are (1) Vairocana, (2) Ratnasambhava, (3) Amitābha, (4) Amoghasiddhi and (5) Akṣobhya. They are the presiding deities of the *Skandhas* or elements and have each obtained a divine consort or *śakti* of his own, namely, Vajradhātvīśvarī, Locanā, Māmakā, Pāṇḍarā and Ārya-Tārā respectively. Each Dhyāni Buddha has a particular Bodhisattva as his son and also a certain human Buddha. Vajrasattva himself has a consort who is variously called Vajrasattvātmikā, Vajravārāhi, Prajñāpāramitā, etc. However, though many deities are found in Vajrayāna, the form of *sādhanā* is the same in all cases, i.e., when a god is worshipped, he is to be meditated on as in union with *Śakti* or *Prajñā*, enjoying great bliss.[3]

In the tenth century A.D., a school known as Kālacakrayāna arose within the fold of Vajrayāna. This is an aspect of Vajrayāna. The supreme deity, according to the school, is called Lord Śrī-Kālacakra.[4] The difference between the two is that in Kālacakrayāna, are found the introduction and predominance, in the system, of a number of gods and their female energies, having awful and terrible aspects, though as powerful as the celestial Buddhas themselves, and of other dreadful fiends known as Dākinīs, all of whom have to be appeased with *mantra* (charms), magic circles, offerings and sacrifices.

In all ages, Hindu gods and goddesses have been adopted in Buddhism. During its later phases, particularly at the Tantric stage, the Hindus also borrowed Buddhist goddesses like Mahācīnatārā, Jāṅgulī and Vajrayoginī and incorporated them into their own pantheon under the names of Tārā, Manasā and Chinnamastā respectively. The deities in Tāntric Buddhism, 'have no independent and real existence apart from the mind of the worshipper and the manner of worship.' They have no external figure, but 'represent purely mental conception of the *sādhaka* who by means of the *sādhanā* undergoes a detailed mental exercise for the development of his spiritual or psychic powers' for the realisation and visualisation of the deity with whom the worshipper is asked to identify himself. In the state of the highest meditation when the individual soul (variously known as Bodhisattva, Bodhicitta and Jīvātman) invokes and combines himself with the Universal or Infinite Soul (variously called Śūnya, Brahman and Paramātman), the deity, i.e., the Śūnya, manifests himself in the mind-sky in flashes and sparks. As the objects or desires of the worshippers are different, the deity appears in various forms, and thus different gods and goddesses are found in the Buddhist pantheon.

Though the Mahāyāna Buddhist mythology alters its nature and form, it has some connection with the mythology of the Hīnayāna Buddhists. The points of such connection are described below.

The Buddha's Supremacy. As we have said elsewhere,[5] the Buddha does not speak of any Creator-God, on account of which Hīnayāna Buddhism is considered not a religion, but an ethical system. The Pali Buddhist literature mentions the Hindu doctrine of the never-ending cycles of creation and destruction and says that the regions from *Vehapphala to Arūpa Brahmaloka*[6] are not subject to destruction which suggests that there is no origin or end of the world. It ever was and will be for ever. On the other hand, Mahāyāna Buddhism is regarded as a religion because it follows the Brāhmaṇical conception of a supreme Creator-God, and the *Guṇakāraṇaḍavyūha*[7] speaks of a supreme primordial Buddha-god (Ādi-Buddha or Ādinātha). He is infinite, omniscient and self-existing (*svayambhū*) and the creator of the universe. He is without beginning and without end. The *Saddharmapuṇḍarīka*[8] says that the Buddha 'has lived since countless aeons in the past, and will live for ever.' In the same work,[9] he says of himself, "I am the father of the world." He is mentioned here as the physician and protector of all creatures.

The Ādi-Buddha was produced from the mystic syllable *aum*[10] which was manifested in the perfect void (*mahāśūnyatā*). At the creation of the world, there was a lotus-flower on which the Ādi-Buddha revealed himself in the form of a flame. This reminds us of the Brāhmaṇical conception of Brahma, the creator-god, who sits on a lotus-flower produced from the navel of Viṣṇu. Ādi-Buddha never descended on earth. He left the creation of the world and direction of its affairs to the active author of creation, the Dhyāni-Bodhisattva. Padmapāṇi (the Lotus-bearer Dhyāni-Bodhisattva),[11] a non-Tantric form of Avalokiteśvara,[12] received from the Ādi-Buddha, through the medium of his spiritual father Amitābha (the Dhyāni-Buddha),[13] the active power or creation and created the actual world.[14] The *Kāraṇḍavyūha*[15] says that Avalokiteśvara created gods out of his own body. The Sun (Āditya) and the Moon (Candra) came from his eyes, Maheśvara from his brow, Brahman and other gods from his shoulders, Nārāyaṇa from his heart, Sarasvatī from his feet, and Varuṇa from his belly.

In connection with the Buddha's supremacy in Mahāyāna, we have to see the position and power held by the Boddisattva Avalokiteśvara because he is an active representative of the Ādi-Buddha. The *Saddharmapuṇḍarīka*[16] says that the Boddhisattva Avalokiteśvara protects his devotees from every danger. At the uttering of his name, all fetters are loosened.[17] If a man falls into a mass of fire, he is saved by remembering Avalokiteśvara. In the same way, one is protected from the current of rivers; the shipwrecked and the caravan attacked by robbers are rescued. Being sentenced to death, if a person prays to Avalokiteśvara, the executioner's sword is broken into fragments. In case the whole triple chiliocosm is teemed with goblins and giants, they would lose the faculty of sight in their wicked designs by the strength of Avalokiteśvara's name. He is worshipped by women for getting a son or a beautiful daughter. By adoring him one is freed from passion, hatred, infatuation and anxiety. If a person falls into the dreadful ocean, the abode of Nāgas, marine monsters, and demons, he is saved by uttering the name of Avalokiteśvara. The devotees of Avalokiteśvara are saved by thinking his name, even if are hurled down from the brink of the Meru, or are surrounded by a host of enemies with swords, goblins, Nāgas, demons, ghosts or giants, fearful beasts with sharp teeth and claws, malicious and frightful snakes, and if rocks of thunderstone and thunderbolts are thrown at their heads. Avalokiteśvara is present everywhere if implored in need and danger.[18] In quarrels, disputes, wars and battles, one can cansubdue the foes by uttering his name. He is a protector, a refuge, a recourse in death, disaster and calamity. Avalokitesvara rescues the beings who are in hell. The *Kāraṇḍavyūha*[19] describes him as 'a lamp for the blind, a sunshade for those who are dying of thirst.' He is a physician to those who are tormented by sickness, and a father and a mother to the unfortunate; he points out the way to Nirvāṇa to those who have descended into hell. He is invoked with the uttering of *Oṁ maṇipadme huṁ*, the 'knowledge of the six syllables', i.e., the protecting and benedictory prayer. According to Winternitz,[20] it is probably a mode of addressing Maṇipadmā, the female counterpart of Avalokiteśvara. The Boddhisattva says, "Whoever will give me the great knowledge of the six syllables, to that man I will willingly give the four continents, filled with the seven kinds of precious stones."[21]

As Avalokiteśvara's father Amitābha is a spiritual son of the Ādi-Buddha, his position and power is also to be stated here to understand the Buddha's supremacy in later Buddhism. The longer *Sukhāvatīvyūha*[22] says that those who have done good deeds, who direct their thoughts to enlightenment and think of Amitābha and his Buddhaland in the hour of death reach the Sukhāvatī heaven. According to the shorter *Sukhāvatīvyūha*,[23] Sukhāvatī is not the reward for good deeds; but one who merely hears the name of Amitābha and thinks of it will go to heaven.

The conception of the Buddha's supremacy is not new in the later Buddhist mythology. It is already found in the early Buddhist mythology. Although the Buddha based his teachings upon reason, the Pali works dealing with the ethical doctrines of early Buddhism represent him as omnipresent, omniscient and omnipotent. In the same way, in the *Mahāyānasūtras*, the Buddha, according to Winternitz,[24] already appears as a demigod in the commentary of the *Brahmajālasutta*. When he starts begging for alms, soft wind sweeps the path before him, clouds pour down a light shower of rain for clearing the dust and then stay upon his head like a canopy, high and low places become even, and lotus flowers spring fourth under his footsteps, and so on. In the *Dīghanīkāya*,[25] the Buddha says that he, whose faith in the Tathāgata is settled, cannot be dragged down by the recluse, Brāhmaṇa, Deva, Māra and Brahman. The *Saṁyuttanikāya*[26] says that those who take refuge unto the Buddha's feet are released from danger. The gods Candimā and Suriya, being seized by the Asura Rāhu, took refuge in the Buddha and uttered the verse—

namo te Buddha vīr=atthu vippamutto si sabbadhi /
sambādhapaṭippanno='smi tassa me saraṇaṁ bhava ti //

"Adoration to thee, great Buddha ! Thou art free from all impurities. I am distressed. Become thou a refuge to me." Then the Buddha addressed Rāhu as follows—

Tathāgatam=arahantam Candimā saraṇaṁ gato /
Rāhu Candaṁ pamuñcassu Buddha lokāṅukampakā ti //

"In the Arahat Tathāgato, the Moon-god, has taken refuge. Rāhu, release thou the moon. The Buddhas are merciful to the world." At this the Asura Rāhu released the Moon-god, went to the place of the Asura chief, Vepacitti and stood in great terror on one side. When the Asura chief wanted to know the cause of his terror, Rāhu replied—

Sattadhā me phale muddhā jīvanto na sukhaṁ labhe /
Buddhagāth-ādhihito='mhi no ce muñceyya Candiman=ti //

"If I do not release the moon, my head would be split up into seven pieces; and were I to live, I would have no enjoyment..." This fact shows that the Buddha is not only a preacher of the Truth, but is also a supreme authority controlling the universe, and protects the good from danger.

According to the *Dīghanikāya*,[27] the Buddha is above all gods and Brahmās. He is supreme and controls the universe.[28] In conformity with this, both the Pali[29] and Sanskrit[30] Buddhist texts state that the Buddha was visited by the gods, Brahmās, Nāgas, Yakkhas, Gandhabbas, Kinnaras, Garuḍas and Asuras in order to listen to the preaching of the Mahāsamaya and Lotus Sūtras.

According to the early Buddhists too, the Buddha is found everywhere. He can travel throughout the universe. Once he reached the Tāvatiṁsa-heaven in three strides for preaching *Abhidhamma* to the gods. The *Brahmanimantanika Sutta* of the *Majjhimanikāya* states that he went to the Brahmaloka for refuting the false views held by Baka, the great Brahmā, that the Brahmaloka was permanent. Besides, he walked long distances in the air for alms.

The Pali texts describe the Buddha as 'world-knower' (*lokavidū*)[31] who knows everything by his supernatural insight.[32] He sees everything by means of the radiance of his body. In connection with these characteristics, the *Saddharmapuṇḍarīka*[33] says that the Buddha is all-knowing and all-seeing. Besides, in the *Dīghanikāya*,[34] the Buddha himself announces his supremacy over the world by roaring the 'lion's roar'. He finds no one equal to him in the world.

Pali literature describes the Buddha as the embodiment of knowledge. According to the *Buddhavaṁsa Commentary*,[34a] the Buddha appears on earth when knowledge is necessary for human and divine life.[34b] He is not born in the early period of a *kappa* when people live longer than one hundred thousand years because, during this period, they are not able to recognise the nature of old age and death, and therefore are not benefited by his preaching. He is born on earth when men live not less than one hundred years and not more than ten thousand. As the Buddha appears in a suitable age for our welfare, he may be regarded as an *avatāra* of the Supreme God (*Bhagavat*).

The Buddha is supreme and *lokottara* because he says himself in the *Aṅguttaranikāpa*,[34c] that he is not a Deva, Gandhabba, Yakkha or man; he is the Buddha. This brings us to draw a conclusion that the Mahāyānists were not the first to regard the Buddha as *lokottara*; they borrowed the conception from the Hīnayānists.

However, on a careful observation of the Buddha's characteristics mentioned in the Hīnayāna and Mahāyāna texts, one may say that the Buddha's supremacy of early days makes the Ādi-Buddha the creator-god in the later period. Likewise, Lakkhī of early mythology, the symbol of the earned merit to the way to *nibbāna*, tends to become the female principle of the Ādi-Buddha in later Buddhism.[34d]

Light from the Buddha's Body. The Hinayāna literature[35] states that all the *cakkavāḷas* are illuminated by the rays of light from the Buddha's body. According to the *Milindapañha*[36] and

Visuddhimagga,[37] after performing the twin-miracle (*yamakapāṭihāriya*) in the Tāvatiṁsa, when the Buddha came to the world of men, he looked at the eastern, western, northern and southern world. As a result, many thousands of world systems (*anekāni cakkavāḷa-sahassāni*) appeared. On that day, the Buddha saw as far below as Avīci and as far above as the Akaniṭṭha abode.[38] And all the inhabitants saw one another face to face (*sabbe sammukhā va aññamaññaṁ passanti*). On another occasion, when the Bodhisattva descended from the Tusita heaven and entered the womb of queen Māyā, a light appeared illuminating the Deva, Brahma and human worlds, etc. The light was so brilliant that the beings of one world could see those of another.

Little wonder if the Mahāyāna Buddhist mythology also on this miraculous conception of the Buddha's light. The *Śatasāhasrikāprajñāpāramitā*[39] says that, when the Buddha, after meditation, glanced over the Buddha-land with his heavenly eyes, radiant light came out from his body and from every pore in his skin, and illuminated all the continents. Seeing this radiance, all beings became clear-sighted and were all confirmed in the unsurpassable, complete enlightenment. At his smile, innumerable rays of light emanated from his tongue.[40] "On each ray there arose lotuses of jewels, shimmering like gold, with a thousand petals, brightly hued, and beautiful to look upon, sweet, golden, with a pleasant scent, delicate and soft." The Tathāgatas sat on these lotuses and preached the doctrine of the six perfections. All beings heard this doctrine and were confirmed in the unsurpassable, complete enlightenment. The *Saddharmapuṇḍarīka*[41] says that when the Buddha sat in meditation, rays of light burst forth from the hair between his eyebrows and illuminated eighteen hundred thousand Buddha-lands down to the great hell Avīci and up to the limit of existence. According to the longer *Sukhāvatīvyūha*, the Buddha Amitābha radiates immeasurable light in the Sukhāvatī-world.[42]

Mahāpurisalakkhaṇā and the Buddha. The thirty-two marks of a great man attributed to the Buddha are found in both the earlier and later systems of Buddhism. In the *Dīghanikāya*,[43] the Buddha is described as flat-footed; he does not toe or heal the ground in walking. On the soles of his feet appear signs of wheel with tyre and hub. He has long fingers and toes. His hands and feet are soft and look like a net. His ankles are like rounded shells and his legs are like an antelope's. He can touch and rub his knees with either hand standing and without bending. His male organ is concealed in a sheath. His complexion is like bronze or gold. His skin is so delicately smooth that no dust sticks to his body. The small hairs on his body turn upward; they are blue-black like eye-paint, and are curling to the right. The front part of his body is like a lion's. There is no furrow between his shoulders. The height of his body is equal to the compass of his arms. His bust is rounded. His taste is supremely acute. He has forty teeth and his jaw is as a lion's. His tongue is very long. He has a divine voice like that of the Karavīka bird. His eyelashes are like those of a cow. A hairy mole appears between his eyebrows, which is white and soft like cotton. His head is like a royal turban.

The Brāhmaṇical literature applied the designation mythology is found in the conception of the Bodhisattvas. Every Bodhisattva descends from the Tusita to earth. He enters into the body of his mother, Māyā, by the right side without causing her any pain; ten months later, he reappears from his mother's body. His birth is honoured by Brahma, Indra and the other Brāhmaṇical divinities.[45]

Cosmology. The cosmology of the Mahāyāna Buddhists is more or less the same as that of Hīnayāna mythology with a little difference. In all periods, the Buddhists speak of the univirse as consisting of innumerable world-systems.[46] According to Pali works,[47] the *cakkavāḷas* are scattered throughout the infinite space, being arranged in groups of three, touching each other, causing a dark region called Lokantarika hell[48] in the triangular space surrounded by three *cakkavāḷas*. Sanskrit Buddhist literature[49] speaks with a little difference in respect of the Lokantarika hells which are said to be situated in all the *cakkavāḷas* and not in the triangular space. However, the *cakkavāḷas* are grouped in different universes. The early Hīnayāna,[50] later Hīnayāna[51] and Mahāyāna[52] mythology mentions three sorts of universes—(1) *sahassī cūḷanikā* (Sans. *sāhasracūḍikā*) *lokadhātu*[53]—a small kind of universe consisting 1,000 *cakkavāḷas*;

(2) *dvisahassī majjhimikā* (*dvisāhasramadhyama*) *lokadhātu*[54]—a middle class universe consisting of 1,000,000 *cakkavāḷas*; and (3) *tisahassī mahāsahassī* (*trisāhasramahāsāhasra*) *lokadhātu*[55]—a large type of universe consisting of 1,000,000,000 *cakkavāḷas*. According to Pali and Sanskrit Buddhist texts, each *cakkavāḷa*[56] or small universe is made of five great elements[57]—the earth, water, air, fire and ether or space, the first four being the substance of all material things. In conformity with the Pali works,[58] the *Abhidharmakośa*[59] and *Kāraṇḍavyūha*[60] state that the earth rests upon water.

In respect of the mountain system, though there is some variation regarding the order of mountains in the different texts, Hīnayāna mythology is interconnected for the following: (a) Mount Sineru or Sumeru is in the centre of each *cakkavāḷa*;[61] (b) it is also called Meru, Mahāmeru, etc.,[62] (c) its height is 1,68,000 *yojanas*, half of which is submerged in the sea,[63] (d) it is surrounded by seven rocky circles—Yugandhara, Īsadhara (Īṣādhara), Karavīka (Khadiraka), Sudassana, Nemindhara (Nimindhara), Vinataka and Assakaṇṇa,[64] each being half the height of the preceding one, commencing from the Sineru; (e) there is an ocean flowing between every two mountains;[65] (f) the four great island continents[66] are situated between the last of the seven rocky circles and the *cakkavāḷa*-mauntain or *cakkavāḷa-silā*.

Both Hīnayāna and Mahāyāna texts state that, in each *cakkavāḷa*, there is a Sun and Moon and a multitude of stars.[67] The commentary on the *Aggañña Sutta*[68] and the *Abhidharmakośa*,[69] state that, at the same time, sunrise, sunset, midday and midnight occur respectively in the four continents. For example, when the sun rises in Apargoyāna, it is midday in Jambudīpa, evening in Pubbavideha, and midnight in Uttarakuru.

Destruction and Renovation of the Universe. The Pali texts of the early Hīnayāna,[70] the *Abhidharmakośa*[71] and *Mahāvastu*[72] of the later Hīnayāna and many other Sanskrit Buddhist texts[73] of the Mahāyāna mythology carry the same view regarding the destruction and renovation of the universe. According to these texts,[74] the universe undergoes many cycles of dissolution and evolution.

The *Visuddhimagga*,[75] *Mahāvyutpatti*[76] and Daśabhūmika *Sūtra*[77] state that the world is destroyed by fire,[78] water and wind. When the world is destroyed by fire, seven suns appear in the sky[79] and all living beings of earth are reborn in the Ābhassara Brahma-world whence they come again on earth during the period of evolution of the universe.[80]

The *Abhidharmakośa*[81] and *Visudhimagga*[82] state that the world is destroyed by fire seven times and the next by water. In this procedure for the eighth time, it is destroyed seven times by water, and seven times again by fire. 'By so much are passed sixty-three cycles. Within this limit, although the turn to perish by water is arrived, it is inhibited, and the wind which takes its turn destroys the world, crushing the Subhakinha whose term of life is full sixty-four cycles.'[82a]

Both the early and later Hīnayāna have the same opinion about the definition of a Mahākappa (great cycle). When the world is under destruction by fire, water and wind, there is in each case a great cycle made of four aeons.[83] The first aeon, from the great world-destroying rain to the cessation of the flames, is called dissolution (*saṁvaṭṭo*). The second, from the cessation of the world-destroying flames to the great rain flooding up the world-system, is called the process of dissolution (*saṁvaṭṭaṭṭhāyī*). The third aeon, from the great world-flooding rain till the appearance of the sun and moon, is called evolution (*vivaṭṭo*). The fourth, from the appearance of the sun and moon to the great world-destroying rains, is called the process of evolution (*vivaṭṭaṭṭhāyī*).[84]

Abodes of Living Beings. The abodes of living beings described in later Hīnayāna and Mahāyāna mythology are almost the same as that of early Hīnayāna. Early Hīnayāna speak of 31 abodes of living beings in each *cakkavāḷa* while the later Hīnayāna and Mahāyāna mention respectively 32 and 33 abodes. But the mythology of all periods state that these abodes are scattered below, upon and above Mount Sineru. They are situated one above another according to the merits and demerits of the inhabitants, commencing from the hell, the lowest place, and divided into four groups—(1) abodes of misery (unfortunate sense-experience), (2) abodes of fortunate sense-experience, (3) the *Rūpaloka* and (4) *Arūpaloka.*

Among these, the first group is fourfold —(1) Purgatory, (2) Animal kingdom, (3) Peta-world and (4) Asura-world.[85] The second group of sevenfold and consists of one realm for human beings and the other six for gods.

As the first two groups of abodes belong to the sense experience, they are taken together as eleven and grouped as the abodes of *Kāmaloka*. Thus it is said that the abodes of living beings generally belong to the three groups—(1) *Kāmaloka* (world of sense-experience), (2) *Rūpaloka* (meterial world) and (3) *Arūpaloka* (immaterial world). Of the 11 *Kāmalokas*, the following six are *Devalokas*—(1) Cātummahārājika (Sana. *Cāturmahārājika*), (2) Tāvatiṁsa (Trayastriṁśa), (3) Tusita (Tuṣita), (4) Yāma, (5) Nimmānarati (Nirmāṇarati), and (6) Paranimmitavasavattī (Paranirmitavaśavartī).[86] The last two groups are devoid of sense-desires. According to the Pali texts, *Rūpaloka*[87] and *Arūpaloka*[88] consist of sixteen and four celestial abodes respectively. The *Rūpa* heavens are divided into four classes—

(A) abodes of the first *jhāna* to which belong three heavens, viz., (1) of Brahmā's retinue (*Brahmapārisajja*, Sans. *Brahmapārṣadya*), (2) of Brahmā's ministers (*Brahmapurohita*), and (3) of the great Brahmās (*Mahābrahmā*).

(B) abodes of the second *jhāna* to which belong the next three heavens— (4) of minor lustre (*Parittābha, Parīttābha*), (5) of infinite lustre (*Appamāṇābha, Apramāṇābha*), and (6) of the radiant gods (*Ābhassara, Ābhāsvara*).

(C) abodes of the third *jhāna* to which belong another three heavens, namely, (7) of minor beauty (*Parittasubha*), (8) of immeasurable beauty (*Appamāṇasubha, Apramāṇaśubha*), and (9) of complete beauty (*Subhakiṇha, Śubhakṛtsna*).

(D) abodes of the fourth *jhāna*, to which belong the following seven heavens: (10) of the gods of great reward (*Vehapphala, Bṛhatphala*), (11) of the unconscious beings (*Asaññasatta, Asaṁjñasattva*), (12) of the lowest *Suddhāvāsa* beings (*Aviha, Avṛha, Abṛhat*), (13) of the serene beings (*Atappa, Atapa*), (14) of the beautiful beings (*Sudassā, Sudṛsā*), (15) of the clear-sighted beings (*Sudassī, Sudarśana*), and (16) of the highest *rūpāvacara* beings (*Akaniṭṭha, Akaniṣṭha*). Of these heavens, 12 to 16 are called pure abodes (*Suddhāvāsā*).

Later Hīnayāna and Mahāyāna have a little difference with the above-mentioned *Rūpa* heavens of early Hīnayāna. The *Abhidharmakośa*[89] and *Dharmasaṅgraha*[89a] mention, respectively, 17 and 18 *Rūpa* heavens, on account of which the total number of abodes increases to 32 and 33 in later Hīnayāna and Mahāyāna respectively.

The *Arūpaloka* is of different grades—(17) the sphere of the conception of infinite space (*Ākāsānañcāyatana, Ākāśānantyāyatana*); (18) that of infinite consciousness (*Viññāṇañcāyatana, Vijñānānantyāyatana*); (19) that of nothingness (*Ākiñcaññāyatana, Ākiñcanyāyatana*); and (20) that of neither consciousness nor unconsciousness (*Nevasaññānāsaññāyatana, Naivasaṁjñānāsaṁjñāyatana*).[90]

Heaven. Mythology of all ages holds the same view in regard to heaven and hell. Heaven is the reward for good deeds and hell is the punishment for evil deeds. Buddhist literature of all periods speaks of some heavens and hells. In respect of heaven, a new outlook is found in Buddhist mythology. Both Hīnayāna and Mahāyāna say that the heavens are divided into two groups of world (1) *Devaloka* (heavens of the gods) and (2) *Brahmaloka* (heavens of the Brahmās). The *Brahmaloka* is divided into two worlds—(1) *Rūpa-Brahmaloka* (material world) and (2) *Arūpa-Brahmaloka* (immaterial world). The number of *Devalokas* and *Arūpa-Brahmalokas* is six and four respectively according to both systems while the number of *Rūpa-Brahmaloka* varies. It is 16 in early Hīnayāna, 17 in later Hīnayāna and 18 in Mahāyāna.

As mentioned above, the lowest heaven is the Cātummahārajika which stands halfway up Mount Sineru, and the next higher heaven, Tāvatiṁsa,[90a] is on the top of the Sineru. In this ascending order, the other heavens stand one above another. Certain texts[91] of the Mahāyāna, viz. *Lalitavistara, Mahāvyutpatti*, etc., draw a difference in regard to the highest heaven of the Rūpa-world. These works place the heaven of Mahāmaheśvara. The Great Lord Śiva, above the Akaniṣṭha, the highest heaven of the *Rūpa*-world are mentioned in the Hīnayāna mythology.

Gods and Goddesses—Both Hīnayāna and Mahāyāna state that the gods of the *Devalokas* and *Brahmalokas* are inferior to the Buddha.[92] The Pali and Sanskrit Buddhist texts mention some important gods who rule over the gods of six *Devalokas*; but none of them is supreme. They are subject to death for which their names are regarded as offices of the kings of gods. At the death of one king, some one who acquires the qualifications of king takes the place of the deceased king. According to the said texts, the kings of the *Devalokas* are as follows—four great kings of the *Cātummahārājika-world*, namely, *Dhataraṭṭha* (Dhṛtarāṣṭra) of the east, Virūḷhaka (Virūḍhaka) of the south, Virūpakkha (Virūpākṣa) of the west and Vessavaṇa (Vaiśravaṇa) or Kuvera of the north, also Sakka (Śakra)[93] of the Tāvatiṁsa-world, Suyāma[94] of the Yāma-world, Santusita (Santuṣita)[95] of the Tusita-world, Sunimmita (Sunirmita)[96] of the Nimmāṇarati-world and Vasavattī (Vaśavartī)[97] of the Paranimmitavasavatti-world.[98] In this connection it may be noted that the four great kings of the Cātummahārājika-world are regarded as four *lokapālas* in both early and later Buddhism.[99]

The heavens mentioned above are named according to the different classes of gods who inhabit them. More or less the same classes of gods are mentioned in the Hīnayāna and Mahāyāna texts.[100] This shows that the later Buddhists borrowed from the early Buddhist literature the conception of the classification of gods in respect of their merits earned through different stages of meditation.

The Vedic tradition of personification and deification of natural phenomenon is recognised in both the Pali and the Sanskrit Buddhist literature. The *Saṁyuttanikāya*,[101] *Lalitavistara*,[102] *Divyāvadāna*[103] and *Mūlasarvāstivādavinaya*[104] are unanimous regarding the following two groups of *Valāhakāyika* gods, namely, (1) *Vassavalāhaka* and (2) *Vātavalāhaka* who are related to rains and wind respectively. The *Dīghanikāya*[105] and *Mahāsamāja Sūtra*[106] refer to some fragile cloud-spirits called *Mandavalāhaka*. Besides, the gods of the earth, air, fire, water, and the Sun and Moon, mentioned in the *Mahāsamaya Sutta*,[107] are found in later Buddhist mythology.[108]

As mentioned above, both the Hīnayāna and Mahāyāna borrowed some Hindu gods. The following names of Hindu gods are common in Pali and Sanskrit Buddhist texts—

(1) Śakra (Sakka),[109] (2) Indra (Inda),[110] (3) Viśvakarman (Vissakamma),[111] (4) Varuṇa,[112] (5) Prajāpati (Pajāpati),[113] (6) Viṣṇu (Veṇhu),[114] (7) Nārāyaṇa,[115] (8) Soma,[116] (9) Skanda or Kumāra,[117] (10) Sīva (Siva)[118] (11) Yama,[119] (12) Kuvera,[120] (13) Sūrya or Āditya (Suriya or Ādicca),[121] (14) Candra (Candimā),[122] (15) Vāyu,[123] (16) Agni (Aggi or Jātaveda)[124] and (17) Pṛthivī or Dharaṇī (Paṭhavī).[125] But, in Buddhism, these gods are treated with certain changes, particularly, in conformity with the Buddhist ideas. According to the early Buddhists, these gods are inferior to the Buddha and subject to death. They follow the teachings of the Buddha and become moral and kind to the good men.[126] The *Saddharmapuṇḍarīka*[127] mentions Śakra, Sūrya, Candra, Samantagandha (Vāyu), Maheśvara (Śiva) and Vaiśravaṇa (Kuvera) as the followers of the Buddha. The *Kāraṇḍavyūha*[128] says that Āditya, Candra, Maheśvara (Śiva), Nārāyaṇa, Vāyu, Dharaṇī and Varuṇa are created from the body of the Bodhisattva Avalokiteśvara. As the Ādi-Buddha appoints Avalokiteśvara as a creator-god imparting power of creation to him, the gods mentioned in the *Kāraṇḍavyūha* may be regarded as the sons of the Ādi-Buddha, for which these gods are inferior to the Buddha.

The *Saddharma-Laṅkāvatāra Sūtra*[129] describes Viṣṇu, Soma, Indra and Varuṇa as some of the countless names of the Buddha. In the same text,[130] a Buddha says that he comes from the Śuddhāvāsa heaven and his father and mother are Brahmā Prajāpati and Vasumatī respectively. The goddess of earth, whether she is called Vasumatī, Pṛthivī or Dharaṇī, is common to the Brāhmaṇical, Hīnayāna and Mahāyāna mythologies.

In both the early and later Buddhist texts,[131] Śakra and Indra are also identical with each other, and Varuṇa, Yama, Āditya, Candra, Vāyu and Agni are personified gods of water, death, sun, moon, air and fire respectively. Śakra is always spoken of as *devānām=indra*, i.e., the Indra of gods (king of the gods). It is a common description of Śakra.[132] But he is not a king of all gods; he rules only over the Tāvatiṁsa gods.[132a]

We have seen Āditya as a son of the Buddha in Mahāyāna mythology. The Hīnayāna also mentions Ādicca as the

Buddha's son. In support of this, the *Saṁyuttanikāya*[133] states that the Buddha speaks of Ādicca as *mama pajā* which Buddhaghoṣa[134] explains as the Buddha's disciple or spiritual son. He also explains Ādicca as the Buddha's *orasa-putta* (breast-born son).[135]

Nārāyaṇa, the Supreme God of Brāhmaṇical literature, is mentioned in the Pali and Sanskrit Buddhist literature[136] as a proverbially powerful personage.

Lakṣmī (Lakkhī)[137] or Śri (Siri),[138] the goddess of good fortune, and Alakṣmī (Alakkhī),[139] the goddess of evil fortune are mentioned in both Hīnayāna and Mahāyāna.

Unlike Brāhmaṇical literature, Pali and Sanskrit Buddhist texts speak of many Brahmās; but none of them is regarded as the highest being. They are inferior to the Buddha.[140] According to the *Kāraṇḍavyūha*,[141] Brahman is not supreme because he is created by the Bodhisattva Avalokiteśvara. Both the early and later Buddhist texts mention Mahābrahmās (great Brahmās); but as they are impermanent and belong to the first *jhāna*, they are not higher than the Buddha. However, the following names of Brahmās are common in Pali and Sanskrit Buddhist literature—(a) Sahāṁpati (Sahampati),[142] (b) Sanatkumāra (Sanaṅkumāra),[143] (c) Ghaṭikāra,[144] (d) Tiṣya (Tissa),[145] (e) Baka[146] and (f) Subrahmā.[147]

Hell. As regards hell, the Hīnyāna and Mahāyāna Buddhists hold more or less the same view. The Jātakas,[148] *Abhidharmakośa*,[149] *Mahāvastu*,[150] *Divyāvadāna*,[151] *Dharmasaṅgraha*,[152] and *Mahāvyutpatti*[152a] mention various kinds of punishments in hells like the following.

1. *Sañjīva.* It is so called because beings are cut to pieces and come again to life for suffering the same punishment.

2. *Kālasutta* (*Kālasūtra*). The inhabitants of this hell are struck down with blazing weapons and are cut to pieces with weapons called *Kālasutta*.

3. *Saṁghāta.* Beings are crushed with burning mountains for which the hell is so called.

4. *Roruva* (*Raurava*).[153] Here the sinners are consumed by a dreadful fire.

5. *Mahāroruva* (*Mahāraurava*). The fire of this hell is fiercer than that of *Roruva*.

6. *Tapana.* It is so called because the sinners have to suffer from a terrible heat in it.

7. *Patāpana* (*Pratāpana*). The heat of this hell is excessive.

8. *Avīci.* It is the most fearful of the *nirayas.* The *Jātaka* commentator[154] says that the hell is so called because there is no cessation either of the fire or of the pain. The *Abhidharmakośa* describes Avīci as the place where there is no happiness. It says that the hell is twenty thousand *yojanas* below the Jambu continent.

According to the early and later Hīnayāna works, the constitution of these hells is as follows. Each hell has four corners and four doors and is divided equally into four divisions. It is surrounded by iron walls on all sides and has an iron roof. Its floor is made of burning iron one hundred *yajanas* around.[155] Besides, there are four minor hells (*utsada*) to each of the four sides of each hot hell. The punishment of these minor hells is suffering from horror and terrible misery.[156] In the *Abhidharmakośa*[157] and *Mahāvastu,*[158] the four *utsadas* belonging to each of the hot hells are (1) *Kukkula,*[158a] the hell of ashes, (2) Kuṇapa,[158b] the hell of dung, (3) *Khuramārga* (*Asipattavana,*[158c] the forest of trees with leaves of swords; *Śālmalīvana,*[158d] the forest of Śālmalī trees, and the place full of Śyāma and Śavala dogs) and (4) the Nadī (*Khārodaka-Vaitaraṇī*). The *Pañcagatidī-pana*[159] mentions the following four *Ussadas*—(1) *Mil̤hakūpa,* the hell of dung, where beings are eaten up by worms; (2) Kukkula, (3) *Asipattavana* and (4) Nadī (*Vetaraṇī*). The *Aṅguttara*[160] and *Majjhima*[161] *Nikāyas* do not mention the eight hells as indicated above. These texts speak of a *Mahāniraya* which, according to some scholars, is identical with Avīci. The *Mahāniraya* has five adjacent hells, wherein the sinners fall and suffer. These are: (1) *Gūtha,* (2) *Kukkula,* (3) *Simbalivana,* (4) *Asipattavana* and (5) *Khārodakanadī.* The four minor hells mentioned in the *Abhidharmakośa* has some conformity with these five. However, both Pali and Sanskrit Buddhist texts contain the same view that the *Mahāniraya* is surrounded by minor hells.

The Sanskrit Buddhist literature[162] mentions eight cold hells—(1) *Arbuda,* (2) *Nirarbuda,* (3) *Aṭaṭa,* (4) *Hahava,*

(5) *Huhuva* or *Hāhādhara*, (6) *Utpala*, (7) *Padma*, and (8) *Mahāpadma*. *The Saṁyutta*[163] and *Aṅguttara*[164] *Nikāyas* and the *Suttanipāta*[165] use the same nomenclature with a few variations and additions which, according to Buddhaghoṣa,[166] are not separate hells, but specified periods[167] of suffering in the Avīci.

As mentioned above,[168] the Lokantarika series of hells described in the Pali and Sanskrit Buddhist works mark the similarity between the Hīnayāna and Mahāyāna mythology. The number of these hells is innumerable because there are many *cakkavāḷas* in the universe. Darkness prevails in these hells.[169] It is tumultuous and dreadful as the light from the sun and moon does not reach it.[170]

Spirits and Semi-Divine Beings. The word 'spirit' is generally applied to those who are dead on earth and are reborn in different worlds in accordance with their earned merit and demerit through various deeds, good and evil. Both Hīnayāna and Mahāyāna follow Hindu mythology and say that spirits who earn merits are reborn in the *Devaloka* and *Brahmaloka* and those earning demerits are born in four *Apāyalokas*, i.e., they are reborn among (1) animals, (2) *Asuras*, (3) *petas* or ghosts and (4) inhabitants of hell.[170a] The *Petaloka* is regarded as a kind of hell because the spirits of the dead suffer here from severe pain owing to their misdeeds of previous births.[171] La Valleé Poussin[172] says that though the *Petas* are found throughout the world of men, they dwell especially in the kingdom of Yama, which is divided into 36 provinces, situated 500 *yojanas* below Jambudīpa.

Besides, supernatural beings are regarded as spirits who become visible at their pleasure and are frequently conceived as good or hostile to mankind. They are divided into two categories, good and evil. The evil spirits are troublesome and terrifying demons. They are Asuras, Yakkhas, Rakkhasas, Pisācas, Māras, etc. But the Yakkhas are sometimes regarded as semi-divine beings. The spirits that dwell in the gardens, houses, hills, rivers, seas, royal umbrellas, waters, etc., are generally treated as semidivine. Of them, those causing anxiety, fear, etc., to mankind are grouped as demons or evil spirits.

As mentioned above,[173] four great kings of the Cātummahārājika-world are the guardian spirits of the four quarters who rule respectively over the Gandhabbas, Kumbhaṇḍas, Nāgas and Yakkhas.[174] These are regarded as lower gods. Besides, the Garuḍas, Kinnaras, etc., are also classed as spirits.

We shall discuss below how the spirits and semi-divine beings of early mythology are borrowed in later mythology.

Nāgas and Garuḍas. According to the early and later Buddhist texts, the Nāgas and Garuḍas are minor deities.[175] The Buddhists, like the Hindus, believed that the Nāgas were in constant terror of the Garuḍas.[176] The serpent-gods became devotees of the Buddha to protect themselves from the attack of the Garuḍas[177] They prayed to the Buddha for protection and the latter appointed the god *Vajrapāṇi*[178] as their special protector.

The Nāgas, in return, protected the Buddha on several occasions. Once a Nāga king protected the Buddha from a heavy storm and rains by spreading his hood above the latter's head like an umbrella.[179] In the same manner, the later Buddhists[180] state that when Māra, the god of evil, began to disturb the Buddha's meditation, Mucilinda (Pali *Mucalinda*), a serpent king, wound his coils about him and spread his hood over his head for protecting him from the attack of Māra.[181] Besides, the Nāgas miraculously multiplied and enlarged their heads and shielded the Buddha from the rays of the sun. This reminds us of Viṣṇu of the Hindu mythology.[182]

Worship of the Nāgas is found in both Hīnayāna and Mahāyāna. According to the Pali texts,[183] the Nāgas are offered sacrifices of milk, rice, fish, meal and strong drinks. As mentioned above,[184] they are the deities of rain clouds and protect the devotees from lightning and bring or stop rains.[185]

Gandhabbas. The Gandhabbas are regarded as semi-divine beings in both Hīnāyāna and Mahāyāna.[185a] Of the Gandhabbas, Pañcasikha was celebrated in the Pali and Sanskrit Buddhist texts.[186] The *Dīghanikāya Commentary*[187] states that Pañcasikha was a favourite of the Devas and of the Buddha. When Sakka visited the Buddha, he sent Pañcasikha in advance for obtaining permission for an interview.[188] The Devas loved him and wished to resemble him. Brahmā Sanaṅkumāra assumed the form of Pañcasikha at the assembly of the gods of Tāvatiṁsa.[189]

Pañcasikha is regarded as an office (lika Sakka) in both Pali and Sanskrit Buddhist texts,[190] because he is subject to death and any one who earns requisite merit on earth is reborn among the Gandhabbas as Pañcasikha.

Devasurasangrama and the Asuras. Both Pali and Sanskrit Buddhist texts state that there was continuous struggle between the Devas and the Asuras.[191] As in the early texts, later Buddhist literature[192] places Rahu and Vemacitri or Vaimacitra (Pali *Vepacitti*) in the list of Asura kings.

Some of the celestial Bodhisattvas, male and female (e.g. Mārici), created in later Buddhist mythology, were fiendish in nature.[193] With the introduction of Kālacakrayāna, we hear of many demons who, according to Waddell,[194] "were monstrous 'king-devils' of the most hideous Śaivite type, with their equally repulsive spouses." They were worshipped when a man attacked by minor demons. This reminds us of Yakkha worship of the early Buddhists.[195] The *Dīghanikāya*[196] says that Karatiya, one of the greater Yakkhas, was invoked by the followers of the Buddha when they were assailed by the evil spirits.[197]

Yakkhas. Both the early and later systems of Buddhism say that the Yakkhas, who are non-human beings, possess different characteristics. Generally speaking, they are semi-divine beings[198] having super-normal powers by which they can influence men and become partly helpful or harmful to them. Even though some of the Yakkhas do not believe in the Buddha and his teachings[199] and molest the followers of the Buddha in their woodland haunts,[200] the *Mahāsamaya Sutta* (*Dīghanikāya*),[201] *Lalitavistara*, *Saddharmapuṇḍarīka*,[202] *Kāraṇḍavyūha*[203] *Suvarṇaprabhāsa Sūtra*,[204] etc., mention the Yakkhas' devotion to the Buddha. The said works also state that the gods of the *Devalokas* and *Brahmalokas*, as well as the Nāgas, Kinnaras, Gandharvas, Garuḍas, Asuras, etc., have devotion to the Buddha.

Māra. The conception of Māra's attack on the Buddha as found in the Pali works is borrowed by the later Buddhists.[205] In support of this, later works like the *Lalitavistara*, *Buddhacarita* and *Mahāvastu* mention elaborately the same conflict of Māra with the Buddha as hinted at in the *Padhāna Sutta* of the *Suttanipāta*.

Māra is generally regarded as the personification of evil spirit trying to prevent Śākyasiṁha from becoming the Buddha.

He tries to turn him from the path of emancipation by threats and temptation.

Māra is often styled Namuci in both the early and later Buddhist mythology.[206] The Pali texts[207] mention five Māras—Khanda-Māra (Skanda-Māra), Kilesa-Māra (Kleśa-Māra), Abhisaṅkhāra-Māra, Maccu-Māra (Mṛtyu-Māra) and Devaputta-Māra. The Sanskrit Buddhist texts[208] refer to the said Māras excepting Abhisaṅkhāra.

Devaputta-Māra[209] holds the position of the head of the Kāmāvacara-world. He is described as a being of great power, with a strong bent for mischief, especially directed against holy men. The *Buddhacarita*[210] refers almost to the same conception and speaks of Māra as Kāmadeva, the god of desire. He strives to tempt the Buddha by the attractions of his three daughters, namely, Taṇhā, Arati and Ragā. Māra and his army take different fearsome shapes and carry dreadful weapons to attack the Buddha. But their attempts are all in vain.[211]

Notes

Chapter V

1. *Buddhist Sects in India,* p. 268.
2. Sarvāstivāda developed with the Mahīśāsakas and the Mahāsaṅghikas (ibid., p. 136) and belonged to later Hīnayāna.
3. We know the actual process of worship and the nature of meditation in Vajrayāna from the description of the particular *sādhanā* of a deity. The Supreme Lord is meditated on with the five Dhāyni-Buddhas first; then flowers are offered. These five with their respective Śaktis are to be worshipped with offerings of flowers, lamp, incense, etc. Then the devotees confess their sins before the Lord and take refuge in the three jewels, viz., the Buddha, Dharma and Saṅgha. After this, the worshippers have to resolve for the deliverance of all and think of the world, both static and dynamic, as All-void, and utter the *mantra,* "Om, I am of the nature of the immutable knowledge, of the void." Next comes the meditation of self as the Lord himself, and that of the various gods and goddesses on either side of the Lord with *mantras,* etc.
4. *Kāla* is the ultimate immutable knowledge (*Prajñā*) or the state of *Śūnyatā,* while *cakra* is regarded as the cycle of world process, or the body of the Lord containing the potency of existence of the universe, which is just the principle of *upāya.*
5. *JAIH,* Vol. III, p. 108.
6. Ibid., p. 109, note 11; see also below.
7. Alice Getty, *GNB,* p. 2.
8. See M. Winternitz, *HIL,* Vol. 11, pp. 295-96.
9. See Chapter XV, Gāthā 21; Winternitz, op. cit., p. 296.
10. Getty, op. cit., p. 2 and note 5.
11. Ibid., p. 58.
12. Loc. cit.
13. Loc. cit.
14. Loc. cit.
15. Winternitz, op. cit., p. 308; P.L. Vaidya, *Mahāyānasūtrasaṁgraha,* Pt. I, p. 285.
16. Winternitz, *op. cit.,* p. 303.
17. Loc. cit.
18. *SBE,* Vol. XXI, p. 407, note 2.
19. Winternitz, op. cit., pp. 308-9.

20. Ibid., p. 309.
21. Loc. cit.
22. Ibid., pp. 310-11.
23. Ibid., p. 310.
24. Ibid., p. 197.
25. PTS, Vol. III, p. 84.
26. See PTS, Vol. I, pp. 50-51; Cf. MAR, Vol. VI, p. 192.
27. PTS, Vol. I, pp. 211-23.
28. *Itv*. p. 15.
29. *Dīg*., Vol. II, pp. 253-62.
30. *Saddharmapuṇḍarīka*, Ch. I.
31. *BME*, p. 116 *In the Ariyapariyesanā Sutta of the Majjhima*., PTS, Vol. I, p. 171 (Dutt, op. cit., pp. 75-76), the Buddha says that he is all-conqueror, omniscient, perfect, etc. (*sabbābhibhū sabbavidū ham=asmi / sabbesu dhamesu anupalitto / ahaṁ hi arahā loke ahaṁ Satthā anuttaro / eko='mhi Sammasambuddho sīti-bhūto='smi nibbuto //*).
32. *BME*, p. 96.
33. Ch. V.
34. See Vol. II, p. 15. (*aggo = 'ham = asmi lokassa, jeṭṭho = 'ham = asmi lokassa, seṭṭho = 'ham = asmi lokassa, ayam = antimā jāti, natthi dāni punabbhavo*). Cf. *sadevakassa lokassa Buddho aggo pavuccati* (*Saṁ*., Vol. I, p. 67).

34a. See pp. 158f.; Malalasekera, *DPPN*, Vol. II, p. 298.

34b. This reminds us of Kṛṣṇa, whom Brāhmaṇical literature calls an *avatāra* of the Supreme God, as saying: "When righteousness disappears and unrighteousness appears, I come on earth to re-establish righteousness by punishing the wicked and protecting the good" (*Gītā*, IV. 7-8).

34c. Vol. II, p. 38; Kern, *MIB*, p. 64.

34d. Getty, op. cit., p. 3. In Hīnayāna mythology, Lakkhī, the goddess of beauty and fortune, possesses wisdom and is a goddess of wisdom, etc., of Brāhmaṇical literature. She is also regarded as the Supreme Goddess because her favour, i.e., 'the earned merit', enables one to get nibbāna, the supreme knowledge (see Haldar in *Foreigners in Ancient India and Lakṣmī and Sarasvatī in Art and Literature, ed.* Sircar, pp. 143-45). According to the later Buddhists, the consort of the Ādi-Dharma (Ādi-Prajñā). In Nepal and Tibet, Ādi-Buddha is called Yogāmbara and his Śakti is Jñāneśvarī (Getty. loc. cit.)

35. *Saṁ*., Vol. I, p. 47; *Maj*., Vol. III, p. 120.
36. *SBE*, Vol. XXXVI, p. 220.
37. PTS, p. 392.
38. See below. They are the highest and lowest of the material worlds.
39. Cf. Winternitz. op. cit., p. 321.
40. Loc. cit.
41. Chapter I.
42. In the said world, there is neither hell nor animals, Pretas and Asuras. It is filled with sweet scent. Jewel trees of different colours

grow there and wonderful lotuses blossom. The country is flat without hills. Rivers of this land yield sweet water. Those who are born here are all endowed with the most beautiful qualities, physical and mental, and enjoy all imaginable pleasures. Men and gods are equal in position. There is no question of day and night. It is devoid of darkness. As stated above, anyone who thinks of Amitābha, pays heed to his good deeds and directs his thoughts to enlightenment is reborn in the Sukhāvatī world. Merely a thought of Amitābha enables one to be reborn in Sukhāvatī. Its inhabitants are not born of women; they appear seated on lotuses and live in happiness and calm, in perfect wisdom and sinlessness.

43. See Vol. II, pp. 17-19; cf. *Maj.*, Vol. II, pp. 136 f; Senart, *Mtu.*, Vol. I, pp. 226-27; *Saddharma*. Ch. III; *Vajracchedikā Prajñāpāramitā*, Ch., XIII; Winternitz, op. cit., p. 323.
44. Keith and Carnoy, op. cit., p. 196; *Lalitavistara*, ed. Vaidya, p. 77 etc.
45. Getty, op. cit., p. xviii; Winternitz. op. cit., pp. 240, 249.
46. Cf. *Vis.*, p. 207; *Vin. Com.*, PTS, Vol. I, p. 120; *Sut. Com.*, PTS, Vol. II, p. 443; *SBE*, Vol. XXI, p. 232; *Abhidharmakośa*, Chap. III. According to some scholars, the *Abhidharma* is an authority of all schools of Buddhism, though it is written from the standpoint of the Sarvāstivāda school of Hīnayāna (Winternitz. op. cit., p. 357).
47. *Dīg.*, Vol. II, p. 12; *Maj.*, Vol. III, p. 120; *Aṅg.*, Vol. II, p. 130; *Saṁ.*, Vol. V, p. 454; *KS*, PTS., Vol. V, p. 382; *Vin. Com.*, loc. cit., *Sut. Com.*, loc. cit.; *Vis.*, loc. cit.
48. This reminds us of the *anārambhaṇam tamas*, 'unsupported darkness', of the *Ṛgveda* (*ERE*, Vol. IV, p. 132).
49. *Mtu.*, ed. Senart, Vol. I, pp. 41, 229, 240; Vol. II, p. 162; Vol. III, pp. 334, 341; *Divyāvadāna*, *ed.* Cowell and Neil, pp. 204-6; *Lalita.*, *ed.* Lefmann, pp. 51, 410; *Saddharma*, *ed.* Kern and Nanjio, p. 163; *Samādhirāja*, *ed.* Régamay, p. 7, line 9; *Śatasāhasrikā*, *ed.* P. Ghosa, p. 102; Winternitz, op. cit., p. 250; *ERE*, loc. cit.
50. *Aṅg.*, Vol. I, p. 228; Rhys Davids, *GS.*, Vol. I, p. 207. Cf. Mc-GOVERN, *A Manual of Buddhist Philosophy*, p. 48; *MB*, p. 8.
51. E.g., *Abhidharma.*, Ch. III.
52. *Mahāvyutpatti*, 3042-44, *Bodhicaryāvatārapañjikā*, II. 14 (*ERE*; Vol. IV, p. 137*a*, note 7).
53. *Aṣṭasāhasrikāprajñāpāramitā*, *ed.* Mitra, pp. 65-66; E. Waldschmidt, *Das Mahāparinirvāṇasūtra*, 31, 46.
54. *Daśabhūmika*. (Gāthā portion), *ed.* Rahder, p. 46; *Aṣṭasāhasrikā*, p. 95; *Śatasāhasrikā*, p. 26.
55. *Mtu.*, Vol. II, pp. 300 ; *Lalita.*, pp. 276, 319, 377; *Saddharma*, pp. 121-23, 156-57, 263-64. 440; *Arya-Mañjuśrīmūlakalpa*, *ed.* Gaṇapati Sastri, p. 343; *Suvarṇabhāsottama*, *ed.* Nobel, pp. 8, 86, 100, 149; *Samādhirāja*, p. 8; *Rāṣṭrapālaparipṛcchā*, *ed.* Finot, p. 2; *Aṣṭasāhasrikā.*, pp. 67-69, 73, 95, 115, 118, 120, 123, 129, 130, 132, 141; *Mahāyānasūtraśaṅgraha*, Pt. I, pp. 79, 85, 87-88; *Daśabhū-*

mika (Gāthā portion), pp. 46, 55; *Śikaṣāsamuccaya*, ed. Bendall. pp. 246-47.

56. *Aṅg*., Vol. I, p. 176; *JPTS*, 1891-93, pp. 123-24; 1884, p. 27; cf. *Mtu*., Vol. II, p. 341; *Saddharma*, p. 316.
57. E.g., *Aṅg*., loc. cit.; *Abhidharma*, Ch. III; cf. *Sikṣāsamucaya*, p. 244; *Ency. Rel. Eth*., Vol. IV, p. 131.
58. *Dīg*., Vol. II, p. 107; *Aṅg*., Vol. IV, p. 312; *Mil*., PTS, p. 68 (*mahāpaṭhavī udake patiṭṭhitā, udakaṁ vāte patiṭṭhitaṁ, vāto ākāsaṭṭho hoti*); cf. *Jāt*., PTS, Vol. III, p. 42; *Vin. Com*., Vol. I, p. 119; *Sut. Com*., Vol. II, p. 442: *Vis*., pp, 205-06; *Dhs. Comm*. PTS, pp. 297-98; Spence Hardy, *MB*, p. 3; cf. D.J. Gogerly, *Ceylon Buddhism*, Vol. I, pp. 19, 21; *ERE*, loc. cit.; Hardy, *LTB*, pp. 85-86; McGovern, op. cit., p. 50).
59. Ch. III.
60. Getty, op. cit., p. 64.
61. E.g., *Aṅg*., Vol. I, p. 227; Vol. V, p. 59; *Abhidharma*, loc. cit.,
62. E.g., *Cv*., PTS, Ch. 42, verse 2; Ch. 37, verse 79; *Maj*., Vol. I, p. 338; P. L. Vaidya, *Samādhirāja*, p. 1.
63. *Sut. Com*., Vol. II, p. 443; *Vin. Com*., Vol. I, p. 119; *Vis*., p. 206; *Dh. Com*., p. 298; *Aṅg*., Vol. IV, p. 100; *Mahāyānasūtrasaṅgraha*, pt. I, p. 272.
64. W. Kirfel, *Die Kosmographie der Inder*, p. 186; *Abhidharma*, loc. cit., *Dharmasaṅgraha*, Sec. 125; *ERE*, Vol. IV, p. 132; *Mahāvyutpatti*, 4 40-48.
65. *Jāt*., Vol. I, p. 64; Vol. IV, p. 125; Vol. VI, p. 43; *LTB*, pp. 84-85; *Abhidharma*., loc. cit.
66. They are Jambudīpa to the south, Aparagoyāna to the west, Pubbavideha to the east and Uttarakuru to the north of the Mahāmeru. The earth consists of these four continents. It is similar to the Purāṇic conception of the four-continent earth (*caturdīpā vasumatī*). See *Vin. Com*., Vol. I, pp. 119-20; *Sut. Com*., Vol. II, p. 443; *Vis*., p. 207; *Abhidharma*, loc. cit.; *Mahāvyutpatti*, 3045, 3047, 3050, 3054, 3057: *Mūlasarvāstivādavinaya* (*Gilgit Manuscripts*), ed. N. Dutt, Vol. I, p. 94; *Dharmasaṅgraha*, Sec. 120; *Aṣṭasāhasrikā*, p. 95.
67. *Aṅg*., Vol. I, p. 227; Vol. V, p. 69; *Abhidharma*, loc. cit.; *Lalita*, p. 75. The number of stars is 28 according to the *Mahāniddesa*, Vol. II, p. 382, and *Mahāvutpatti*, 3186-214; but Hardy mentions 27 stars (*MB*, pp. 23-24).
68. *Dīg. Com*., Vol. III, pp. 866ff.
69. Ch. III.
70. *Dīg. Com*., Vol. III, pp. 84; cf. *Vis*., p. 414; *MB*, pp. 28.
71. Chap. III.
72. *Mtu*., Vol. I, pp. 63, 229, 268; Vol. II, pp. 133, 284.
73. *Lalita*, p. 345; *Maṇḍavyūha*, ed. Suzuki and Idzumi, p. 277; *Mahāvyutpatti*, 8279-80; *Bodhisattvabhūmi*, ed. Wogihara, 253-14; Edgerton, *Buddhist Hybrid Sanskrit Grammar and Dictionary*, Vol. II, s.v. *vivarta*.

74. Loc. cit.
75. See p. 414.
76. *Mahāvyutpatti*, 8285-87.
77. See 91. 27; Edgerton, op. cit., *s.v. saṁvartanī*, Cf. *Śikṣāsamuccaya*, p. 246.
78. Cf. *Aṣṭasāhasrikā*. p. 180.
79. *Aṅg.*, Vol. IV, pp. 100-03; *Vis.*, pp. 414-15 *Abhidharma*, Chap. III. In the same manner as the *Vis.*, the *Śikṣāsamuccaya*, p. 247 says that, when the destruction begins, the second sun appears and dries up the small streams; the third and fourth suns dry up, respectively, great rivers and great seas.
80. *Aṅg.*, Vol. V, p. 60; *Dīg.*, Vol. III, pp. 84-85; *MB*, pp. 28, 30-31; *Vis.*, pp. 415-20; *Abhidharma*, loc. cit.; *Mtu.*, Vol. I, pp. 52, 63, 338. In the same way as the Pali texts (*Dīg.*, *op. cit.*, pp. 84-96; *Vis.*, pp. 417-20), *the Mtu.*, Vol. I, pp. 338-48, describes how the universe renovates itself after a period of dissolution (cf. *Abhidharma.*, Chap. III). The *Śikṣāsamuccaya*, p. 247, has also some connection with the renovation theory of early and later Buddhist mythology and says that, at the beginning of the recreation of the universe, the universe of 1,000,000,000 *cakravālas* are covered with clouds which pour down a sea of water.
81. See Ch. III.
82. See pp. 421-22.

82a. *Path of Purity*, PTS, Vol. II, p. 488.

83. *KS*, PTS, Vol. II, p. 123; *Abhidharma*, Chap. III; cf. *Mtu.*, Vol. I, p. 63.
84. *Aṅg.*, Vol. II, p. 142; *Vis.*, p. 414.
85. *Pet.*, PTS, p. 66; *Aṅg.*, Vol. I, p. 37; Vol. V, pp. 269-70, etc.
86. *Dīg.*, Vol. I, pp. 215-23; *Maj.*, Vol. I, p. 289; Vol. III, pp. 100-03, 147; *Aṅg.*, Vol. I, pp. 210, 227-28; Vol. III, p. 287; Vol. IV, pp. 119, 240ff.; *Mtu.*, Vol. I, p. 212; Vol. II, p. 16; Vol. III, pp. 223, 319; *Divyāvadāna*, pp. 68, 140, 367; *Avadānaśataka*, ed. Speyer, Vol. I, p. 5; *Lalita*, pp. 364, 366, 396, 401, 441; *Mahāvyutpatti*, 3078-83; *Dharmasaṅgraha*, ed. Müller, Sec. 127.
87. E.g., *Maj.*, Vol. I, p. 289; cf. *Lalita*, pp. 30, 99, 219, 250, 413; *Mtu.*, Vol. I, p. 159; *Mahāvyutpatti*, 3085-3108, *Dharmasaṅgraha*, sec. 128.
88. *Maj.*, loc. cit.; cf. *Dharmasaṅgraha*, Sec. 129; *Mahāvyutpatti*, 3110-13.
89. Ch. III, cf. *ERE.*, Vol. IV, p. 136.

89a. Sec. 128.

90. E.g., *Aṅg.*, Vol. I, p. 41; cf. Kern. *MIE*. pp. 57-59; *Dharmasaṅgraha*, Sec. 129.

90a. The *Mtu.*, Vol. I, p. 32. *Divyāvadāna*, pp. 194-95, and *Mahāvyutpatti*, 4194-97, follow the Pali texts (*Aṅg.*, Vol. III, p. 40; *Dhammapadaṭṭhakathā*. Vol. I, pp. 271-75; Vol. II, p. 266; *Jāt.*, Vol. I, p. 204; Vol. V, pp. 385-86; *Vim. Com.*, p. 94) and state that the following four parks, namely, Pāruṣyaka (*Pali Phārusaka*), Citraratha (Cittalatāvana), Nandanavana and Miśrakāvana (Missakāvana) are in the Tāvatiṁsa (Trayastriṁśa) heaven.

91. *ERE.*, Vol. IV, p. 136.
92. See above, notes 29 and 30; also see Vaidya, *Suvarṇaprabhāsa.*, intro., pp. 7, 9, 11; *Mahāyānasūtrasaṅgraha*, Pt. I, p. 258; *Laṅkavātāra*, trans. Suzuki, p. 216.
93. Cf. *Gaṇḍavyūha*, p. 119.
94. Ibid., p. 216.
95. Loc. cit.
96. Loc. cit.
97. Ibid., p. 117.
98. *Dīg.*, Vol. I, pp. 217-19, Vol. II, pp. 207f., 257-58; Vol. III, pp. 146, 194f.; *Aṅg.*, Vol. I, p. 242; Vol. IV, pp. 242-43; *Saṁ.*, Vol. IV, p. 280; *Buddhacarita*, Chap. XVI; *SBE*, Vol. XLIX, p. 187; *Dharmasaṅgraha*, Sec. 7; *Mahāvyutpatti*, 3136-39, 3146-49; *Saddharma.*, pp. 46f; *Lalita.*, pp. 217-18, 302; *Mtu.*, Vol. III, pp. 306-09; *Suvarṇabhāsottama.*, ed. Nobel, p. 64.
99. Vaidya, *Samādhirāja*, p. 62. The *Dharmasaṅgraha* (Secs. 7-10) mentions the above four and also enumerates eight, ten and fourteen *lokapālas*. The eight *lokapālas* are—(1) Indra, (2) Yama, (3) Varuṇa (4) Kuvera, (5) Īśāna, (6) Agni, (7) Nairṛta and (8) Vāyu (see also *Mahāvyupatti*, 3146-49, 3152, 3154-59). The ten *lokapālas* are—*aṣṭalokapāl-ādhikam-ūrdhve Brahmā, adhaḥ Kṛṣṇaḥ*. The fourteen *lokapālas—tadyathā daśa-lokapāla-sakalam, candra, sūrya, pṛthvī* and *asura*.
100. *Maj.*, Vol. III, pp. 100ff.; KV., PTS, 207, 208; *Abhidhammatthasaṅgaha*, 21; *Mahāvyupatti*, 3075ff; *Dharmasaṅgraha*, Sec. 127ff; *Mtu.*, Vol. II, pp. 314, 358; *Lalita*, p. 150; *Avadāna*, Vol. I, p. 5; *Divyāvadāna*, pp. 68, 138, 167, 568; *Boddhisattva bhūmi*, ed. Wogihara, p. 61; *Gaṇḍavyūha*, p. 249; Edgerton, *op. cit.*, Vol. II, p. 270. In this connection, it may be noted that Susīma-devaputta of the *Saṁ.*, Vol. I, p. 217, is mentioned in the *Mahāvyutpatti* 3136.
101. Vol. III, pp. 254ff. Cf. *Mil.*, PTS., p. 191 (*Ghanikā*, cloud-spirits).
102. See p. 273. The *Mtu* , Vol. III, p. 324, mentions only the *Varṣavalāhaka* gods.
103. See p. 127.
104. Vol. I, p. 243.
105. Vol. II, p. 259.
106. Waldschmidt. *Kleinere Sanskrit Texts*, 4, 185.2 (see note 3).
107. *Dīg.*, Vol. II, pp. 253-62.
108. Getty, op. cit., p. 125; *Mahāyānasūtra*, Pt. 1, pp. 258, 285.
109. See above, notes 93 and 98; also see Winternitz. op. cit., p. 334.
110. *Dīg.*, Vol. I, p. 244. Inda is mentioned here with Soma, Varuṇa, Īsāna, Pajāpati, Brahmā, Mahiddi and Yama as a god whom the Brāhmaṇas invoke. Also see ibid., Vol. II, p. 274; *Sut.*, verse 310. For Mahāyāna texts, see *Lalita*, p. 62. *Mahāvyutpatti*, 8022; *Saddharma-Laṅkāvatāra*, Ch. III; Winternitz, loc. cit. Īsāna (Īśāna), one of the chief gods of the Brāhmaṇas, is mentioned in the *Dīg.*, Vol. I, p. 244, and *Dharmasaṅgraha*, Sec. 8.

111. *Dīg.*, Vol. II, p.180, *Jāt*, Vol. IV, pp. 323, 325, 489, 499; Vol. V, pp. 132, 190-91; Vol. VI, pp. 12, 29, 72, 211, 519f.; *Dīg. Com.*, Vol. III, p. 855; *Bud. Com.*, p. 280; *Aṅg. Com.*, Vol. I, pp. 126f; *Mahāvyutpatti*, 4310; *Laṅkāvatāra*, trans. Suzuki, p. 216.
112. *Saṁ.*, Vol. I, p. 219; *Dīg.*, Vol. I, p. 244; Vol. II, p. 259; Vol. III, p. 204; *Jāt.*, Vol. VI, pp. 500-01, 586; also above, note 15; *Śikṣāsamuccaya*, p. 169; Winternitz, op. cit., p. 334; Getty, *op. cit.*, p. 125.
113. *Saṁ.*, loc. cit.; *Dīg.*, Vol. II, p. 274; *Maj.*; Vol. I, pp. 140, 327, 329; *Jāt.*, Vol. V, p. 28; Vol. VI, pp. 568, 571; Winternitz. loc. cit.
114. *Dīg.*, Vol. II, p. 259: *Āryā-Mañjuśrī*,, p. 625; Winternitz, loc. cit.
115. See below, note 136.
116. *Dīg.*, Vol. I, p. 244; Vol. II, p. 259; Vol. III, p. 204; Winternitz, op. cit., p, 334.
117. *Udāna Comm.*, p. 351 (Malalasekera, *op. cit.*, s.v.); *Mahāvyutpatti*, 4761. He is regarded as a demon because he causes drought. He may be identical with his Brāhmaṇical namesake who causes diseases in children (Edgerton, op. cit., s.v. *Skanda*).
118. *Saṁ.*, Vol. I, 56; *Samanta.*, PTS, Vol. III, p. 626, *CV.*, Ch. 74, verse 193; Ch. 93, verses 9, 10; Winternitz, op. cit., p. 334.
119. *Maj.*. Vol. III, pp. 179ff.; *Dīg.*, Vol. II, p. 259; *Dham. Com.*, Vol. III, p. 337; *Dīg.*, *Com.*, Vol. II, p. 690; *Aṅg. Com.*, Vol. II, p. 228; *Mahāvyutpatti*, 3155, 3328; Winternitz, loc. cit.; Getty, op. cit., 125, 145; *Dharmasaṅgraha*, Sec. 8.
120. *Dīg.*, Vol. III, p. 201; *Dīg. Com.*, Vol. III, p. 967; *Jāt.*, Vol. VI, p. 270; *Sut. Com.*, Vol. I, p. 369; *CV*, Ch. 37. verse 106; Ch. 39, verse 5; Ch. 80, verse 5; Ch. 87, verse 31; see above, note 98.
121. *Dīg.*, Vol. III, p. 196; *Dīg. Com.*, Vol. III, p, 963; *Mahāyānasūtra*, Pt. I, pp. 258, 285; see also above, notes 15 and 108; Getty, op. cit., p. 125; *Suvarṇaprabhāsa*, p. 89.
122. *Dīg.*, Vol. II, p. 259; *Saṁ.*, Vol. I, p. 50; *Jāt.*, Vol. I, p. 172; Vol. IV, pp. 1, 63, 69; Vol. V, pp. 386, 412; *Suvarṇaprabhāsa.*, loc. cit., see above, notes 15 and 108; Getty, loc. cit.
123. See above, notes 15, 108.
124. *Jāt.*, Vol. I, pp. 214, 285, 494; Vol. III, p. 17; Vol. V, p. 452; Vol. VI, pp. 201-02 etc. The *Naṅguṭṭha Jātaka* (ibid., Vol. I, pp. 494-95), says that the Bodhisattva refused to worship the fire-god because the latter has no power to protect his offerings. See also ibid , Vol. II, pp. 43, 45. Getty, loc. cit.
125. See above, note 123; see also *Suvarṇaprabhāsa.*, p. 87.
126. *Dam. Com.*, Vol. I, pp. 17f. The Jātakas contain many instances where Sakka rescued the good people in distress; cf. the cases of Dhammaddhaja, Guṭṭila, Kaccāni, Sambulā, Kusa, Mahājanaka's mother, etc.
127. See Ch. I.
128. See above, note 15.
129. See Chap. III; Winternitz, op. cit., p. 334.
130. See Chap. X; Winternitz, loc. cit.

131. *Jāt.*, Vol. III, p. 146; Vol. V, pp. 115, 409-12; Vol. VI, p. 568, Sec. *Dīg.*, Vol. II, p. 274, where Vāsava, i.e., Sakka, is addressed by Gopaka as Inda. Winternitz, loc. cit., *Lalita.*, pp. 62-66; *Saddharma*, p. 69.
132. E.g., *Aṅg.*, Vol. III, p. 89; *Dīg.*, Vol. I, pp. 21ff; Vol. II, pp. 221, 275; *Saṁ.*, Vol. I, p. 219; *Lalita.*, loc. cit.; *Saddharma.*, loc. cit.; *Aṣṭasāhasrikā.*, pp. 69-70, 72-73, 95, 112, 140, 190; *Mahāyānasūtra.*, Pt. I, p. 258.
132a. Both Pali and Sanskrit Buddhist texts (*Dhammapadaṭṭhakathā*, Vol. I, p. 273; Vol. III, pp. 216ff.; *Jāt.*, Vol. IV, pp. 180, 265; (*Divyāvadāna*, pp. 194 95; *Avadāna.*, Vol. II, p. 89; *Mahāvyutpatti*, 7127) mention Paṇḍukambalasilā (Paṇḍukambalaśilā) as the throne of Indra. In connection with Sakka's family, it may be noted that the *Sudhābhojana Jātaka* (*Jāt.*, Vol. V, pp. 399-405) and *Mtu.*, Vol. II, pp. 57-59, mention Śrī or Śirī (Pali Siri), Śraddhā (Saddhā), Āśā (Āsā), and Hrī (Hirī) as four daughters of Śakra who are personifications, respectively, of glory, faith, hope and modesty. They are called *Devakumārikā* in the *Mtu.*, Vol. III, p. 309 and *Lalita*, p. 391.
133. Vol. I, p. 57.
134. Malalasekera, op. cit., Vol. I, p. 245, s.v. *Ādiccabandhu.*
135. *Vim. Com.*, (PTS) p. 116. Buddhaghoṣa also, in the same way as the Vedas (Macdonell, *Vedic Mythology*, p. 30), says that Āditya is Aditi's son (Malalasekera, op. cit., Vol. I, p. 245, s.v. Ādicca).
136. *CV*, Ch. 47, verse 25; Mahāvyutpatti, 8214; *Lalita.*, pp. 109-10, 202, 291; *Saddharma.*, p. 428; *Mūlasarvāstivāda.*, Vol. I, p. 271. *Nārāyaṇabalam*, a certain measure of physical strength, is used as the strength of the Buddha in many Sanskrit Buddhist texts. This shows that Nārāyaṇa, in later literature, is none other than the Buddha. In this connection, it may be remembered that Viṣṇu is one of the countless names of the Buddha. As Viṣṇu and Nārāyaṇa are identical in Brāhmaṇical literature, the application of these names to the Buddha in Mahāyāna mythology is intelligible. But in some other later texts, Nārāyaṇa is regarded as inferior to the Buddha. For example, the *Kāraṇḍa.* (see above, note 15) shows that Nārāyaṇa is produced from the Buddha. The *Mahāparinirvāṇa.* (ed. Waldschmidt), 31. 12, says that the Buddha possess power of many hundred Nārāyaṇas.
137. See Haldar in *Foreigners*, etc., pp. 142ff; Getty, *op. cit.*, pp. 61, 103; *Suvarṇaprabhāsa*, p. 48.
138. *Jāt.*, Vol. III, p. 259; *Suvarṇāprabhāsa.*, intro., p. 11.
139. *Jāt.*, loc. cit., *Suvarṇāprabhāsa.*, p. 87.
140. *Dīg.*, Vol. I, pp. 211-23; *Mahāyānasūtra.*, Pt. I, pp. 258, 265; see also above, notes 29, 30, and 92.
141. See above, note 15.
142. *Saṁ.*, Vol. I, pp. 137f.; Vol. V, p. 233; *Bud. Com.*, p. 287; *Mtu.*, Vol. II, p. 63; Vol. III, p. 381; *Saddharma.*, Ch. I; *Mahāyānasūtra.*, Pt. I, p. 258; *Divyāvadāna*, pp. 613, 652, 655; *Avadāna.*, Vol. I, pp. 305, 311,

317, 329, 337, 343; Vol. II, p. 198; *Lalita.*, pp. 73, 83, 130, 274; *Suvarṇabhāsottama*, pp. 84-91; *Bodhisattvabhūmi*, pp. 75, 295. The commentaries on the *Maj.* (PTS, Vol. II, p. 372) and *Buddhavaṁsa* (pp 12, 29) explain him as Sahakapati and the *Lalita.*, pp. 44, 61, 63, 69-70 and other Sanskrit Buddhist texts speak of him as Sahāpati.

143. Malalasekera, op. cit., Vol. II, p. 1022; *Dīg.*, Vol. II, pp. 200-19;. *Mtu.*, Vol. II, p. 197; Vol. III, pp. 212, 344.
144. *Dham. Com.*, Vol. I, p. 380; *Jātaka*, Vol. I, p. 65; *Sut. Com.*, Vol. II, p. 382; *Vim. Com.*, p. 314; *Mtu.*, Vol. I, p. 319; Vol. II, pp. 150, 152; *Mūlasarvāstivāda.*, Vol. I, p. 217.
145. *Dīg.*, Vol. II, p. 261; *Mahāsamāja.*, 191. 11.
146. *Maj.*, Vol. I, pp. 326-31; *Jāt.*, Vol. III, pp. 358ff.; See Lévi, *Mahākarmavibhaṅga and Karmavibhaṅgopadeśa*, 34.8. Baka is described as one of the Mahābrahmās in Pali texts, but in the *Baka-Pratyekabrahma*, he is regarded as a Pratyeka-Brahmā.
147. In the *Saṁ.*, Vol. I, pp. 146ff., he is regarded as a Pacceka-Brahmā; but the *Lalita.*, pp. 359-60, describes him as a leader of the Brahmākāyika gods.
148. E.g., *Jāt.*, Vol. V, pp. 266-75; *JPTS*, 1884, pp. 154-56.
149. Ch. III.
150. Vol. I, pp. 5, 9, 13, 21, 42, 337; Vol. II, p. 350; Vol. III, pp. 274, 454.
151. See pp. 67, 138, 366.
152. Sec. 121; cf. *Mahāvyutpatti*, 4921-23, 4925, etc.; *Gaṇḍavyūha*, p. 157; *Avadāna.*, Vol. I, p. 4.

152a. 4920-27.

153. The *Raurava* and *Mahāraurava* are mentioned in the Sanskrit texts. The Pali texts state that the name of the *Roruva* hell is derived from the proper name *Ruru*. It has been devided in the Jātakas into (1) *Jālaroruva*, the hell of flame, and (2) *Dhūmaroruva*, the hell of smoke. But the *Pañcagatidīpana* mentions *Roruva* and *Mahāroruva*. The *Saṁ.*, Vol. I, pp. 92-93 (cf. *Dhammapadaṭṭhakathā*, Vol. IV, p. 79) refers to *Mahāroruva*.
154. *Jāt.*, Vol. V, p. 271.
155. Cf. *Catukaṇṇo catudvāro vibhatta bhāgaso mito /*
ayopākāra-pariyanto ayasā paṭikujjito //
tassa ayamayā bhūmi jolitā tejasā yutā /
samantā yojana-sataṁ pharitvā taṭṭhati sabbadā ti //
(*Jāt* , Vol., V, p. 266; *Aṅg.*, Vol. I, pp. 141-42; *Maj.*, Vol. III, p. 183; *Abhidharma*, Chap. III).
156. *Jāt.*, Vol. I, p. 168; Vol. IV, p. 493; Vol. V, p. 272.
157. See Ch. III.
158. Vol. I, pp. 5, 6, 11; Vol. III, pp. 185, 369, 455.

158a. *Mahāvyutpatti*, 4931.

158b. Ibid., 4938.

158c. Ibid., 4942.

158d. Ibid., 4941.

159. JPTS, 1884, pp. 155f.
160. Vol. I, pp. 141-42.
161. Vol. III, p. 185.
162. *Abhidharma*, Chap. III; *Dharmasaṅgraha*, Sec. 122; *Divyāvadāna*, pp. 67, 138; *Mahāvyutpatti*, 4929-36; *Avadāna*, Vol. I, p. 4.
163. Vol. I, pp. 149-52.
164. Vol. V, p. 173.
165. See p. 126; *SBE*, Vol. X, p. 119; Kern, op. cit., p. 58; *ERE.*, Vol. IV, p. 133.
166. *Aṅg. Com.*, Vol. V, pp. 61-62.
167. *Abbuda, Nirabbuda, Ababa, Aṭaṭa, Ahaha, Kumuda, Sogandhika, Uppala, Puṇḍarīka*, and *Paduma* are counted in a geometrical progression of twenty (*i.e.* twenty *Abbudas*=one term of *Nirabbuda*, twenty *Nirabbudas*=one term of *Ababa*, etc.). An *Abbuda* was reckoned as the time taken to remove twenty Kosalan Khāris (equal to a cartlord) of *tila* seeds, taking one seed at the end of each century. See also *KS*, Vol. I, p. 190 notes 1 and 2. The *Sutta. Comm.*, Vol. II, p. 447, gives an *Abbuda* as equal to 100,000 *ninnahutas* and 20 of it are one *nirabbuda* ((*Aṅguttara, Comm.*, loc. cit.).
168. See above, notes 47-49; also *Mahāvyutpatti*, 3062.
169. E.g., *Dīg.*, Vol. II, p. 12; Edgerton, op. cit., s.v. *lokāntarika*.
170. *Jāt.*, Vol. VI, p. 247; Edgerton, loc. cit.
170a. E.g., *Pet.*, p. 66; *Mtu.*, Vol. I, pp. 30-31; *Mahāvyutpatti*, 4749-52.
171. B.C. Law, *Buddhist Conception of Spirits*, p. ,viii; *Jāt.*, Vol. VI, p. 595; *Mtu.*, Vol. II, p. 324; Winternitz, *op. cit.*, pp. 307-08.
172. *ERE*, Vol. IV, p. 134.
173. See note 98.
174. Loc. cit., *Dīg.*, Vol. II, pp. 407f.; 257-58; Vol. III, pp, 194f.; *Divyāvadāna*. pp. 126, 182.
175. *Jāt.*, Vol. I, pp. 497f.; Getty, op. cit., p. 155.
176. *Dīg.*, Vol. I, p. 54; *Saṁ.*, Vol. III, p. 240; Vol. V, pp. 47, 63; Getty, loc. cit.; *Jāt.*, Vol. II, p. 13; Vol. III, p. 103.
177. *Mahāvaṁsa* and *Mahābodhivaṁsa* (Malalasekera, op. cit., Vol. II, p. 1355); Getty, loc. cit. The Garuḍas were virtuous (*Jāt.*, Vol. VI, pp. 178, 184, 261f.).
178. According to Grünwedel, Vajrapāṇi is identical with Śakra or Indra, the Indian god of rains. He is 'both the ferocious emanation of Vajradhara and the spiritual reflex, the Dhyāni-Bodhisattva, of Akṣobhya'; but Alice Getty is of the opinion that he is mentioned as a minor deity in the early Buddhist legends (Getty, *op. cit.*, p. 48) Buddhaghoṣa (Malalasekera, *op. cit.*, Vol. II, p. 808) identifies Vajirapāṇi with Sakka. There is no doubt that Sakka of the early Buddhist mythology is inferior to the Buddha; but he may not be regarded as a minor deity because, as the king of the Tāvatiṁsa-gods (see above), he holds an important position in the *Devaloka*.
179. *MB*, p. 182.

180. Getty, op. cit., intro., p. xx.
181. Ibid., p. 154; cf. *Lalita.*, p. 379; *Mtu.*, Vol. III, p. 300.
182. Getty, op. cit., loc. cit.
183. *Jāt.*, Vol. I, pp. 497f.
184. See notes 29 and 30.
185. Getty, op. cit., p. 155.
185a *Dīg.*, Vol. II, p. 212; *Mahāvyutpatti*, 3219.
186. *Dīg. Com.*, Vol. III, p. 699; *Mahāvastu*, Vol. III, pp. 197, 215; *Avadāna.*, Vol. I, pp. 95, 113; *Samādhirāja.*, pp. 19, 37; *Ārya-Mañjuśrī.*, 46.1.
187. Vol. III, p. 699.
188. *Dīg.*, Vol. II, pp. 263ff.
189. *Dīg. Com.*, Vol. II, p. 640.
190. *Jāt.*, Vol. IV, p. 69; *Mtu.*, Vol. II, p. 49.
191. For details about *Devāsurasaṅgāma*, see *Saṁ.*, Vol. I, pp. 216ff.; *Mtu.*, Vol. I, p. 30; Getty, op. cit., p. xxii, note 1.
192. *Saṁ.*, Vol. I, p. 222; Vol. IV, pp. 201ff.; *Jāt.*, Vol. I, p. 205; Malalasekera, op. cit., Vol. II, p. 924; *Mahāvastu*, Vol. III, pp. 138, 254; *Lalita*, p. 241; *Divyāvadāna*, pp. 126, 182; *Saddharma.*, p. 5; *Gaṇḍavayūha*, p. 250; *Avadāna.*, Vol. I, p. 108; *Ārya-Mañjuśrī.*, 655. 11; 663.21.
193. Waddell, in *ERE.*, Vol. IV, pp. 571-72; Getty, op. cit., p. 134.
194. *ERE., loc. cit.*
195. *Vim. Com.*, pp. 224, 333.
196. Vol. III, pp. 204f.
197. Several direct references to sacrificial offerings to the Yakkha demons are mentioned in the Jātakas (Vol. II. p. 149; Vol. III, p. 146). The *Suvarṇaprabhāsa.* (ed. Vaidya, intro., p. 11 says that the Yakśas and demons protect the listeners of the *Sūtra.*
198. *Saṁ.*, Vol. I, p. 205; *Amitāyurdhyāna.*, Pt. IV; *SBE*, Vol. XLIX, p. 201. Northern Buddhism also speaks of the worship of the Yakṣiṇī as a giver of children (Getty, *op. cit.*, p. 75) According to the *Mtu.*, Vol. I, p. 30, three classes of Yakṣas—(1) Karoṭapāṇi, (2) Mālādhara, and (3) Sadāmatta supported the Devas in their fight with the Asuras because of which they were regarded as Devas. This conception is also found in Mahāyāna Buddhism as the *Mahāvyutpatti*, 3150-52, includes the above classes of Yaksas in the list of *Devātas*. Though the Mālādhara and Sadāmatta classes are not mentioned in the Pali texts, the *Dīgha.* (see above, note 197) mentions Karatiya as a protector of the followers of the Buddha.
199. *Dīg.*, Vol. III, pp. 194f.
200. *Udāna*, PTS, IV. 4.
201. Vol. II, p. 256; also above, notes 29 and 30.
202. Ch. I.
203. *Mahāyānasūtrasaṅgraha*, Pt. I, pp. 258, 265, 269, 277, etc.
204. *Suvarṇaprabhāsa.*, intro., p. 11.
205. Ling. op. cit., p. 48; Getty, op. cit., pp. xx and 9.

206. Ling. *op. cit.*, p. 56; *Mtu.*, Vol. I, p. 264; Vol. II, pp. 238, 413; Vol. III, pp. 254, 381; *Lalita*, pp. 261, 302, 311, 328, 357; *Divyāvadāna*, p. 393; *Diśabhūmika*, pp. 28, 90 ; *Ārya-Mañjuśrī*, p. 171; *Samādhirāja*, p. 19; *Rāṣṭrapāla*, p. 58.
207. E.G., *Vis.*, p. 211; Malalasekera, op. cit., Vol., II, pp. 611, 613.
208. E.g., *Mtu.*, Vol. III, pp. 281ff.; also see *Saṁ.*, Vol. I, pp. 103f., 273; *Saddharma*, p. 290.
209. *Aṅg.*, Vol. II, p. 17; also *Lalita*.
210. See Ch. XIII; *Saṁ.*, Vol. pp. 124f.; *Mtu.*, loc. cit., *Dhammapadaṭṭhakathā*, Vol. III, pp. 195f.
211. Loc. cit.

Bibliography

A

1. *Abhidhammatthasaṅgaha* (Journal), Pali Text Society (PTS), London, 1884.
2. *Aṅguttaranikāya*, PTS, Vols. I-V.
3. *Aṅguttaranikāya Commentary*, PTS and SHB.
4. *Apadāna*, PTS, Vols. I-II.
5. *Buddhavaṁsa*, PTS.
6. *Buddhavaṁsa Commentary*, PTS,
7. *Culavaṁsa*, PTS,
8. *Cullaniddesa Commentary*, SHB.
9. *Dāṭhāvaṁsa* (Journal), PTS, 1884.
10. *Dhammapada*, PTS.
11. *Dhammapada Commentary*, PTS, Vols. I-V.
12. *Dhammasaṅī*, PTS.
13. *Dhammasaṅgaṇī Commentary*, PTS.
14. *Dīghanikāya*, PTS, Vols. I-III.
15. *Dīghanikāya Commentary*, PTS, Vols. I-III.
16. *Itivuttaka*, PTS.
17. *Itivuttaka Commentary*, PTS.
18. *Jāṭaka*, ed. Fausböll, Vols. I-VI.
19. *Kathāvatthu*, PTS.
20. *Mahābodhivaṁsa*, PTS.
21. *Mahāniddesa*, PTS, Vols. I-II.
22. *Mahāniddesa Commentary*, SHB.
23. *Mahāvaṁsa*, ed. Wilhelm Geiger, PTS.
24. *Majjhimanikāya*, PTS, Vols. I-III.
25. *Majjhimanikāya Commentary*, PTS and SHB.
26. *Milindapañha*, ed. Treckner, Williams and Norgate.
27. *Nettippakaraṇa*, PTS.
28. *Paṭisambhidāmagga*, PTS.
29. *Paṭisambhidāmagga Commentary*, PTS.
30. *Petavatthu*, PTS.
31. *Petavatthu Commentary*, PTS.

32. *Suttanipāta*, PTS.
33. *Suttanipāta Commentary*, PTS.
34. *Theragāthā*, PTS.
35. *Theragāthā Commentary*, SHB, Vols. I-II.
36. *Therīgāthā*, PTS.
37. *Therīgāthā Commentary*, PTS.
38. *Udāna*, PTS.
39. *Udāna Commentary*, PTS.
40. *Vibhaṅga*, PTS.
41. *Vibhaṅga Commentary*, PTS.
42. *Vimānavatthu*, PTS.
43. *Vimānavatthu Commentary*, PTS.
44. *Vinaya Piṭaka*, PTS, Vols. I-V.
45. *Vinaya Piṭaka Commentary*, PTS, Vols. I-IV.

B

46. *Abhidharmakośa*, ed. Vasubandhu.
47. *Ārya-Mañjuśrīmūlakalpa*, Vols. I-III, ed. Ganapati Sastri, Trivandrum, 1920, 1922, 1925.
48. *Aṣṭasāhasrikāprajñāpāramitā*, ed. Rajendralal Mitra, Calcutta, 1888.
49. *Avadānaśataka*, Vols. I-II, ed. Speyer, St. Petersburg, 1902, 1906.
50. *Bodhicaryāvatārapañjikā*.
51. *Bodhisattvabhūmi*, ed. Wogihara, Tokyo, 1930-36.
52. *Buddhacarita*, ed. Asvaghosa.
53. *Daśabhūmikasūtra* (Gāthā Portion), ed. Rahder and Susa.
54. *Dharmasaṅgraha*, ed. Max Müller, Oxford, 1885.
55. *Divyāradāna*, Cowell & Neil, Cambridge, 1886.
56. *Gaṇḍavyūha*, Suzuki and Idzumi, Kyato, 1934-36;
57. *Gītā*.
58. *Kleinere Sanskrit Text*, ed. Waldschmidt.
59. *Lalitavistara*, ed. Lefmann, Halle 1902 (See also P.L. Vaidya's edition).
60. *Laṅkāvatārasūtra*, D.T. Suzuki, Routledge & Kegan Paul Ltd., London, 1932, 1956.
61. *Mahākarmavibhaṅga* and *Karmavibhaṅgopadesa*, ed. Lèvi, Paris, 1932.
62. *Mahāvastu*, ed. Senart, Paris, 1882, 1890, 1897, Vols. I-III.

63. *Mahāvyutpatti.*
64. *Mahāyānasūtrasaṅgraha*, Pt. I, ed. P.L. Vaidya, Mithila Institute, 1961.
65. *Mūlasarvāstivādnvinaya* (Gilgit Manuscript), ed. N. Dutt.
66. *Rāṣṭrapālaparipṛcchā*, ed. Finot, St. Petersburg, 1901.
67. *Saddharmapuṇḍarīka*, ed. Kern and Nanjio, St. Petersburg, 1912.
68. *Samādhirājasūtra*, ed. Régamay, Warsaw, 1938.
69. *Śatasāhasrikāprajñāpāramitā*, ed. P. Ghosh, Bibliotheca Indica, Calcutta, 1902ff.
70. *Sikṣāsamuccaya*, ed. Bendall, St. Petersburg, 1897-1902.
71. *Sukhāvaṭivyūha*, ('Larger' and 'Smaller'), ed. Müller, Oxford, 1883.
72. *Suvarṇabhāsottama*, ed. Noble, Leipzig, 1937.
73. *Suvarṇaprabhāsa*, ed. P.L. Vaidya, Mithila Institute, 1967.

C

74. Getty, Alice, *The Gods of Northern Buddhism*, The Clarendon Press, Oxford, 1914.
75. Gogerly, D.J., *Ceylon Buddhism*, Colombo, Wesleyan Methodist Book Room; London, Kegan Paul, Trench, Trubner & Co. Ltd., 1908, Vols. I-II.
76. Hardy, R.S., (a) *Manual of Buddhism*, Williams and Norgate, London and Edinburgh, 1860; (b) *Legends and Theories of the Buddhists*, Williams and Norgate, London and Edinburgh, 1866.
77. Hare, E.M., *The Book of Gradual Sayings*, Vols. III-IV, PTS, London, 1934-35.
78. Hastings, James, *Encyclopaedia of Religion and Ethics*, Vol. IV, 1935.
79. Keith, A.B., *The Mythology of All Races*, Vol. VI, Boston, Marshall Jones Company, 1917.
80. Kern, H., *Manual of Indian Buddhism*, Strassburg, 1896.
81. Law, B.C., (a) *Buddhist Conception of Spirits*, London, 1936; (b) *Heaven and Hell in Buddhist Perspective*, Calcutta, 1925.
82. Ling, T.O., *Buddhism and Mythology of Evil*, George Allen & Unwin Ltd., London, 1962.
83. Macdonell, A.A., *The Vedic Mythology*, Varanasi, Indological Book House, 1963.

84. Mackenzie, D.A., *Indian Legend.* The Gresham Publishing Company, London, 1913

85. McGovern, W., *A Manual of Buddhist Philosophy*, Vol. I, London, Kegan Paul, Trunch, Trubner & Co. Ltd., New York, E.P. Dutton & Co., 1923.

86. Rhys Davids, Mr. and Mrs., *Dialogues of the Buddha*, Vols. I-III, PTS, London, 1899-1921.

87. Rhys Davids, Mrs., (a) *Psalms of the Sisters* (Vol. I. of the *Psalms of the Early Buddhists*), PTS, London, 1909; (b) *Psalms of the Brethren* (Vol. II of the *Psalms of the Early Buddhists*), PTS, London, 1913.

88. *Sacred Books of the East*, Vol. X, 2nd ed., Oxford University Press, London, 1924; Vol. XXI, reprinted by Motilal Banarsidass, Delhi 1965; Vol. XXXVI, Clarendon Press, Oxford, 1894; Vol. XLIX, Clarendon Press, Oxford, 1894.

89. Sircar, D.C., (a) *Cosmography and Geography in Early Indian Literature*, Calcutta, 1967: (b) *Foreigners in Ancient India and Lakṣmī and Sarasvatī in Art and Literature*, Calcutta, 1970.

90. Winternitz, M., *A History of Indian Literature*, Vol. II, Calcutta, 1933,

91. Woodward, F.L., *The Book of Gradual Sayings*, Vols. I, II and V, PTS, London, 1932-33 and 1936.

92. Woodward, F.L., and Rhys Davids Mrs., *The Book of Kindred Sayings*, Vols. I-V, PTS, London, 1917-1930.

D

93. *Journal of Ancient Indian History.*

94. *Journal of the Royal Asiatic Society.*

INDEX

D

R

T